Lifted by Hope:

How I Overcame Barriers by Becoming the First Immigrant Woman from Africa Ordained by the Presbyterian Church USA

Rev. Dr. Jemimah Ngatia

In Him we Trust.

[signature]

7/3/18

Published By: Lulu www.lulu.com

Edited By: Jean Johnston

Scripture quotations, unless otherwise specified, are from the New Living
Version of the Bible (taken from the website www.biblegateway.com)

ISBN 978-1-387-77055-7

9 781387 770557

90000

Lifted by Hope:

How I Overcame Barriers by Becoming the First Immigrant Woman from Africa Ordained by the Presbyterian Church USA

"How can we sing a new song in a new land?"

-Psalm 137:4

Forewords

Lifted by Hope tells the story of Jemimah Ngatia's life. But it does more than that. It describes the influence she exerts on hundreds of African refugees that come to Colorado each year. She lifted my life when we first met - she visited me in the hospital. I have seen firsthand her capacity, as chaplain and pastor, to joyfully love and encourage others. Hers is a story of hope, the power of God's love toward those in need, and one that will inspire many with the life-lifting truth that, with God, all things are possible.

-Dr. Ted Travis, Author, Building Cathedrals: Urban Youth Discipleship That Works

It has been my pleasure to know and serve alongside Rev. Dr. Jemimah Ngatia. She is a wise woman, with wisdom gleaned from relentlessly pursuing the Lord's calling on her life over two continents and overcoming life's challenges along the way. She is a woman of great courage, and a strong and humble leader in the church. Rev. Dr. Ngatia's love for Jesus Christ, her Lord and Savior, is evident in every area of her life. Anyone would do well to follow her lead.

~ Helen Kaminski, Providence Bible Church/ Cross Purpose Ministries

I am truly honored and blessed to call the Rev. Dr. Jemimah Ngatia my friend. She is a true minister of the gospel of Jesus Christ. Jemimah has a special gift of befriending strangers, reaching out to those on the margins (including immigrants and refugees) and loving those around her in beautiful ways. Because she loves others so well, many people (including myself) consider her family. She has given me the honor of the nickname "Nyawira" (a Swahili word roughly translated "hard worker" - a name she calls her own daughter). I do not take that lightly – it is a true honor! I have learned much from her seasoned experiences and her years of walking with Jesus. It has been my sincere pleasure to help my friend Jemimah edit her story (that has been forged over a lifetime). Rev. Dr. Jemimah Ngatia reminds me of Jesus in many ways. To God be the glory! Hers is a story well worth reading!

-Jean Johnston, Editor, _Lifted By Hope_ Cru High School Ministry, Senior Field Staff

Jemimah Ngatia and I are sisters in Christ: African sisters. She is a lovely black woman from Kenya in East Africa and I am a white woman who spent about 17 years in Senegal, West Africa (so she accepts me as her African sister). One of the first things she will tell you is that she loves Jesus and he is her personal Savior. Jemimah also loves people, and it shows in all she does. She makes friends wherever she goes. Her life story is rich in experiences of walking with Jesus. All of us have things we can learn from reading about her life in _Lifted By Hope._

-Dottie Wire, Providence Bible Church

Jemimah Ngatia has been a faithful servant of the Lord Jesus Christ for her entire life. She has served the Lord and His church by comforting the grieving, supporting the weak, visiting the sick, teaching the Word, leading God's people, and loving her family. It has been my joy to know her and to walk with her through the mountaintops and valleys of life. You will enjoy reading her life story.

-Jason Janz, Elder of Vision and Teaching
Providence Bible Church

Pastor Jemimah's story, <u>Lifted by Hope</u>, is fascinating, startling, frightening, invigorating and full of hope. She enables us to enter the beautiful and painful scenes from her life in Africa and in the United States, in such a way that we feel informed, invited to grace and inspired to take hold of the promise. "Weeping may last for a night, but joy comes in the morning!" I'm glad I read this book and eager to commend it for others.

-Zack Eswine, Pastor of Riverside Church
Webster Groves, Missouri

Jemimah's journey has not been an easy one. She has lost loved ones, faced prejudice and had to adapt to a new and strange culture. Jemimah's impressive accomplishments have been the result of hard work, inspirational perseverance and an unwavering faith. The most remarkable aspect of her difficult journey is the constant joy that she exhibits and spreads to those around her. Jemimah's warmth impacted me the first time I met her, and I know that I am not the only acquaintance that has become her "brother" (in a matter of minutes). I know that you will be inspired and challenged by the remarkable story and the contagious, joy-filled faith of this amazing woman.

-Reid Hettich, Pastor of Mosaic Church of Aurora
Chair of the Benson Memorial Family Center

Rev. Dr. Jemimah Ngatia is a God-fearing leader who believes in Church planting. She has planted several churches in different states throughout the United States. Jemimah has taught me that Church planting is an exhausting, but exciting, venture of faith. I remember her encouraging words when I was starting a church plant in Dallas. She told me "whenever people put on pioneer garb and ride off the wilderness; they have entered the realm of faith." This means that they, like Abraham, must move outside their comfort zones (of certainty and security) and enter an unknown world. This always involves taking risks, which is easier for some than for others. Yet faith and risk go hand in hand. Anything of authentic spiritual significance is accomplished through faith! The writer of Hebrews affirms that "without faith it is impossible to please God" (Heb. 11:6a). Those who enlist in launching new churches must be men and women of strong, stretching faith in God. Jemimah's example is one of both believing in and Trusting in God.

-Rev. Dr. Cyprian Kimathi Guchienda, Pastor of All Nations Highland Park Presbyterian Church (in Dallas, Texas)

Upon meeting Jemimah, I knew it would be a lasting and impactful (albeit unlikely) friendship. I was a white adoptive single mother of a four-year-old Haitian daughter (shell- shocked by the wonderful demands of motherhood and in need of the wisdom of a woman who loved the Lord). Jemimah understood the challenges of being a strong Christian woman of color (challenges my daughter would soon face). It is a blessing to get to know Rev. Dr. Jemimah Ngatia on a deep level (I became her family overnight). Jemimah was the first to meet my husband. Jemimah and Benson's 56 years of marriage was a great example to us of how to do it right. Deep friendships flourish when forged in hard times. Jemimah and I have shared in joys and celebrations and have supported each other through the darkest of times. Jemimah is a faithful friend, strong mentor, giver/receiver, fallible human, caring pastor and dear sister. I can confidently say that Jemimah is a blessing and she will bless you as you learn her story.

-Meredith Bishop, Accenture Global Human Resources

Jemimah creates happiness with every contact. My family is blessed to have her in our lives. She is a supporter, advisor and friend to every member of our family.

-Kim Barnhill, Biomedical Engineer
California

Rev. Dr. Jemimah Ngatia is not just grandmother, but a mover and a shaker. There is no mountain too high that it is unclimbable and no valley too low that it is impassable. The key to overcoming barriers has been represented by the faith that Rev. Dr. Jemimah Ngatia has lived out. Two covenants that have been passed down in our family from my great grandmother (Bilhah) to Jemimah (my grandmother) to me, and now to Jemimah's great grant kids are found in Joshua 24:15 ("For me and my house we shall serve the lord") and Hebrews 11:6 ("Without faith it is impossible to please God").

-Benson Jr. Ngatia, Grandson of Jemimah,
on behalf of my family
(Rochelle Ngatia, Hezekiah Ngatia (6),
the late Hannah Jane, and Josiah Ngatia (1))

My Mum is very inspiring, loving, hopeful, faithful and above all, a God-fearing person. She has been very persistent and will rarely accept a "no" for an answer. My Mum overcame many challenges in her life by trusting that anything is possible, as long as we trust in the Lord.

- Joy Nyawira Njogu, Jemimah's Daughter

My Grandmother is very kind to everyone and loves everyone. She has a very big heart and cares for others

– Zawadi Wangui Njogu (15), Jemimah's great-granddaughter

Grandmother (Cucu) is a nice and caring person who loves everyone

– Zahra Wanjiru Njogu (12), Jemimah's great-granddaughter

Cucu is a loving Grandmother that is kind and generous

– Armani Muita Njogu (10), Jemimah's great-granddaughter

My friend and sister Jemimah, is a Proverbs 31 woman. Meeting her for the first time, I immediately knew before we spoke a word that she was a woman of noble character. We first met in a vintage furniture store as she set about her work for God's kingdom vigorously. Her arms were strong for her task. She mentioned a cross I was wearing around my neck. She was kind, and Christ-like. I quickly discovered that she loved Jesus and she would love me, too. Our conversation continued into the parking lot, where her husband Benson was waiting patiently for her to return. My impression of Benson and Jemimah as a couple during my initial meeting them were "their smiles are so warm, they embraced me with genuine love and compassion. I realized I had made some new friends". Jemimah truly possess the characteristic of a wife of noble character. Benson while alive had full confidence in her and lacked nothing of value. I had the great opportunity to observe her take care of Benson as he battled with cancer that eventually took to be with Jesus. She exemplifies Proverbs 31:10-14. Benson, a man of God exemplified being in God's image. Jemimah and Benson met no strangers. They went about their lives loving people, the way God said for us to love. I honor them both and I am grateful God placed them in my path.

-Deborah Simonds, Counselor, Prison Ministry

When I think of Jemimah, the first word that comes to mind is "family". Everywhere she goes, she makes new family. She is a mom, a sister, a "shosho"/Cucu (grandma) to so many people. She has such a big heart and cares for people so deeply. I'm excited that now people get to read her story and be inspired by such an amazing and strong woman.

-Joshua Proemmel, Mentee and Honorary Son

I am very thankful for people who enrich my life in ministry. One of those persons is the Rev. Dr. Jemimah Ngatia. Jemimah has served in the Presbytery of Denver as an Organizing Pastor for a New Worshipping Community, an African Swahili language Ministry for two years. Church planting is not an easy task, but Jemimah is passionate to reach out and to share the good news of Jesus Christ. I admire her tenacity, faithfulness and perseverance; it has been a great joy to journey together as companions serving the living Christ.

Rev. Amy Mendez, Denver Presbytery

Acknowledgments

First of all, I want to thank my lord and savior Jesus Christ. I also want to thank my beloved late husband Benson Ngatia Wanjau, my father (the late Norman Kabuga), mother (Bilha Ngima Kabuga) and all my loving family. My family includes my late daughter Jane Ngatia, daughter and son-in-law Joy and Joe Njogu, grandchildren Benson Jr., Rochelle, Zawadi, Zahara and Armani, great-grandchildren Hezekiah, (late) Hannah, Josiah, late five brothers and late two sisters and my living sister Cecilia Kamau, late nephew Alex Kabuga, Pauline Kabuga (and their family), late nephew Benson Mwangi, my sisters-in-law Priscilla Wanjari Gitonga and Shelmith Githinji. I also want to honor Sister Patricia Bombard (BVM), Father Gerry Kreb, last Moderator Rt. Rev. Jesse Kamau, the late Jack Hanford and Joanna Hanford. I would like to honor Rev. Amy Mendez from the Presbytery of Denver, Rev. Felix Kimathi, Pastor Jason and Jen Janz, Terry and Marsha Bratton (and all the elders of Providence Bible Church) as well as Rev. Dr. Cyprian Kimadhi. I would also like to thank the Rev. Dr. Linda Shugert of Giddings-Lovejoy Presbytery and Pastor Paul Macharia of Covenant Church in St. Louis, Missouri. I also want to acknowledge Rev. Dr. Jane Nyambura Njoroge (from the WCC-the World Church Council), the Rev Dr. Terry Empling and Annie Empling (former Stated Clerks in the Giddings-Lovejoy Presbytery), Rev. Dr. Emmah and Robert Rasoarivojjy and family. I want to thank the Stephen Minsters (Care-Givers) at Bahati Presbyterian Church in Nairobi, Kenya. I want to honor the board members of the Benson Memorial Family Center Ministry in Denver, Colorado (Pastor Reid Hettich, Ted and Shelly Travis, Meredith Bishop and Chris Macey, Dave and Dottie Wire, Jean Johnston and Josphat Ombacho). I want to thank Josh Prommel, Heather Ledford, Helen Kaminski, Pam and Nate Austin, Schatzie Barnhill, Kim Barhill and the Barnhill Family, Lavern and Kathy Yutzy, Lilian Wanjuku Mwaniki, Sarah Karanja, Gladys Biamah and Samuel Mwangi and Nancy Mwangi and Priscilla Wangari Waigwa and Wambui Waigwa.

Chapters

1. Introduction

On November 12, 2005, I became the *first* immigrant woman from Africa to be ordained as a minister of Word and Sacrament by the Presbyterian Church USA.

I have served at the United African Presbyterian Church at the Presbytery of Giddings-Lovejoy, St. Louis Missouri. The United African Presbyterian Church is formed by the people from Africa (and some members are Americans from the community). I have been a full-time minister of this church.

I currently serve in Aurora and Denver (Colorado) as an organizing Pastor for a Presbyterian Church serving new immigrants and refugee families from African countries.

We conduct our Worship Services in English. The services are also interpreted into African languages, including Swahili, because not all our members understand the English language.

We worship God using African traditions (just as we worshipped in Africa). We use different languages in our singing, prayers, testimonies, reading the word and worshiping God. It is all in the purpose of inviting God's spirit to come down into the center of our worship. Our worship lasts several hours (having lunch after the worship together with the women of the church each bring their popular dish to share with others after the service). We hold our church service the way we used to worship back in Africa before we came to the United States.

Our church has been a powerful and meaningful connection to our cultures. Our worship experiences have been a tremendous blessing to us. We did not expect to be able to worship God in our native tongue in America. Sometimes it feels like a dream, but it is real. The Presbytery of Denver has supported us and allowed us to connect with each other and with God in this way, worshipping in our mother tongues.

We welcome everyone in our Church service, and most Sundays we worship with people from several different African countries. It is not unusual for new people to come and join us, particularly when we have special events. People from Africa like to join us to share our worship and share our members' food. They also come to have fellowship after the worship service. They enjoy singing African songs and hearing the different African languages. The food we share reminds them of the food they used to eat before they came to the United States. Worship brings them home.

2. The Beginning of My Journey: Childhood

By the time my older siblings and I were born, my parents already were old (well into their 50s). We were the first generation of my family to be born into a Christian home (my parents were some of the first children in our community to have been taught by missionaries). They were taught to read and to write by Presbyterian missionaries from Scotland. My parents were also the first couple in the community to ever get married in the church. As you continue to read this book, you will read about my relationship with my father and my mother.

My mother had her first child in 1924, when she was about 23 years old. The rest of us (we totaled five sons and four daughters) followed. I was my mum's last baby daughter. I was born seventh out of nine children. My siblings' names were: Gregory Mwangi Kabuga, John Mina Kabuga, Phyllis Wamuyu Kabuga, Royce Muthoni Kabuga, Naftali Macharia Kabuga, Cecilia Wanjeri Kabuga, (Jemimah Wambuga Kabuga), Geofrey Githaiga Kabuga, and Jotham Maranga Kabuga. My mother actually birthed eleven children altogether, but two died before me. She named me after her sister Wanjiriu (Chiru), but my mom loved to call me Wambugo as my nickname. To everyone in the community (including my schoolmates and my family), I was known as "Wambugo Kabuga". I was my parents' baby daughter, baptized as an infant and then given the name Jemimah, which is a biblical name that means "dove". In the story of Job, Jemimah was one of Job's daughters born after God restored him. The first daughter born in Job's second generation of children was named Jemimah (the second was Keziah and the third was Keren). *"God also gave Job seven more sons and three more daughters. He named his first daughter Jemimah, the second Keziah, and the third Keren. In all the land no women were as lovely as they daughters of Job. And their father put them into his will among their brothers." (Job 42:14)*

In the community, I was known as the daughter of my father Norman Kabuga Gichuru and my mother Bilihah Ngima Kabuga. My parents were the founders of our local Karindudu Presbyterian Church East Africa (PCEA) in the Karindudu Nyeri District in Kenya. My mother and father would eventually die twenty-three years apart. My father would die in 1970 (he suffered a short time with stomach cancer and passed away at the age of eighty-four years). My mother survived much longer - she died on May 5, 1993, when she was 103 years old!

I was born at a Presbyterian hospital in the community which was founded by the same Presbyterian missionaries from Scotland who had reached out to my parents. The Presbyterian missionaries first came to Kenya in 1891 and arrived at a place called Kimbezi. Many of those missionaries lived their whole lives in Kenya, died there and were buried there (in fact, there is a historical cemetery where their still bodies lay). Missionaries who survived later went on to the Kikuyu Kiambu District (my family community). The work of God also expanded to other places like Tumutumu in Nyeri District and Chogoria Meru District. One of the many hospitals the missionaries founded is where I was born (Tumutumu Hospital).

When I was old enough to understand it, my mother told me a story about what happened during the time of my birth. Immediately after her delivery, she was shown her new baby. Later, she was taken away to a different room. The nurses again brought a baby to her, but the baby they brought to her was not her baby! When she saw the baby, she immediately screamed, "This is not my baby! The beautiful baby I delivered was brown with long legs. This baby is too dark and has small legs!". She noticed right away that the baby given to her was not me. My mother saw the little baby tired with a little knitted shawl and she frantically explained to the nurse who brought the infant, "This is not my baby! My baby – the one I was shown right after delivery -- was brown!" My mother was a short woman and her skin color was brown; my dad was a tall man and his skin color was also brown (that means that I took after both of my parents' brown complexion and my father's height). After she screamed long enough, the nurse returned the darker baby back to her own mother. Finally, the nurses brought my mom's real baby (me) into her arms where she began breastfeeding

During the time I was born, there was a famine in our area (called Ng'aragu Ya Mianga, which means "the famine of the cassava flour"). There was no food – it was a time of hardship. That is the reason why my parents kept birth records. The birth records correlated with the time of the famine between 1943 and 1944 (which is when I was born). During the famine, my mother had to go to a different community where they searched for cassava, brought it home and ground it up to make flour. With this flour, she could prepare cassava porridge ("uji") to feed her children and family. The other record of the time I was born was confirmed because my parents were educated (they knew how to write and to read as they were taught by the Presbyterian missionaries). They kept good records of the dates when each of their children were born, which was rare in our community (most could not keep records of when their children were born).

I grew up loved by both of my parents and all the members of my family. I had a deep relationship with my mother and her friends (other women) in the community. My mother was always caring, and she was a friend to many women. My mother would take me everywhere the women were gathering. She used to feed me with soft food and took great care of me. There is a very famous saying about the power of community "it takes a village to raise a child". In my case, I was literally raised by the community of our village!

My childhood was full of joys and surprises. It seemed every day there was a story being told about Jemimah. My mother would often share the story about my birth (and the switch up) to the other women in the community. She did this to warn them to be careful when they went to the hospital to deliver their own babies. My mother wanted to be sure that the same thing would not happen to them. Many women used to deliver their babies in their homes (being assisted by the by "Traditional Birth Attendants" or TBAs in the community). Because my mother was a Christian and a missionary in her own community, she discouraged women from delivering at home. She knew that many babies died in childbirth at home, and mothers would also sometimes die because of prolonged bleeding in labor or after delivery (without medical care). My mother still believed it was better to go and deliver in the Hospital than to deliver at home, despite the risk of switching babies.

My work as a young girl in my community was to help my mother with housework: fetching water from the spring, fetching firewood and preparing food for my sisters and brothers who were working at the farm. My mother trusted me to be left at home with the other children. I would cook for everyone and when my mother came back home, she would find everything in order.

Being the youngest daughter, I had responsibilities to do house work (but not heavy work in the house). I had light duties. My duty was to prepare the food and keep the house clean. When the food was ready, I was to take to the food to the garden/fields to my mother and other children working there. I remember doing my work while singing choruses of praise and memorizing bible verses while the food was cooking. This always brought great joy and happiness to my heart. This meant that I grew spiritually while I was doing my chores.

My main work was to prepare the house for our guests and to keep it in order. My parents used to host ministers and church workers who would come to our village. My dad organized bible studies, and I started seeing Presbyterian ministers and church elders coming to our home to fellowship with my parents. To this day, when I see a church minister, it reminds me of the relationship between those church workers and my parents. During that time, I learned to be humble and respect elders and the visitors who came to visit my parents. In our community, children like me were taught to give the way for and respect the elders. This was a message for every child in the community.

My other duties included taking care of the sheep and goats and bringing them home from the field (as well as putting them where they were supposed to be in the afternoon). I was to milk only one cow if I needed milk - to prepare hot tea for the other children who were working with my mom in the fields. I was given permission to milk that one cow anytime I needed to get fresh milk. The cow I milked was so polite. She was called "Kageni", which means "little visitor". She was so very easy to milk. I would treat Kageni specially and bring her treats to eat. I took care of all the calves (feeding them away from their mothers, so the cows could produce more milk), lambs and cows. Kageni was always my favorite!

3.   My Christian Life

My Christian life in my community inspired me to become who I am today in my work as a church Minister of Word and Sacrament. Being the daughter of the founders of our church helped me to understand that the last children who are born are often not known as well in the community. The family sometimes forgets that there is a child outside taking care of the cows, sheep and goats. Sometimes, even when the visitors would come to our home, I was the last child to be introduced to the visitor. It was only when I was told to bring the firewood from outside that everyone would see me and ask about me. I would hear the voice of my mother saying, "Ask

Wambugo to bring some more firewood in the house."
That would be just the time I would appear in the
presence of the visitors. It reminds me the story of David
as the youngest child and how he had to shepherd the
sheep while his siblings were called by Samuel. *"In the same
way all seven of Jesse's sons were presented to Samuel, but Samuel
said to Jesse, 'The Lord has not chosen any of these.' Then Samuel
asked, 'Are these all the sons you have?' 'There is still the youngest,'
Jesse replied. 'But he's out in the fields watching the sheep and
goats.' 'Send for him at once,' Samuel said. 'We will not sit down to
eat until he arrives'"* (1 Samuel 16:10-11)

After a few years, I was to join my brothers and sisters in
the fields during the coffee picking days. My dad was a
good coffee farmer. Indeed, he was the very best coffee
grower in the whole community. He planted a lot of
coffee in our community (and he also had many milk
cows from which he would sell milk every morning). As
his children working in the fields, we could not go to
school for days during coffee picking season

My father did not want us to attend school during the
coffee picking days. My father was the chairman of the
parents' board at our school, so the principal (headmaster)
knew that during coffee picking days, Mr. Norman
Kabuga's children were not supposed to come to school.
They would be picking coffee two days during the school
week. When the chairman of the parents' board (my
father) spoke, no one dared to ask why the Mr. Norman
Kabuga's children did not come to School. They already
knew. The coffee was to be picked three days a week (two
of which were during the school week) and during the

other three days we could still go to school. My parents
had a coffee farm to work and it could not wait. This was
just the way it was. There were three days (Tuesday,
Thursday and Saturday) to pick coffee. On these days,
everyone had to go to out into the fields to pick coffee
and take it to the factory the very same day. Saturday was
good because school in the community was out anyway.
However, on Tuesdays and Thursdays we had to miss
school. This was frustrating, challenging and painful. It
was painful because our coffee farm was near the school.
As we walked by, we would see the other children going
to school and playing outside while we were working hard
harvesting coffee. I wanted so badly to be in school with
them. The children from school would tease us as we
passed by. I was so tired of doing that (over and over
again) day after day, with a lot of challenges in the
community. I felt shame seeing other children that got to
go to school while I had to labor in the fields. You see,
my parents' home was very close to the school compound
where the other children could see me in the coffee field.
I did not like that. When the children were going home
after school, they used to pass near my home walking on
the side of the road shouting my name, "Jemimah!
Jemimah! Are you still picking that coffee? We had fun at
school! We were taught new subjects!" At that time, I
wanted to hide under the coffee trees. I did not want the
students to see me, but I could still hear them shouting
my name. My life in my parents' home was hardened by
picking the coffee. Every family that grew coffee plants
acted like they were living in the fields during the harvest
(some families even literally slept in their fields at night).
Those who had never belonged to a family of coffee
growers could not relate to or even understand this. I
hated doing it.

The coffee factory was called "Kiangaruru (Karatina) Mathira Nyeri District Central Province". After each of the children picked coffee, we each had to deliver the picked coffee to the factory. I was frustrated, because I was so small. To be given the heavy responsibility of picking coffee and taking it to the factory was very hard for me. The distance from my home to the factory was about five miles (each way, not counting all the work we were doing in harvesting). Walking to the factory was serious business because we had to walk at such a fast pace with coffee on our backs. There was a narrow time window we had to make before factory would close. We did not want to miss the deadline to get our coffee in. The rest of my family always reached the factory before me. My dad would come back looking for me, wondering where I was (because everyone else had already reached the factory). I used to walk slowly because the coffee was heavy for me to carry on my back. My siblings were older and bigger than I was (and stronger). When my dad would come back looking for me, he would find me still walking and I would know his thoughts. I knew he was mad at me because others had already reached the factory. The first words from his mouth to me were "WHY WERE YOU WALKING SO SLOWLY LIKE THAT?!" I would start crying because I was tired, frustrated and suffering. I was walking five miles each way carrying the bag of coffee on my back, and I had no one to help me. I remember walking slowly (being left far behind) with my coffee. Sometimes my mother would arrive first to the factory and she would walk back looking for me. When she found me, she helped me to get my bag to the coffee factory. However, my dad never helped me.

It was not an easy job for me, especially because the other children in the community were seeing me caring the heavy, heavy bag of coffee and being left behind because I was too small and skinny (not yet able to carry the heavy bags of coffee fast enough reach to the coffee factory in time). But it did not matter, I was required by my father to do it anyway. One day, I remember telling myself that "someday this will come to the end!" During these days, I felt like I was a slave in my family. I did not want to grow up repeating the same fate with my own future family. My prayer to God was, "please, please my God, you are faithful! My dread is that I will meet a nice boy who picks coffee. I do want to get married, but NOT to a coffee grower. I am sure, God, that when I grow up, you will bring a boy in a place where they do not grow coffee." My goal was not to marry for wealth or education. All I wanted was just wanted a Christian, humble man who was NOT A COFFEE GROWER! I did not want to move from picking coffee with my parents only to go to another problem and family and pick coffee all the time. God is good! Let me tell you, after I grew up, God answered my prayers. God later blessed me with a handsome, humble, Christian husband whose parents did not grow coffee (but they did grow tea leaves). I would tell myself "I will overcome this one day. I will not be picking this coffee forever." I still have these memories even now. I told myself, "one day I will get married and go away like other my sisters." I thought of scriptures that encouraged me that this hard work would not last forever. I came to learn that God was not unjust *"God is not unjust; He will not forget your work and the love you have shown him as you have helped his people and continue to help them (Hebrews 6:10)" "For our light and momentary troubles are achieving for us an eternal glory that far outweighs them all. So, we fix our eyes not on what is seen, but on what is unseen, since what is seen is temporary, but what is unseen is eternal (2 Corinthians 4:17-18)"*

Although my father was at times a hard man, I knew he still loved me. I remember one day my mother came from the fields with my siblings and some children from the community. They brought home the ripened bananas from the garden where they spent most of their time. She divided the bananas to give every child one to eat. Every child but me, that is. I did not get a banana. I realize now that that this, of course, was not on purpose. It was just that there were not enough bananas for each child to get their own (instead my mom gave me a sweet potato because I was the youngest). My mother had a compassionate heart for children in the community and wanted to bless them (she lived out loving her neighbor as herself and modeled that for me since I was born).
"…Love your neighbor as yourself" (Matthew 22:39b). I went outside the house and sat under the tree where my father found me crying. He asked me what happened. I told my dad the whole story and he told me "let us go in the house." When my father took me back in the house, he asked my mother "why didn't you provide the banana to *each* of the children?" Before she even answered the question, my father told each of my siblings to cut the banana twice. "Each of you give Jemimah half of your banana!" He instructed. At that, my brother was taking a long time to cut his banana. My mother started calling each of my siblings by their names. Finally, I ended up eating more than all of them combined (plus the sweet potato which my mom originally game me)! I ate even

more bananas than I would have if I had gotten an equal share at the beginning. I saw my dad fight for me that day! What this story taught me in my journey today is that when things become hard, we need not to fight for ourselves, because God has good plans for us and He will fight for us. When things sound hard, God will always send someone to us like the way God sent my father at the right time before my brothers and sisters had started eating their bananas. We need to be patient – it pays off! *"The Lord Himself will fight for you, you need only be still (Exodus 14:14)"* This scripture encourages me that God is a provider. The same thing is true in the Kingdom of heaven. We may feel forgotten by people, families, friends and the community, but our father in heaven gives us far more than we can expect. *"Now all glory to God, who is able through His mighty power at work within us, to accomplish infinitely more than we might ask or think." (Ephesians 3:20)* Sometimes, the last children get overlooked in the family. The Bible tells us about the story of the children of Jesse, the father of King David. Nobody remembered David – He was often still outside watching over the animals. But God ALWAYS saw him! While many overlooked him, God called Samuel to anoint David as the King of Israel. The story of David helps me on my own journey, especially when I read Psalm 23 *"God is my shepherd, I shall not want. He makes me to lay down beside still water. He sets my table in the presence of my enemies. Though I walk through the valley of the shadow of death, I will fear no evil, for God is with me. His rod and staff comfort me. He anoints me with oil. My cup is overflowing." (Psalm 23)*

Since I was a little girl, I was taught to obey my parents and big brothers and sisters. I was taught that when my mother or my father sent me, I was not to ask any questions, just to obey. If they asked me to do something I did not want to do, I was to do it anyway and then come back and ask questions (but not before I had done what they asked).

My Christian life in the community grew my faith when I started attending Sunday school and attending the youth activities in our church programs. My mother and my father helped me to love the ministry of the church and I ultimately came to know Jesus as my personal Lord and Savior! The bible reminds me, *"For it is with your heart that you believe and are justified, and it is with your mouth that you profess your faith and are saved (Romans 10:10)"* This became my identity and purpose: to tell my family and friends that Jesus can save and sustain! Today, I have a powerful testimony of seeing God's faithfulness over many years. I have had the privilege of witnessing to many people and I have gotten to see many people come to know the Lord as people have heard about God's faithfulness through my own journey (through happiness, sadness, struggle and everything). God has been faithful! During my life, my testimony has been a powerful tool in my ministry. God has sustained me in difficulties and in happiness to see people growing spiritually. I have seen the heart of the Lord in my life and in my ministry (and through my family).

I experienced many difficulties in my early education. My family was the only family in the area where whose children shared the same single school uniform. My sister and I shared it. Since our home was in the valley, I used to meet with my sister at the water spring and change into the uniform (my sister, who was older, went to school in the morning, and I used to go in the afternoon). So, my sister would give me her uniform for school, and I would give her the dress I had. She would go back home with the dress I was wearing the whole morning, while I would head off to school in the uniform. Sharing a single uniform was a shameful thing, especially since my father was on the school board and was a leader in the Christian church. It was not a good example to those who were not Christians in the community. Let me tell you something interesting. My mother knew how to stitch, and when our uniform was torn, she was able to sew patches over the tears so often, that you could not tell what color the original uniform actually was. We used to make money from picking coffee, but my dad was so stingy with the money he made, that my mom could not buy us uniforms. He viewed having a uniform for each child as a waste of money. My father was known in the community as a man who had a lot of money, but it was still hard for him to buy his own children uniforms. I remember one day he told our mother to meet in our local town and buy us uniforms. When we reached the store, my mother was busy fitting us in our uniforms. We later came to find out that our dad did not have small enough bills, and he did not want to break the note for our uniforms! We left the store sad and without what we came for.

In addition to sharing my school uniform with my sister, I had to walk each way to school (8 miles each way, so 16 miles round trip each day). I had to carry my lunch, my books and the gardening tools (we learned about farming in school). Did I mention that we did not have shoes? It's true! I walked all those miles to school each day and did all this barefooted! My father was often the last parent in the community to pay his school fees for his children. He was not able to buy kerosene for our lamps for light (to do our homework in the evening) . Instead, we burned firewood to create light to do our homework and study at night. The good news is that we still got our educations and finished school, despite all of the unnecessary hardships (coffee picking, uniforms, walking miles, shame and so on). This taught me a lesson. Going through this (with the lack of support through my early education) did NOT stop me. The hardships did not stop God's blessings for my education. Even now, I am writing this book and I have overcome barriers to live, prosper and be lifted by hope. This lesson was not just for my education, but it was a powerful lesson for my spiritual journey as well. I learned that life and dreams do not always come easy, but the journey is worth it. That hardship came to be something that gives me strength and power today. I can encourage people even today who go through different kinds of hardship. From the depths of my heart, I still remember that God was with me and I knew that He had good plans for my future. Hardship does not prevent us from receiving blessings from our mighty God. The goal is not to get ease and comfort, it is for God to make us holy and humble. We learn through hardship – it is a process that forms us. *"For I know the plans I have for you, declares Lord. Plans to prosper you and not to harm you. Plans to give you a hope and a future." (Jeremiah 29:11)*. My prayer is to be a good model and to demonstrate to my family, friends and believer that with God, you can make it! Even if you go deep into the valley, God is there with you. The same God who empowered Moses, is still the same God today.

On my journey, God opened the doors for me to not only succeed through early education, but to go on to earn my bachelor's degree (in 1997), 2 master's degrees (in pastoral counseling and a Master's in Divinity) and my doctorate (of ministry in church leadership D.Min). During my studies later in life, I had an opportunity to complete seven units of Clinical Pastoral Education (CPE). Finally, I became the first new immigrant woman to be ordained by the Presbyterian Church USA from Africa.

l prayed to God that I would work hard to provide necessities for their education when I had my own children. I wanted to support them (by all means) to achieve their educational goals. I did not want any of my children to suffer the way I did during my early education. I wanted to enable them to study for their own higher education. I wanted to be able to provide for their comforts and their needs. Instead of the model I had of my father being the last parent to pay the school fees, I would be the first parent to pay the school fees for my children (and I would work with them on their homework and take care of their needs during their schooling).

Growing up, we would remind our father about his teachings to the people. He was a leader in teaching other people. When I was growing up, I was praying that our father. I prayed that God would change him, so he would truly be a good model in the community as a leader. You see, our father was a preacher and he wanted the people to do what he was preaching, not what he was doing. We wanted him to walk out what he preached. This meant that my father was a leader in our community and many parents were coming to our home for help. Indeed, my father helped them in many ways, but never with money. Many people would come to work at our home and my father would go away for the whole day. I remember these people were waiting for my father until evening (for dad to pay them as they had agreed). My mother had a lot of difficulties in the community. Mom often visited needy families to share with them resources and God's word. *"Where two or three are gathered in my name, there I am in the midst of them." (Matthew 18:20)*. Every family she visited, they always talked about her husband (she had a hard task of defending our dad to others). She would humbly and strongly remind the community members to pray for her husband. Married women were called to be advocates for their husbands – this would increase love in the family and be a good witness to the rest of the community about God. My mother demonstrated well what it looks like to be an advocate for her family. God calls us all to this. *"…but as for me and my family, we will serve the Lord" (Joshua 24:15b)*

My mother was a peacemaker to everyone who was angry at our father. She tried to cover for our father and protect the way we looked at him. She would even talk to us and share with us, "maybe your father does not have the money to buy your uniform". My brother Naphtali Macharia would ask my mother "what about the milk we are selling and the coffee we are picking?" My brother would say, "He is being paid good money!" Mother told her story that even the time our dad was walking in town he provided for us, but when he did not have money, he could not buy us anything. My mother always was defending our father and sharing good things about our father saying, "your father will do now what he has not done before." My mother was known in the community as peace maker in the family. I learned a lot from my mother. I learned that I should defend and respect my husband, so that I can bring peace into my family.

My sisters and my brothers struggled in our education, but finally each of us finished a little academic education. As I shared earlier, I remember when I was in primary school, I used to walk sixteen miles a day. As I shared earlier, at that time, during our gardening education, we had to carry tools to work in the garden (agricultural class was one of our subjects), and I had to carry my heavy school bag and my lunch. Walking all those miles each day, carrying what was required by our class teacher. I used not to wear shoes for all those miles and we used to walk on the rough road.

I prayed and told God that if I had a family someday, I would not do to them what our father did to us. I wanted to be generous, not stingy. God later gave me the ability to meet all of the school needs of my children, and to be there for them; to enable them to become professionals. I wanted to be very supportive and loving. I have told this story to my own children, and I am sure that my children will treat their own children in a more merciful and compassionate way than my dad did with us. Although our dad did not give what we felt we needed, we still knew he loved us. I cannot forget that our dad did provide for us in other ways. Besides that, He helped me to see that if we seek God's Kingdom first, God will provide everything else we need (in His timing). *"Seek first God's kingdom and his righteousness, and all these things will be given to you as well" (Matthew 6:33).* I humble myself when I talk with my children. It was not that my parents did not love me, but it was because they did not have all the resources (I would drop my children to school and pick them up because I had a car. My kids did not have to walk even a minute to get to the car - they themselves got driven to school and had everything they needed, including money for lunch). I thank God that I was later able to educate my children and support them (by all means). By God's grace, my husband and I were able to do whatever we could to support them for their education. When I have shared these stories with my own children, they could not believe it or relate to it. "It was unbelievable that mom would walk sixteen miles without shoes!"

I grew up in a community where there were not many other Christians. Many families used to not visit us very often because my parents were not liked by the (non-Christian) community. This was because my parents were against some of harmful cultural practices of the community at the time. My father encouraged parents to educate their children, which was not common. My parents encouraged other parents to take their children (sons and daughters) to school. My parents were teaching the families in the community not to perform ritual circumcision on their daughters. There was a belief in the community that if you did not circumcise your daughter, she would not get a man to marry her in the community (because all the girls who were circumcised were known in the community – this was a community ritual). The other practice my parents fought against in the community was marriage enforcement of the girls who were underage.

Some families were forcing young girls to be married to the rich men in the community (wealth was defined as families having many goats and cows). The wealthy man's family would exchange some cows and goats as a dowry for the girl, which was seen as a gain for the family. Families in my community did not educate girls because they believed that if the girls were educated, they would not get married to the rich men who were known in the community. Missing out on marrying into a wealthy family was viewed as a loss to the parents and to the whole family. The families believed it important to educate only the sons (because even if the sons were educated, they still would remain at home with their parents). All of these cultural practices were against the teachings of the Church. The practices were in conflict with the Christian teachers and missionaries. This was offensive to those who were not Christians in the community and especially to those who were taking part in some of these cultural practices. Yes, some young girls used to die because of excess bleeding after circumcision. In different families, it was believed that the woman who was not circumcised would never became mature (and that was the reason why was difficult to marry a girl who was not circumcised). They believed that if a girl was not circumcised, she would continue to talk like a child and act like a young boy (climbing on trees, etc).

During my childhood, my siblings and I were protected from friendships of children from the non-Christian families in the community. We were really protected too much (overprotected) by our parents, and we used to miss out on playing with our peers in the community because our parents would not allow us to visit with kids from our age group in the community. If our mother was to go somewhere, she would give us enough homework to occupy us until she came back home. We did not have time to go out and play or have fun with the other children outside. We were protected against having friendships with other girls and boys in the community (especially those who are not coming to church or who were in their parents' practices). I used to secretly go out to seek kids my age from the community so that we could play together and talk in our own languages. Our parents always wanted us to interact only with the other children in our church (Christians only), not the greater community.

We grow up being isolated in the community because my parents were the only Christians there. Christians were the minorities in the community and my parents did not want their children to have any relationships with families who were not Christians. The fear was that the non-Christian children would not behave well (even as children, we were isolated, especially as girls. We used to be protected even more than the boys because of the false marriages and female circumcision). My parents had a lot of fear regarding the abuse of young girls.

In my village, I was known as a happy little girl and I would greet everyone socially who came on my way. When I was in grade one, my teacher used to call me "Makena" (which means "happy girl"). Something that I cannot forget is that I deeply wanted to help the old women. If I happened to see an old lady going to fetch water from the spring, I would run to her and ask her if I could go down to the river and bring some water for her. I believe some of the things I did in my community to serve older women led me to the ministry I have today.

The other thing I can remember is that when we were watching our cows and goats in the field with other children, we used to play very much. We loved jumping over the logs. We would have competitions to see how many times in a row we could jump over the logs.

Another thing I cannot forget is that one day we were too busy arguing over who did more log jumping. While we were arguing, the cows and the goats went into my neighbor's garden and ate all of their crops! This happened because at that time no one was taking care of the cows and goats (it was supposed to be our job). It was our responsibility to take care of them and we instead were playing. Unfortunately, we forgot that, and continued being busy playing. We did not realize that already the cows and goats were in the neighbor's garden eating up their crops.

Let me tell you that when the owner of the garden came, he removed the cows from his garden himself. He called us softly and he grabbed us by our arms, one by one, and he held our hands, too. He could do this because we were not big; we were little girls. He took a very hot plant (called "thabai") and he whipped us with it. We were beaten very well and since we did not have underwear then, you can imagine how hot it was on the backs of our thighs. I remember my skin reacted and I was not able to sit down for at least a few hours.

When we went home, my mom told me to sit down. I said, "I want to stand up". I was hiding because if I told her that we had been beaten (and the reason why), my mother might have beaten us a second time. After a short time, the owner of the garden came and asked where our mother was. When I saw him, I jumped outside and hid myself in the banana tree leaves. You know what, my brother went straight there and told my mother "Jemimah is hiding over there near that banana tree!" My mother came out to me and she pulled me from the leaves. She did not ask me any questions. Instead, she just started beating me, pulling my ears and my cheek. I had not yet told her the reason I was not able to sit down. The old man was still there watching my mother beating me, and he said to my mother, "that is enough, because I have done it before you." She did not know that he had already given us discipline first.

Then my mother asked me, "were you beaten by Baba Muchina?" I said "yes", then she looked at my skin and she felt sorry. She took me in the house and washed me with warm water and with salt. It was more painful than before. I started crying, calling my mother and shouting saying "Maitu! Maitu!" (which means "mother, mother"). "It is ok, I will never repeat that again" she said. I cried until I slept on the floor. Since my mother had loved me so much, she said to me "I know you are a good girl, but why did you go to play with the children of Baba Karebe?" She continued, "I know they are the ones who influenced you to play outside rather than taking care of the cows and goats (until they went to eat our neighbor's crops)". I had learned my lesson. My mother finished,

"You will never repeat that again. You have learned a good lesson today."

I remember at that time, my two little brothers were laughing at me saying "Jemimah okay Wambugo okay" (Wambugo is my middle name). "Umeshika hadafu" (Swahili words, meaning "you are now disciplined"). The following day, I took our cows to the same spot, and my mother called and told me "Okay, are you going to do what you did the other day?" I just kept quiet because I did not want anyone to remind me of that day. Everyone in the community knew that I was beaten by the owner of the garden (and at the same time my mother did the same). It was not a good picture since, I was known as a good Christian girl and I went to church every Sunday (especially because the children I was playing with were from a non-Christian family).

While I was still there taking care of the cows and goats, the same girls came from their homes, but I did not talk with them. They were asking me if I could play with them. My mother had observed me from very far away. When I came home, she came and asked me, "okay, your friends have come again?" I replied politely "no, I did not talk to them." My mother asked me "Jemimah, did you forget what happened the other day?" At that time, my mother wanted to remind me that she had refused the company of those girls in our community. It was a shame that I stopped to play with those girls my age. Although I made a poor choice, it was painful for me because those girls would still pass by where we used to play. They could come there to show me that they still continued to play the games that we had played together. I was grieving to be rejected by my old friends (because I was to show them that I needed to obey my mother's rules). *"Honor your father and mother. Then you will live a long, full life in the land that the Lord your God is giving you" (Exodus 20:12)*

Another thing I cannot forget to mention in this book is that during that time, children were not allowed to drink tea with sugar. The children's drinks were only porridge (this is something like hot oatmeal) morning, afternoon and evening. Every day the porridge was the children's drink. One day, my mother forgot to lock the drawer where she kept the sugar. That day, she come home and cooked tea (but for us, no sugar). That evening I sat where I usually sit (near my mother's drawer where she kept the sugar and salt). You know what, mom's tin of sugar and salt looked alike! I put my hand quietly into the drawer, and I reached the tin of salt, thinking that it was sugar. I did that very fast before my mom noticed, but I made a mistake! I had put salt in my tea instead of sugar! The reason I was doing that is because we were not allowed to taste sugar. Because it was forbidden, I wanted to taste the sugar! After putting the salt, I took a drink of my tea. The taste was horrible! My mother did not notice, and that was the end of the story (because nobody saw me putting my hand into my mother's tin and I was not about to let on that my drink tasted so badly). I was never caught by my parents, but God saw everything that happened. We need to remember that the things we do in darkness, God always reveals. *"The time is coming when everything that is covered up will be revealed, and all that is secret will be made known to all." (Luke 12:2)*

Another time, I was helping my mother carry some bananas to our open market to sell. My parents had a lot of bananas in their garden (and we used to sell bananas for my parents to get money to pay school fees for my elder brothers who were at school). My late brother Naphtali Macharia was a beloved son by my dad. I can remember my mother selling bananas, but the money was not enough to cover his school costs. My dad had to sell a cow (which was giving the family milk and was a sacrifice) simply because his beloved son needed to be educated. *"I will never fail you. I will never abandon you"* *(Hebrews 13:5)*

4. Sports

I was born as the seventh child of my parents. I was so small in body that you could count my ribs. I was also taller than all my brothers and sisters. My mother was short, and her body was small, so I was very different from her physically. I used to be selected in the community as the best athlete. My height really helped to reach where the short girls in the community could not reach.

What I remember (when I was between 8 to 10 years old) is that I used to help my mother in collecting the firewood, fetching the water from the spring and cooking. I would also help to serve the elderly women in the community (I would fetch firewood for them). Any time I was sent by my mom to do all of those activities, I would go running and jumping all the time (over and over). So, when I grew older, it made sense that I got involved with sports - it was fun and reminded me of my childhood.

Being involved in track and field (particularly high jumps), reminded me of the way I was used to play as a child (over jumps and high jumps). My teacher nicknamed me "impala" in Track and Field, because I ran like the very fast animal in Kenya. I was the fastest.

I used to win most high jump competitions (and other short races) which gave me confidence from winning races. I was selected from my community and my school to represent us and compete against other athletes.

The following were my favorite games (and I was known as an expert in): high jump, long jump, 100-yard track, 220-yard track and 440-yard track relay. These were the games that I excelled in (and I was known as the best athlete in the community for these events). Among these, the 100-yard dash was a challenge to me because I did not use the proper sports shoes (once again, my father could not afford to buy the shoes for me or pay the athletic fees). Sometimes the other runners had the proper shoes, but not me. I was barefoot. After I finished the 100-yard race, I remember my whole body would shake (like someone who had been in the cold) and my feet could hurt very much because the track field was rough (not smooth), with small stones. We had to run very fast - 100 yards full speed in racing was a challenge, especially without shoes.

My teenage life was full of sports achievements. I was the topmost in my community. Most of the things I enjoyed were the celebrations after the competitions. Many young people would carry me high. holding my awards and presents (gifts like basins, bar soap, machetes, and so on). They would hold me up, carrying green tree branches (which signifies success) singing the victory of my winning trophies in those sports. People were proud of me because I was representing our community.

This reminds me of how many people will hold us up when we get into heaven, after the victory of struggling, we will receive the trophies of the race of this world. That celebration is what we focus on in our spiritual journey. After winning (in being faithful to God), the angels and saints before us will celebrate. *"Therefore, since we are surrounded by such a huge crowd of witnesses to the life of faith, let us strip off every weight that slows us down, especially the sin that so easily trips us up. And let us run with endurance the race God has set before us. We do this by keeping our eyes on Jesus, the champion who initiates and perfects our faith, because of the joy awaiting Him, He endured the cross* (Hebrews 12:1-3)"

My coach used to tell us to focus on the finishing tape. We were not to look to either side or pay attention to the crowds around us. The end of the race was our goal. As believers, we are called to focus on the goal as well. We are not to get distracted by what is around us, but we are to push toward the prize He has called us to. *"Not that I have already obtained all this, or have already arrived at my goal, but I press on to take hold of that for which Christ took hold of me. Brothers and sisters, I do not consider myself yet to have taken hold of it. But one thing I do: forgetting what is behind and straining*

toward what is ahead. I press on toward the goal to win the prize for which God has called me heavenward in Christ Jesus" *(Philippians 3:12-14)* It is a wake-up call because it does not matter how difficult it is on our journey. We are called to focus on Jesus.

In addition to track and field, I was also quite good at basketball (go figure). I was a defender and a shooter. When my team was being defeated, I would go to defense and turn the game around so we would win. Our team would win so much, that one day the opposing team said, "we will not compete if Jemimah plays. It is not fair. She is so tall - she shoots, and she defends!" One day, the school leadership had a discussion about this. They decided not to let me play anymore. I was crying, and I was so sad. My father came to me and said, "that's okay, you're still my daughter". This reminds me of the way God comforts us as His children. When we are rejected because of our success or our ability, God comes to us and comforts. Our success today as believers is to be lifted by hope and to live out the gospel of Christ. Not everybody will like us or cheer for us when we succeed and do our best. *"Now may our Lord Jesus Christ himself and God our Father, who loved us and by his grace gave us eternal comfort and a wonderful hope, comfort you and strengthen you in every good thing you do and say." (2 Thessalonians 2:16-17)*

5.   My Christian Life in the Village

My Christian life in my village was overwhelming. There were a lot joys, and most of the time there were challenges. This is because my family was known as the

"church family" (which meant we could not do most of the things other young people were doing over the weekends).

Saturdays and Sundays were the time for the young boys and girls to meet and talk and share fun for the day. Most of the other children's parents were not Christians, so their parents were okay with them spending time outside. Unlike my parents, the parents of non-christian families did not ask, and they were not concerned about where their children had been. Our parents were overprotective.

I cannot even now tell you what those kids were doing out there (because I was not there and I did not see), but some of the children at school would share with me about what they were doing (when we would meet at school during our break times). The girls would tell me how they went to the bush to meet with boys to dance. They had homemade instruments (guitars, drums and other traditional instruments) to play music while they danced. The girls at school shared with me that at these dances girls and boys would dance together! This dancing together was just for fun, it was not romantic. Boys and girls in my community could not have boyfriends or girlfriends because they would have to marry who their family set them up with anyway later.

The girls in my community used to marry very young because marriage, not school, was not the family's priority. These marriages were called "enforcement marriages" or arranged marriage. Those parents wanted to see that the girls were getting married to boys from rich

families (with many goats and cows). The families (not the boys or girls) would arrange the marriages. The future husbands and wives did not have the choice of who they were to marry. When it was time for the girl to get married, the parents of the girl expected a dowry from the boy's family. Once boys and girls were married, they stopped going to school. So, this demonstrated that education was not important to many of the families in our community.

When a boy turned around 17, his parents would build a hut (thingira) outside, close to their own home. The boy would begin to sleep there in the hut until the parents selected the girl they wanted him to marry. Once the girl was chosen, they would instruct the other youth in the community to lay in wait for her while she was going to fetch water in the spring near their home. When they saw her, they would physically grab her and carry her up high. They would bring her to the boy's hut. Once the boy's parents were informed, she been taken to his hut. The parents would take a goat and a lamb and deliver them to the parents of the girl. They would inform her parents that their daughter was not lost – they were coming to report that she was safe. At this point, the two families would meet to negotiate the dowry for their daughter. This was typically in the form of cows and sheep. Once this was agreed upon, the traditional marriage ceremony followed, and the boy and girl would start their new family together.

6.   Church Activities

My parents were taught by the Presbyterian missionaries from Scotland. The Presbyterian missionaries came to Kenya in 1891. They were a medical doctor, a pastor and a school teacher. They started treating people, educating and evangelizing. They first came to a place called Kibwezi. After some of the missionaries died and were buried there, others traveled to a placed Kikuyu, where they also started teaching, serving and evangelizing. They later went to a place Tumutumu. They spread out in the community and came to place called Kirindundu where they started ministry there as well.

My parents lived in Kirindundu and this is where they came to our community and where they found my father and my mother as teenagers. My parents started coming to the missionaries' class. My mother told me the story. My mother would be given salt so that she would not miss the next day's class. My dad was given sugar for the same reason. My mom told me her teacher was a woman named Phoebe. They would not miss the class because it was exciting. My mother was also given a head scarf by the missionaries. My parents were taught Christianity. Because my parents went to the missionary classes together, they got to know one another. They were taught how to read the bible and they were baptized (my mom and dad were baptized at the same time).

The missionaries did the first wedding in the community…with my parents! After they married, my parents were blessed with their first child, a son, in 1922. My parents continued being taught by the missionaries. After their firstborn, my parents were blessed with ten more children (and two died before I was born).

Altogether, my parents were blessed to raise five sons and four daughters. I was the seventh born and the baby daughter of my mom. I was a special daughter in the family.

As I was "mom's girl". Growing up, I used to follow my mother to many of the Church fellowship meetings for women and to other places where my mother was volunteering (to help the needy in the community). During this time, I learned a lot from my mother and from the women who were friends with my mother. I started to learn how to provide and care for those who needed care in the community. I remember my mother sending me to take food to a family she knew needed food. My mother was a hard worker and what I remember is that we used to prepare food each day. I loved helping my mother cook, fetch firewood, draw water from the spring and to serve. When I came to seminary, I reflected on what my mom was doing. I came to realize that my mother had actually been a pastoral care giver to members of her community. Observing my mother and her activities in the community helped me to become the pastoral care giver that I am today. I learned to become a caregiver during the time I was working and serving with my mom - to give pastoral care to the community. She modeled it for me and showed me how to do it. When God later called me into full-time vocational ministry, my mom's story was always on my fingertips.

My mother used to pray for the food every morning. She would often ask one of us to pray for the food before we ate our breakfast. She used to pray for God to take care of as we went to school and coming back home. She used to cook a lot of food and keep it outside in a store which is called (Ikumbi). That food would last for two or three days and not go bad. Anytime someone in our family was hungry, they could go to that store and get some food. If we had a friend with us, we could also get food for them.

During that time, I learned how to serve in the church activities. I learned that I should not complain while Church activities, because my mother taught me that if I do something grudgingly and complaining, there would be no blessings from it. I wanted to be blessed, so I would not complain (I truly wanted blessings from God). This is what my mother taught me. I never heard my mother complaining about the church activities, even though she had so many responsibilities.

Every Saturday, my family would go to the spring and wash our clothes so that we would have fresh, clean clothes to wear on Sunday for church. After our mom prepared our clothes for church, we would then go to the church building and clean it to make it ready for the next day's church. I remember every Saturday, I would go with my mother to clean the church and dust the pews for the preparation of Sunday worship. After that, we would pass by people in the community and remind them about the coming Sunday worship. "Church is tomorrow!"

On Sunday morning, we would wake up early to have prayers and eat breakfast. We were given corn, eggs, or potatoes to bring to the church as our offering. Each Sunday, my mother always made sure we brought our offering to the house of the Lord. In Sunday school, I would sing choruses of songs and recite memory verses in Scripture. When I later went to seminary, my Sunday school training (songs that taught me the books of the bible and truths from God's word) were a great blessing. God's word was written on my heart from a young age. I still know those songs to this day. One such chorus was a song that helped me to learn the books of the New Testament. This is one of the most memorable songs I learned, *"Mathago, Manko, Luca, Johana, Atumwa, Roma, Akoronitho ni'en', Agaratha, Aferso, Timotheo nayo ni en, Jaknkbu, Petero nao ne atatu, Petero nao ni atatu, Judasi, Kugurririo"* It was in Sunday School, that I also learned and memorized John 3:16 *"For God so loved the world that He gave His only begotten son, so that whoever believes in Him will not perish but have everlasting life."* *(John 3:16)* In Kikuyu, that same verse is *"Tondu Ngai niguo endire kinndi gia guku thi niguo mundo owothe ndakore no agie na muoyo watene natene (Johanna 3:16)"*

Most of the time, my mother would lead prayers during the worship service and my father would give the announcements. Of course, my father never forgot to remind farmers of the days for picking the coffee. The days to pick coffee in the community were Tuesdays, Thursdays and Saturdays. He also made announcements encouraging farmers to take care of their cows. He also shared any other announcements that were good for the community to know. My uncle Jotham Maranga (Dad's brother) would read the scriptures and conduct the singing. Uncle Jotham used to sing a Kikuyu song. It went, "uka, uka hari kwi jesu uka hari we oriu…" This song meant, "come, come to Jesus right now." Even today, that song is still in my heart. Something I cannot forget is that every Sunday, my mother gave her children something to bring to the house of God as an offering. Some Sundays, we brought whole corn (white maize). Other Sundays we might bring one egg each, or little bag of beans.

After Sunday School, in the evenings during dinnertime, my dad would ask each of us what we learned that day in Sunday School. We would have to tell him, but before we shared, he asked us who our Sunday School teacher was that day (it was funny because our teacher was always my father). We had to share with our dad that night what we had been taught by the "Sunday School teacher". He asked us so that he knew we were paying attention (understanding and taking his messages to heart). My father believed deeply the truth in proverbs that says, *"Train up a child in the way he should go, and when he is old, he will not turn from it." (Proverbs 22:6)* He was asking us the questions, and there was a consequence for not knowing the answers. Whichever of his children did not know the answers, had to stay home the following Sunday and cook food for the others to come and eat after church. We did not want to miss church, so we tried hard to pay attention.

The foundation that was laid in my youth continues to motivate me today. My life has been filled with surprises. Because of the church activities of my youth, I remember that when my children were growing up, if someone called my house to say they wanted to come visit, the children would tell them to come directly to the church "because my mom is always in church".

All my life, I have been very active life with church activities. This has been true in Kenya (in rural areas, and in city Presbyterian churches). Places like Karindundu Karatina, Endarsha Muiga Nyeri, Karunaini Ihururu Nyeri, and Bahati Nairobi city Kenyan Presbyterian churches. I have also been active with church activities in the United States. American churches I have been a part of have included Southminster Presbyterian Church in St. Louis, Missouri; Hyde Park Presbyterian Church in Chicago, Illinois; Mishawaka Presbyterian Church in South Bend, Indiana; United African Presbyterian Church in St. Louis, Missouri (under the Giddings-Lovejoy Presbytery); Neema African Refugee Presbyterian Fellowship in Denver, Colorado (under the Denver Presbytery); Providence Bible Church in Denver, Colorado; Neema African Refugee Fellowship in Denver, Colorado.

I have served in various roles in the Presbyterian Church USA and Presbyterian Church East Africa (PCEA). The following are some positions I have served in:

- Deaconess – Hospital Chaplain
- Giddings-Lovejoy Presbytery Staff
- Evangelist
- Church Elder
- Preacher
- Woman Leader
- Hospital Staff Leader
- Leader of the Department of Hospital Chaplains

- Children's Sunday School Teacher
- School Parent Board Member
- Representative of New Immigrants Presbyterian Women Churchwide (USA)
- Ordained Presbyterian Minister
- Spiritual Leader of United African Presbyterian Church
- Stephen Ministry Leader and Trainer
- Spiritual Director Leader
- Coordinator of Values-leadership Nairobi Kenya
- and more and more.

I thank God that He has given me a compassionate heart. By God's grace, I have touched many souls during the time of my church leadership in my life. Presently, my passion is to walk the journey of refugees from Africa who are arriving to the United States in my community. I will comfort them, cry with them, support them, listen to their struggles, help them to overcome culture shock, and to love them (because I had friends who loved me when I first arrived in America from Kenya). My husband (Mr. Benson Ngatia Wanjau) was very supportive and compassionate to all of God's ministries I have done. He has always been a part of my ministry.

7. The Marriage Process Begins

As you continue to read this book, I hope it will give you an idea of the way marriage is viewed in the Kikuyu culture. I also pray that my story gives you insights into some of the traditions practiced by different people in the world.

My marriage story is very interesting. I got married without knowing what I would experience in life. I did not know what to expect about being a wife and a mother.

My older brother Naftali Macharia was living in Nairobi City. He had recently bought a new car. He left his old car at his house and the older car had been stolen (from where he had parked it) when he left. You see, he had come home to show off his new car in the countryside (Karatina Town, where he was born and raised). That night, some robbers came to steal his old car. Unfortunately, those same robbers then used his stolen car to go on a crime spree – they did several other robberies in the area using my brother's car! The robbers were chased by the police, but they got away and were not caught.

When my brother returned home, he discovered his old car was not where he had parked it. He went to the police station to report his stolen car. At the police station, he was interrogated (because his car had been used in robberies). He had to prove that when the car was stolen, he was out of town. When he gave his statement (at the Central Police Station in Nairobi), the officer that took his report sent a message to the Karatina police station. They passed this information on to the Karatina police station to verify whether or not Naftali was telling the truth. At that time, Benson Ngatia (my future husband) was a police officer working in a crime investigation department at the Karatina police station. Benson was sent to my brother's home to interview people and confirm my brother's whereabouts during the time of the crimes. As a part of the investigation, Benson came to my parents' home. There he saw my dad. That first meeting was also the first time that Benson saw me. It was ultimately proven that my brother was indeed out of town when the car was stolen (and there was no longer a case against him).

After that first meeting, Benson became a friend to my dad and he would come to visit my father regularly after that. He quickly became like part of our family. At the same time Benson was befriending my father, he also began pursuing me (I did not know this at first). Benson often used my sister Cecilia Wanjeri to call me without my parents knowing about it. Benson continued coming back to my house again and again until he finally went to his parents and told them about me.

As I mentioned earlier, I got married when I was so young because I wanted to move out from my parents' home. I did not have any career before I got married, but my father took me to a school (called "Singer Tailoring School") where I learned how to sew clothing for women. I was trained to make and to cut dresses and children's clothing. Knowing how to make the clothing was my first job, and I received my own money. I had opened a small sewing business. I used my earnings to support my mother and to buy the only salt in our home. Even though I was making some money, I was not making enough money to pay for the clothing materials and for the monthly store rent. I was struggling to keep the business afloat. Benson once brought his trousers out to be mended by one of the tailors in the store where I worked.

I was not sure whether to get married (I was not ready or prepared). I wanted to start my new marriage away from my parents because of hardship, but I was not quite sure what my marriage might be like or how to approach it (because I was still very young). I did not know where to start. I was not ready to get married, but circumstances encouraged me to start thinking about getting married and moving out of my parents' house.

The desire for marriage at first was like a secret between me and Benson. Benson never actually asked me to get married, but I came to know he was truly interested in marrying me for the first time when he eventually brought his parents to meet mine. Usually, when the family of the groom comes home for negotiations, the bride is not supposed to be present for the talk. However, I was there. I still remember when they came to our home. My parents had no idea why they had come (in fact, at first, my dad thought they must just be there because Benson was friends with my dad). Benson's parents told my parents that Benson was "interested in one of their daughters." Since my other sisters were already married, my dad said, "all of my daughters are already gone. There is just Jemimah and she is still very young". My father was not ready to accept the message that Benson's parents were coming for *my* hand in marriage. My parents still viewed me as a child and they were not ready to admit that I was old enough to be approached by a man. When

Benson's parents came, I saw them coming through the gate. Just like it was a surprise for my parents, I also did not know why his parents were coming or where they were coming from. I had never even seen them before (and of course my parents had not seen them either). They came from a far away and different community than our own. I had never seen them before, but when I looked at them, I thought they were weird (the way they dressed was different – not like my parents). The other thing about Benson's parents was that they were not Christians. They did not have proper clothes and shoes (like my dad and mom). Instead, they wore homemade sandals made from car tires called "Nyamuga". Benson's mother was not wearing a dress (she was wearing a wrap). She had recently shaved her head, and her scalp was shiny because she had put oil on it. Only Benson was dressed "properly." The rest of his family seemed peculiar to me.

I was not present for what followed, but I was told later that they sat down over a lot of food. They began negotiating with my parents. Benson's parents were told to bring the dowry they had agreed upon on their next visit. Benson's family was told to bring a goat and a lamb so that the families could continue negotiations.

After they left (several days later), Benson came back to me and told me that he was interested in marrying me (I did not know this until then). So, he invited me for dinner where he expressed his intentions to me. He told me he had been praying that when he approached me to be his wife, I would not turn him down. God answered his prayers and I said yes. I was excited because he was a handsome man. He was so smart and well-dressed (as a police officer). I loved many qualities about him, especially that he loved the Lord. The journey of Benson and I truly began on this day. We talked and agreed that we wanted to get married. He agreed to take me to his family and go through the next steps. Before I would be taken to meet his family, I decided to share this with my mom. It was then that she revealed that she had already known that Benson was interested in me (and had already spoken with his parents).

Soon after, I was taken to Benson's home to see his family. I grew up in the countryside. Benson also grew up in the countryside, but it was a totally different area. His family was excited to meet me there. I remember hearing the women in the house talking amongst themselves behind my back ("look what Benson has brought us!"). They made fun of me because I was so skinny and looked very young. They had cooked a lot of food because Benson told them "our special guest is coming". I felt sad when I heard this. When I came, there was too much food (and too many people). There were many women from his community preparing food. They were excited because Benson had never told them before about bringing a friend home to meet the family. One thing I remember was that they had also prepared homemade alcohol. It used to make them drunk. The women in the community wanted to go to the forest and fetch firewood to brew the alcohol. They used sugar cane, honey, tree leaves called "Miratina" (which was something like pawpaw which grows in the trees) and water. They would mix the ingredients together in a giant pot. They would pour the concoction into pots and place them around the fire. The process lasted several days. This preparation was a big job in the community. Every woman in the area needed to go the jungle to fetch water and firewood for the liquor. (Later, it would become difficult for me to fetch these things in the jungle because I knew it would be used to brew the alcohol). This distressed me. I later shared about it with my mom and dad. I wondered if this was the kind of life I, too, would have if I married into Benson's family and community. Since my parents did not want me to get married (they believed I was too young), they felt bad for me and had mercy on my situation because of what Benson's family was doing.

Finally, Benson's parents brought the dowry. The came again a third time, this time asking for permission to hold the wedding. They were given permission. Benson and I agreed about the date. Benson and I were wed in the same church that my parents were married in (the Presbyterian church that had been founded by the Scottish missionaries). The wedding was so colorful! It was the "wedding of the year" in our area! There was so much food!

After the wedding, I had still some sadness in my heart and fear about what I might be entering into. I had no idea what marriage had in store for me. After I got married, we stayed together for one year and then he took me home to stay with his parents. I was living with his mother, his father and his relatives.

When I got married, I did not have a job. My work was to cultivate the land with my mother-in-law and Benson's family. His family taught me a lot because there many things about the home I did not learn from my mother (like fetching water the way they did, gathering fire wood from the jungle and also picking tea leaves). I tell you, it was a blessing to me that I was not picking coffee any longer! One of the things I did with my mother-in-law was to go to the open market to sell vegetables (potatoes, beans, and so on). I was her helper. We would go together two days per week. I would help her carry all the goods we sold in the market.

My in-laws were not Christians. My father in-law was the oldest person in their household, so many people would come to the home to drink the liquor they prepared. I did not like this. Only my husband was baptized (he had been the only Christian in his family). It was difficult for me to interact with them (not praying and not reading the bible together). There were no spiritual practices in the community. It bothered me so much. This was very difficult and hard for me to live in the community without this fellowship. I cried out to God and asked Him why He brought me into this kind of family. I heard God share that He placed me into that family so that I could shine Christ's light there. I remember that song, "this little light of mine, I'm gonna let it shine." I started praying for God to show me how to reach them spiritually. It was a grief for me to see them without Christ. I asked God how I could share with them. I struggled and prayed.

I began sharing with my in-laws, and many of them come to know Jesus Christ as the Lord of their lives. I began holding house prayers and bible studies with the family. At that time, I introduced myself to the nearby

Presbyterian church ("Karikaruini Presbyterian Church"). I met with the elders and the pastor and they welcomed me. It was a special day in that congregation. I told them the story of my spiritual journey and they received me as a member of the church. I continued evangelizing in my new community (both within my extended family and in the community). Since I knew how to sew, I took the wrappers from my mother-in-law and I made her a dress. I also invited her to come with me to church. We continued going to church and praying together. Finally, my mother in-law trust in Jesus and was baptized (she was called 'Mercy Wanjugu Wanjau"). She started coming to church with me. She also became member of the church women's guild. When she eventually died, there was a celebration of her going home to God as a Christian. Also, my father in-law also came to trust Christ and he was baptized ("Peterson Wanjau Muthui"). When he eventually died, he also died as a Christian (but it just took longer for him to come to know Christ than his wife). Benson's parents went to be with the Lord when they died. They had become strong Christians!

God blessed Benson and I with a daughter in 1961. On April 15 of that year, our precious daughter Jane Ngatia was born. I taught her how to pray when she was still a baby. She would later become a prayer warrior. Benson left me home with his family and he returned to his work as a police officer. I was left at the home to care for our daughter. I was also caring for Benson's nephew (who was a young child at the time).

After some years, my husband removed me from his parents' home to a new location (called "Endarsha Muiga

Nyeri"). My husband built a very nice house for us. I started raising cows and pigs and planting and cultivating the potatoes, beans, corn, cabbage and wheat. My responsibilities included waking up at 3:00 a.m. and bringing the milk to be collected in the community for sale. During that time, my husband was working and living in town most of the time. He used to come home at the end of the month. When he came home, he used to bring us sugar, tealeaves, bar soap, cooking oil and bread for the children. One of the important gifts he brought to me (that I cannot forget) were the Gumboots (rain boots). I was wearing them every day until they give me a mark on my legs. I loved them. Even before he brought me the boots, I was known as the only one in the community to have shoes.

8.   Working in the Community

Since I was educated, when I took our milk to the collecting center, I used to help the clerk write in his ledger. I used to spend time there and I was well known to the other farmers. As I brought the milk to the collecting center, I would help the clerk register the farmers and record who had brought milk and how much each time (I noted how many pounds – we literally hung the milk on scales). I knew a little bit of English then, and I used to spend lots of time there helping out. I was a young, beautiful and intelligent woman!

There was a community general meeting in the area. The Community Development Officer came to visit our community. I was selected to give our gift to him and I spoke in front of everyone. We gave him fresh carrots, which we grew in the area. Several days after the meeting, the community leaders came to my house and asked whether I could start a day care for the children in the community. I waited for my husband to come back and asked whether I could do that. He gave me his permission, and I opened the daycare. I remember that I had 25 children (alone – no other adult leaders). I taught songs, bible choruses, drawing, ABCs, and other things to the children.

During the time I was teaching preschool, there was primary school called Charity Primary School. The headmaster (David Mwaura) was a Presbyterian. We discussed how we could start a bible study fellowship together. We then gathered people from the community to begin studying the word together. I met some likeminded people named Esther, Rahab, Milka, Joseph Kangethe and Peter Ndungu (I also talked with some parents of the children from the daycare). Like me, these were Christians who also did not yet have a good place to pray with other believers. They were excited for the community fellowship and Bible study. The headmaster and I were given a room to start the worship inside of his school building. We announced that we were starting worship and we continued every Sunday. Then we invited the Reverend Barnard Muindi to come and see us. He helped us to get organized. Of course, I was one of the leaders of the church (alongside the headmaster and other leaders). Very soon after the founding of the fellowship, we had the first wedding (Mr. and Mrs. Peter Ndungu Kanini). The headmaster and his wife were the best man and matron of honor, respectively. And I was the Master of Ceremonies– officiating the cutting of the cake. The church grew and grew. To this day, Charity Presbyterian Church still exists and it has so many members worshipping together!

Community leaders used to come and visit the daycare to see how everything was going. One day, the Community Development Officer came to visit our center. We had practiced songs for the children to sing for our guest. The children also shared bible verses they had memorized. He was so impressed. He loved to see how quickly the preschool had grown since we started.

After two days, I got a letter from him. I had been promoted from being a day care teacher to a Kiene West Community Development Assistant (CDA). I again asked my husband Benson for permission to accept this position, and he gave it again. My brother-in-law, on the other hand. had a harder time with me accepting this promotion. This was because I had been doing work for the family (in getting up each day at 3am to milk the cows and bring the milk to the collection center). Benson's brother knew that by accepting this position, it would mean more work for he and his wife to take on.

I became a leader of the zone we were in. I was given a scholarship to attend a training (Wambugu Farmer's Training Center) where I was taught to organize community development projects. There I was trained in cooking and I was taught to cook carrot soup and birthday cake. I started prayer group for the women in the community and I taught them to prepare the carrot soup and to bake bread. I went back to the community and I started helping people in my area launch self-help projects. This included churches, youth centers and women's groups. I led athletics for the young people (including track and football and soccer) and I organized adult literacy classes. I organized these projects and brought leaders in to teach them. We also had health centers where I would go and teach the women about personal hygiene, balanced diet and child care.

As you might imagine, I became very popular because of what I was doing in the community. I was given a bicycle with the registration of Kenya Government (KG). This empowered me travel to visit different projects throughout the community. I started making good money to help my family and members of the community. I was able to start community development projects all over. I helped the community start Presbyterian churches and Catholic churches (through the catholic priest serving those communities). I also opened more schools and health centers in the community development work I was doing. These projects were sponsored, supported and supervised by the government, and I was a government employee. There were other government employees in the community as well. We used to work together to share ideas with one another for the development of our community.

My work as a Community Development Assistant (CDA) was to supervise and empower the leaders of all the projects. My work was training the project leaders, bringing the women to the table and into leadership, finding resources for grants (for the mentioned community projects), and supporting and working together with the other leaders in the community. I needed to secure resources and funding to build leadership for schools, community educators and sports coaches.

After many years of involvement with the women and the youth in the community, my name was again proposed and recommended to be given another job – this time as a "Family Planning Motivator." For this position, I was given an office in town and I traveled to different areas helping women to understand family planning practices (birth control). I joined a family planning team. This was hard because I was hired by an organization called International Planned Parenthood Federation (IPPF). This was an organization from the United States of America (I did not know at the time all that Planned Parenthood represented in the United States and the controversy – I was only involved with specific aspects of what they were doing in my community with education and preventative birth control). I qualified for this position because of my previous experiences in community development. It was difficult because women did not want to space their children out. Birth control was something new to the parents – they had never heard of it before. My community did know about this foreign organization from the United States, and they did not understand what they were doing meddling in the affairs of Kenyan families. Additionally, the introduction of family planning was not understood by the men in the community either. I was sponsored to go to a training to be competent in this new system regarding family planning. In our context, family planning meant spacing out time between having babies so that people could have a stronger, healthier family. This organization believed that family planning helped build a healthier and stronger community (less children, they thought, would mean more resources to support the ones they did have. The idea was that family planning could help alleviate poverty). I believed in health education. I related the work I was doing to the scripture *"the people are destroyed from lack of knowledge" (Hosea 4:6).*

During the training, we talked about health education. We were given a different approach for Maternal Child Health (MCH). It was proposed that the government could implement this new approach of Maternal Child Health (MCH). This approach involved instructing mothers in our communities to come to the MCH center for their "total health education." Often, mothers would come to bring their children in for immunizations. Since they were already there, they would get an opportunity to obtain family planning supplies (birth control) discreetly.

I would speak at churches and community meetings to help the community understand the importance of spacing out their family. I shared that this would help families to not be overwhelmed with too many children (children they might not be unable to provide for financially). As you might imagine, this was a very private matter. Women who were practicing family planning did not want it to be publicized in the community. It was kind of a secret. Because of this need for discretion and confidentiality, I also used to do home visitations and share with both the husband and wife the importance of spacing out their children. This approach was helpful because some of the families could not ask questions in public.

My role was met with resistance from some. Many fathers (in refusing birth control) would refer me to the Genesis passage in the Bible that says, *"be fruitful and multiply" (Genesis 9:1b)*. I started now trying to approach this from another angle so that the families could grow healthier families by spacing out their children. I thought it was a good idea to train the trainer (TT), thus forming communities locally (rather than attempting to personally visit all of families in different communities). Leaders who were already known and trusted in their own communities were trained so that they could bring the information to their own relatives and their neighbors. That was a good model. It was effective for the leaders of the community to understand why this program was important for their own people. They also knew their own culture and values and could translate the information in ways they were uniquely equipped to do.

In 1975, my husband was given a transfer to come to Nairobi City to serve in the police force there. I was also offered a job at Kenyatta National Hospital in the department of Health Education in Nairobi. My work was to motivate the women about Maternal Child Health (MCH) in the department of Health education. I was attached to a unit of the children's department (Pediatric Unit). I taught the following trainings: children's immunization, family planning, personal hygiene, balanced diet and home visitation.

I had earned a diploma in nutrition from Karen Nutritional College. Because of this, my new job was to work with mothers whose children were admitted after being diagnosed with Kwashiorkor and other malnutrition diseases (like Melisma's). These diseases were caused by a poor diet. Mainly, Kwashiokor was caused by only feeding children a diet of carbohydrate-filled foods. Malnutrition was caused primarily from feeding children not getting enough to eat and becoming underweight. This led to Edema (the body getting bloated with water). Since I had compassion for children, the job greatly stressed me out. It was hard to see innocent children suffering. Fortunately, the hospital supported me with lots of resources.

This position developed in me a great concern for the lives of the poor mothers who could not get enough food to feed the families. I went back again to receive more training to help the mothers. I learned how to instruct the mothers about feeding balanced diets to their children, so they could prevent some of the diseases. I did not want to see their children in hospitalized again for something so preventable. I also went to some of their homes to demonstrate cooking balanced diets to make sure the mothers really understood how to do it.

All new patients with underweight children were referred to my care. It was my duty to offer the training so that the mothers would carry the knowledge home to prevent having malnourished children again. When a child was admitted, the hospital kitchen prepared a special balanced diet for those who came in suffering with Kwashiorkor or

Melisma's and then they were brought to our unit for training.

I worked with compassion as I saw the children suffering in the pediatric units. I was acquainted with the pediatricians, doctors, nurses and public health workers in the department. Sometimes, I was invited to give a presentation to the fourth-year medical students in our pediatric unit about the causes of diseases which attack children and the way to prevent those two diseases: Kwashiorkor and Melisma's. These were sometimes fatal, but preventable diseases which were common in some of our communities, mostly in families with low incomes.

I would do my demonstration to mothers about how they could create a balanced diet using local food like fish, vegetables, beans, fresh fruits, eggs, milk and all kinds of meat. Sometimes, I would pay a surprise visit to their homes (during lunchtime) to find out what they had prepared for the children that day. When the children were discharged from the hospital, the mothers were referred to me. I discharged them armed with the new balanced diet training and I provided them with powdered milk and beans to take home with them (this food was provided by the hospital). I would also refer them to their local health center in their own community. If the child needed immunizations, these would also be given before the mother and the child were released.

I would remind the mothers about personal hygiene and would also share family planning advice. Some of the mothers took home family planning supplies (birth control) and would be instructed to go to a follow-up appointment at their nearest health center. After I educated the women on health education, sometimes (especially if the parents had come from far away and needed the transportation) I used to refer the mother to the nearest health clinic with discharge notes. This was a great blessing to have a job seeing children who had come into the hospital literally dying and in serious condition, and then after the treatment, seeing children go home healthy, well and with a smile on the face!

9. God's Call on My Life

I am telling my story to encourage those who feel like they are at end of the road or they have hit the wall. I want them to know that our God knows what is good for us and that His timing is the very best. We do not know what God is keeping for us and when something is going to happen. Let us focus on waiting for God. *"I waited patiently for the Lord; He turned to me and heard my cry"* (Psalm 40:1).

When I was visiting the families, my call was to encourage them because these two diseases were the killer diseases. Some of these parents had lost their children in the hospital. I remember holding these moms and giving my shoulder for them to cry on. I was there to encourage them in that difficult moment.

I worked in the hospital, but during my free time and my lunch time, I used to volunteer to visit with the patients in different units of the hospital. I would pray with the patients, encouraging them in the midst of their pain and suffering from their illnesses. They touched my heart spiritually. I continued during my lunch breaks. I went to the hospital's medical unit and kept on visiting the patients, bed by bed. I carried the patients in my heart - to see whether they were suffering and how they were doing spiritually. Some of these patients did not have anyone to visit with them during the hospital visiting time. I remember walking slowly, looking for those patients with no visitors. Many times, I would listen to the feelings of the patients (and many of them touched my heart). The patients were heavy in my heart, and from that time my life changed. Some of them were Christians and they needed someone to pray with them. Unfortunately, the medical staff's roles were only to care for the patients' medical needs. There was no one to care for their spiritual needs. I heard that some of them had been discharged, but since they did not have money to pay the hospital (and their families did not come). They were waiting to see whether the hospital could waive their hospital bills to allow them to go home. I used to help with my little money I had and even purchased (out of my pocket) basic items for the patients to use while they were in their hospital beds. When they were waiting, I heard how long they were there and had been waiting. I would often try to advocate for them in the administration to request that some of their fees be waived. I would share about my faith in God. It would become so hard. I felt humble before God. I remember crying (and not knowing why I was crying), especially when I was praying alone. I started experiencing the presence of God more than ever before as I went before the Lord in the midst of the suffering I was seeing. God continued talking to me when I saw how these mothers and families were suffering.

During this time, I continued visiting the patients until I reached one woman. She had been referred from Chogaria Hosptial Meru to Kenyatta National Hospital. I went up to her bed and she looked up at me. She began crying. I asked her "why are those tears flowing like that?" When I looked at her, I saw that her tears were so heavy. She said "Jemimah, I'm so glad you came to pray with me. Before I fell sick, I had a testimony that Jesus Christ is my personal savior. During my time in the hospital, I had not been able to share this. My name is Jerioth Kawira and I am from Meru Chogaria Hospital. I love Jesus Christ as my personal savior. I listen to the word of God. I accepted Jesus and then told others about Him, too. Since I came here, I was not able to share my testimony with others. Jesus died on the cross for my sins. I am his witness." After I heard this testimony, it touched me. I told her who I was. We prayed together. I also shared my own personal testimony with her at her bed. I gave her a hug. I wanted to stay with her longer, but I had to go back to work. This woman touched my heart deeply.

From that time on, my heart was broken. I started crying and praying. I continued visiting patients and praying with them. Anytime I shared my testimony, I would cry. This went on for a long time. I could not sleep at night. My voice was changed whenever I could share my testimony. I could feel God's presence in the valleys and in the mountains. I could see myself everywhere. I felt God's light. Then I would wake up and it would continue like that. For three months, I did not have spiritual peace. My heart was heavy. It was too much to bear. I wondered if I was not doing enough for the Lord since I was not sleeping, even at night. This reminded me of the scripture where God was calling Samuel. I could not sleep for three months and I had dreams of patients looking for someone who would listen to their stories. During this time, I was not really sleeping until I truly listened to God's voice. I relate this dream (and not having sleep at night) to the story of Samuel. *"Then the Lord came and stood and called as the previous times. 'Samuel, Samuel!' Then Samuel answered "speak, for your servant is listening"" (1 Samuel 3:10-11)*

When I was still wrestling with this, I had a dream one night in which I was visiting the patients. In my dream, there was one woman I visited. She looked very sick (with tubes all over and no one beside her bed). I sat near her bed and she opened her eyes and she shared with me that since she was admitted to the hospital, "no one has listened to my testimony". This was because when she came to the hospital, she had a testimony that Jesus Christ was her personal savior. She knew Jesus as her Lord and Savior! After she told me that, she went back to sleep. In my dream, I stood there and wept, not having words to say. I remember praying a special prayer then that even if God took her life, I would share her testimony and share with others that "she loves Jesus!" The following day in my dream, I went back to her and she was happy to see me. She said to me "I'm glad that you came to visit me and that you listened to what God has done in my life. Even now, I'm waiting upon God." She asked me to pray for her as well. I prayed a special prayer, and I left her smiling! She told me "Jemimah, come again and pray with me". I went back and found that she was well and ready to be discharged. We hugged, and I left her. Immediately she was discharged and went home. This was a powerful dream.

That dream stayed with me and disturbed me so much for about three months. I knew that it had something to do with me and my spiritual journey.

One day, there was a retreat in my church. When the speaker was talking about the mission and about transformation, it touched me. When I talked to the speaker, I was still crying and shaking. He was the Rev. Dr. Chege Kimani. I told him how I had struggled over the last three months. My tears were flowing as I was talking with him. He told me "Jemimah, God is calling you. I want us to pray. You just need to say, 'here I am, Lord'". He prayed for me and blessed me to serve the Lord. I said to God, "yes, Lord. Use me. I accept you for who you are". It was a deep, deep, painful prayer. I continued praying, asking my prayer group to help me and for God to show me the meaning of this dream.

After a while, the dream became clear to me. *God was calling me into full-time ministry!* So, my story started there. *"Then I heard the voice of the Lord saying, 'whom shall I send and who will go for us' and I said 'send me!'" (Isaiah 6:8)*. This was in 1984. When I said "yes, Lord", I was relieved. I was free because I realized God was calling me into His full-time ministry. I accepted that call because I heard the voice of God. I felt like God was saying "go, wake up and listen to the stories of the patients. Pray with them and give them encouragement. Do this because I am God". After I realized that was God calling me, I became free, powerful and ready to go and do the ministry! Then, I was like a newborn baby – I was a new person.

My question is, "what does all of this mean?" God was calling me to be humble and to differentiate his voice from other voices. I saw that God was penetrating the hearts of people. For me, it took a lot of time to recognize that God was calling me. I want to let you know that He is the same God today that He was then. Open your heart and allow Him to direct you!

After that, the next steps of my life became easy. It was easy for me to testify about how much God had been faithful to me. I felt loved by God more than ever before. I shared about my dream with my family, and I finally went to my pastor about it. When I shared with the church, I had been an active member of Bahati Presbyterian Church in Nairobi. My pastor encouraged me! He called a meeting of the church leaders for me to tell my story. I went and met with the pastor and church leaders and they prayed for me. They encouraged me to start the preparation for full-time ministry. After our meeting, I went to the hospital (where I was then working on staff with nutrition). I told the hospital supervisors about my call. They listened to me and then they invited me into a staff meeting. When I spoke, I told them what God showed me. I said, "There are Christian patients in this hospital who came with a testimony to share, and there is no one to listen." I told them that I believed my purpose was to listen to them. I wanted to hear their stories and to share mine with them. The hospital also called another meeting to discuss and share my story. After a week or so, they agreed to reassign me from the Pediatric Unit (as Health Educator) to the Hospital Chaplain Department.

I did this for two weeks, and then I received a letter from the National Director of the hospital. This letter stated that I had been promoted into a position as the head of the Chaplaincy Department in the hospital. My salary was also increased! At this point, I was also given a big office. I cried at this confirmation and I continued asking God to use me. As I directed this department, I began my regular schedule. I started on the first Sunday and began preaching for Sunday worship in Swahili. I had seven pastors from different denominations assigned to the hospital. I helped organize their visitation schedules. I held meetings with them and began planning together with them. We started some programs together. Most of my work involved scheduling and coordinating the pastors.

My ordination process really began from that time forward. I met with the church pastors, leaders and elders in 1984 at the Nairobi Presbytery. I met with them and I shared my story. They voted for me to start the ordination process. After two days, they called me to start the process for ordination. (I became ordained 2005. I would never have guessed that my ordination process would take me twenty years! I am glad I did not know that yet).

10. Opportunity for Theological Study in America

After several months of serving in the hospital as a chaplain, there was a Presbyterian pastor who came to visit his mother. He came to my office first. He had returned to Kenya from the United States and his name was the Rev. Dr. Muroko. I escorted him to see his mom (I had already previously visited her). We went there together and visited with her. The mother told us her story and we listened together. After that, I prayed for his mother. The patients were in my heart (including his mother). This pastor appreciated and saw how meaningful my presence was to them. We all prayed together and went back to the office, where he told me "You know, Jemimah, if you add a little theology on top of what I already see you doing, you can be even more effective in your ministry. I loved what I saw you do with my mom and what I know you are doing in this hospital for the patients. I am going back to USA where I am a theological seminary student and I will request for a scholarship for you to come to my seminary for one-year theological studies." He himself was a student at Eden Theological Seminary in St. Louis, Missouri. He told me that he was going back to his seminary that week, and he said he would ask if they would grant me a scholarship to study there also.

He talked to the Admissions office and he was given application forms, which he sent me when he returned to the United States (he also gave me directions on how to fill them out). When I received the application forms, I showed my family. My husband said to me "No, you cannot go to the United States. I cannot see you going". This broke my heart. My children were teenagers at the time (I was also already a grandmother by this time). They started laughing at me. They said "you are not educated. You need to have enough education in Kenya first before you can study abroad. Do you even qualify?" I responded that this was a different kind of education, and that God had opened the door. The qualifications were different. I reminded them that when God opens the door, no one can shut it. My family did not like that. *"So then, God's choice is not dependent on human will, nor on human effort, but on God, who shows mercy" (Romans 9:16)* I gathered a group of women who were my prayer partners. We prayed together about this matter. My family's doubts planted seeds of inadequacy in my heart, but God's call was still there.

About a month later, my husband came to me and said "where are those papers? Let us fill them out." Before I sent in the forms, I went to the hospital and spoke to the staff about this opportunity (before I went to the hospital, I prayed about their response). They shared how rare it was to have such an opportunity and they blessed me by pledging to pay for my air ticket. They also asked what else I needed! After this, I went to the Presbyterian Church East Africa General Assembly office. I shared with them about the seminary opportunity and what God had done in my life. They were excited. They gave me their blessing and had written a great recommendation for me. I sent all the requirements into to the seminary. I filled out the forms and I sent them back to Eden Theological Seminary. They sent back a letter of admission and I cried! *"For with God, nothing is impossible"* *(Luke 1:37)* My sisters and brothers in Christ and my colleagues encouraged me very much. God does not change. People can change and even friends can change, but God never changes.

I was accepted for one year of Theological Seminary with a scholarship! It was unbelievable for me to travel to the United States for theological studies! God is good. I was accepted by God for this opportunity so that I could travel to the United States and study His word.

I want to encourage you that God is there to give you direction. Where are you right now? It takes time to know what God is doing through you and in your community. Where are you? No matter what is out there, remember God walks with us and works with us.

I started getting ready. During that time, one of my friends told me "Jemimah, do you think you are going to understand American English?" I jokingly told her not to worry. If I didn't understand and would have to come back, I would still get to go and see what America was like. I could come back and share aspects of America (like snow even). I knew that God would make a way. He would enable me to understand. Whether or not I knew American English, I knew that God knew all languages and He lived in me. Nothing is impossible with Him!

11.   Saying Goodbye

My hospital paid for the air ticket and my church gave me pocket money to use when I got to the seminary. This was a joyous time for my family, friends, my prayer group and my church members. I remember we had prayers in my home to send me off. My family prayed and was excited. After the prayers in the house, I was escorted to the airport by many people. My mom was among them (at the time, she was 103 years old). Since she was living with me, she came to the airport with the others. I was escorted (by my family friends and my pastor) to the airport on August 22, 1992. My mother gave me a big hug and told me to and study the word of God and continue preaching the word. She looked at me with sorrow in her eyes and she told me, "If you come back and find me dead, I will go to heaven and wait for you after you finish God's work in this world." I did not like hearing that from my mother. I started crying and screaming! I called my friend who was there with me, and I told her listen to what mom was saying to me. My mother repeated the same words again and called me by the name she used to call me ("sister in Christ"). She repeated, "you can go and study the word. When you come back, and you find I have died, I will go and wait for you in heaven. I want my sister to continue with the work I started with a lot of difficulties in my community. Continue being faithful to God." I felt a knot in my stomach and I started crying. My mother would not release me until it was time for me to board my flight. She would not let me go until the last second. She had to be forced to let me go. My mother's words turned out to be prophetic. That was the last time I ever saw my mother alive. She would die the next year (when she was one hundred and three years old) on May

5, 1993. This would happen when I was doing my finals exams in my preaching class, before I would finish my sermon (I would fall at the pulpit and lose consciousness at the exact same time my mother passed away in Kenya). As you continue reading this book, you will learn more about the details of this story.

I checked into the flight, still with tears in my eyes. Everyone who had escorted me was so sad to see my heavy tears. When I got on the flight (my first ever flight), the airhostess thought I was crying because I had lost my travel documents. The flight attendant asked whether I had lost my travel documents or my luggage because I was visibly upset. I responded that I was okay, but just missed my mom. I still had tears in my eyes as my plane took off into the air and I saw Kenya from above.

12.   My First Days in America

I arrived at Lombard airport in St. Louis, Missouri on August 22, 1992 at 4:00 pm Eastern Time. My flight came through JFK airport in New York before my final leg to St. Louis. I was surprised to see so many flights landing and taking off in New York. It reminded me of the heavy traffic from all of the cars in Nairobi city in Kenya – instead these were not cars, but airplanes (there were so many!). The other thing that surprised me was that there were many African Americans (black people) were working at the airport. I did not know that there were so many black people in America! Most of the Americans I knew were white. Up until that time, I had only met two African Americans in my whole life.

I was not well informed about African American history yet, but I was beginning to see that my picture of America was not exactly like the reality. After my layover in New York, I arrived in St. Louis, Missouri. I was greeted by Professor Hale Sweher (the Dean of Common life at Eden Theological Seminary). He was the one who picked me up at the airport and drove me to Eden. He met me at the gate and he said to me "Are you are Jemimah Ngatia from Kenya?" I said to him "yes, yes, I am Jemimah." He gave me a hug and gave me a warm welcome to America. He then escorted me to baggage claim to pick up my suitcases. Then he drove me in his car to the Seminary.

Before we reached the seminary, he drove me to the grocery store to pick up some items I would need in my room. When we went in the store (called "Schucks"), he told me to pick out what I wanted. In that store, there was nothing I could relate with (only the cabbage, potatoes and breads were familiar). Then, he took me to the aisle and shelves where could pick out laundry detergent as well as soap for my body. Unfortunately, I could not pick out anything because I was not accustomed to the American products. The professor asked, "what do you use in Kenya?" I told him "Lux and Cussion's soap, but I cannot find them here in this department" Then, I asked the professor "Which one do you use?" He then picked out the Ivory brand soap for me. I replied, "I will take that one and will go and try it".

After our shopping trip, he took me the seminary where he showed me my room. I walked around the bedroom and he showed me the kitchen and laundry area. He took me to one of the senior student's rooms. She welcomed me there. She was in her room, and she said she could show me any other places I would need to know at the seminary. The professor left me with that student and we sat down to share our stories. She once again repeated my name. I spoke slowly. I was so nervous. At that time, I started getting worried because the dorm was so quiet. This senior student kept on saying that she liked my accent. Whenever she mentioned my accent, it triggered my insecurities. This brought to mind the words of my friends who said I may not be able to understand American English. No other students were there because they had not yet come back from the summer holiday (I arrived 2 weeks before the term began). The student looked at me and said to me "you look worried. Is your family okay back home?" I started crying because she could not understand my English, and I could not understand all of what she was saying to me either. One thing I did understand was her asking me, "Jemimah, what can I give you to drink?" I told her "tea." She repeated to me "tea?" I nodded, and then she brought me a glass of iced tea (which I had never seen before or tasted). I said to her "I want tea with sugar and milk" so she went back to her kitchen and brought me the iced tea with ice cubes plus milk and sugar together. I was like "whoa, not like this! I want *hot* tea with milk and sugar" I asked her if I could come to her kitchen. At that time, I was craving Kenyan tea. I started missing my family and my country.

She allowed me to come with her in her kitchen and I prepared a cup of hot tea (but the tea leaves not like the ones I am familiar with). I brought my tea back into my room and we started a conversation. She wanted to know more about the size of my family, the work I had been doing in Kenya, and my church. I felt she wanted to get to know me so that she could help me to settle down and feel more comfortable with her.

Then it was time for dinner and she asked me what I wanted to eat. I thought to myself "if the tea was a problem, what about food?" In Kenya instead of saying "dinner is ready", we say "supper is ready." When she said it was time for dinner, I did not respond because I did not know what she was talking about. I kept quiet to see what was next. She picked up the phone and ordered a pizza to be delivered to our room. I did not understand what she said on the phone, but after a few minutes, I heard a knock at the door. She got her pass and opened the door and then pizza was brought to me. I had never had pizza before. To me, it looked like chapatti, but different. It had food (tomato sauce and cheese) on top of the bread. I had never seen this before. She put it on the table and I waited to see how she was going to eat it. I also picked up a piece to try. I did not like it because it had too much cheese. Then, I decided to prepare another cup of tea and drink it with the bread the professor bought for me from the store. That was my dinner in America.

After dinner, I was very tired because my flight from Kenya had taken sixteen hours (from the time of leaving my country until I arrived in St. Louis). I went to bed, but I did not sleep well. I had too much on my mind. I was thinking about home and my family and church friends. I was thinking about all of the people who I had not seen or talked to since arriving the day before. I did not sleep that first night because I was experiencing jet lag, culture shock and frustration. This was not at all like I had expected. I prayed that God would give me peace.

In the morning, I got ready and I went to my friend's room. I knocked on the door and she welcomed me in and asked me how my night was. I told her it was okay, but that I did not sleep well. She told me the other students would start coming tomorrow and they would be happy to meet me. I was able to share my testimony with the first people I interacted with "My name is Jemimah, Jesus Christ is my personal savior and I am from Kenya. That is my identity. I am here because I love Jesus." I got to share this often.

On the day the students arrived, I got a roommate. I prepared lunch and we ate (all of us). This was a good time. Everyone was intrigued to ask me any questions they had about Kenya. ("There is a student from Kenya" This is the way my friends introduced me to others at Eden). After lunch, some of the students decided to take me out for ice cream (that was another world altogether).

When we got to the ice cream shop, I sat with my friend and she ordered ice cream and donuts for me. We ate while talking (but I was busy trying concentrate so that I could understand the stories they were sharing). They already knew one another, and they were telling stories about what they did over the holiday vacation. They loved laughing loudly and telling fun stories about different movies they had seen and activities they had done. I did not understand their jokes or their stories, and I felt left out. The time came to pay the bill, and I did not know how much my ice cream and donuts cost because my friend had ordered them for me. My friend told the waiter to give individual tickets. I had never heard of this before. In my culture, when someone invites you for dinner, the one who invites you is the one that pays. In America, I was invited for ice cream and I was expected to pay for my own. I did not understand what was happening (also, I did not know how much money I was supposed to pay for my ice cream). I opened my purse and I gave the waitress twenty dollars because I did not have small change or other money. After that day, I got to know more students at Eden and my life changed completely. I had never been away from my family before.

13.   Culture Shock

I was born in and raised in the countryside (including growing up and going to school). I married into a different community in many ways, but this was still similar to the community where I was born (it was still in the Kenyan Countryside). The cultural differences I had to adjust to were very minor compared to the differences I experienced when I came to the United States.

On August 22, 1992, I arrived in St. Louis, Missouri. It was my first time in the United States. Little did I know, I would be entering into a *completely different culture* (different in almost every way from where I was born and raised). To say that coming to America brought culture shock to my system is an understatement!

Coming to America taught me a great deal about different cultures (especially the western culture that is so different from my own). I have learned that my own culture is very communal, and that western culture is much more individualistic. America has a very fast culture - they do things so quickly that most of the time I am left behind (in many ways).

In my culture, people in the community meet all the time. This is especially true during events like weddings. If there is a wedding in the community, *everybody is welcome* (and you are encouraged to bring friends). There is no such thing as an RSVP or making a reservation in my culture. You just come. The community usually cooks more than enough food for everyone to enjoy. Not only that, but everyone attending the wedding also goes home with extra food or drinks ("to carry") for later. The community provides everything that is needed in the wedding (this includes transportation for the families and food donated by the members of the community). Traditionally, women cook the food (assisted by the men). While the women handle most of the food, grilling meat is typically the work of the men in the community. Creating and putting up decorations is most often the work of the youth in the community. The whole community is responsible for a wedding (and the community leaders start the work well before the wedding day for the arrangements). *A typical*

Kenyan wedding takes more than seven hours! During the ceremony in the church, choirs sing choruses and family from both sides speak and bring gifts for the new couple.

I have learned that when weddings happen in the United States, it is a much more exclusive and individualistic event. Sometimes, a wedding may happen and even the neighbor right next store might not even know that there was even a wedding at all! This is unbelievable to me! Many times, I would hear that so and so got married (some of these people would even be people I knew well!), and there was no sign of it at all. Sometimes, I would receive an official formal invitation to a couple's wedding. Friends would send me an invitation card in the postal mail. The card would state the details of the wedding celebration (date and time, location of the church, and so on). The card instructed me to return a special card that would indicate whether I would be attend their wedding (RSVP). I found this all to be very formal and far less communal. When you would arrive at the wedding, everything would already be planned out (many times, the couple had paid lots of money for things like flowers and food. It was did not come from the community who had rallied together; it instead came from hired services).

Another cultural difference I have noticed between Kenya and America is the way we approach funerals. If someone dies in the Kenyan community, the whole community takes the responsibility of the funeral arrangements (meeting every day in the home of the grieving family and pulling together until the funeral is done). Sometimes, it takes one week or two weeks before the funeral is held.

Even after the funeral, the community continues visiting the family. This is because in our culture we believe that *after* the funeral is real the time that the family needs support (of food, prayers and helping them to grieve). One time in America, I was surprised to learn from my neighbor that her husband had died. I saw her sitting outside on her porch. It was summertime, and I used to see her sit with her husband. This time, I noticed that she was outside by herself. I went and greeted her. Before I could ask her about her husband, she told me "my husband died. We buried him five days ago." I was so surprised! There was no outward sign in the neighborhood that there had been someone grieving in the neighborhood. It was all very private and hidden away.

When I arrived at Eden Theological Seminary, I was shocked by what I experienced. I met many people who could not even fathom or understand my culture (likewise, I could not understand the American culture at first). I experienced culture shock in various ways as I continued to study as a student in seminary. One thing I was struck by was the pace of life here. It was truly overwhelming having to learn so many new things all at the same time. For me, this included not only the academic courses, but also learning how to assimilate into American culture and how to connect with Americans.

On my first day of class at Eden, I dressed up just the way I used to dress in Kenya when attending church meetings and other meetings related to church. I dressed nicely as a show of respect for the place of learning I was in. I soon discovered that I was very overdressed for their casual environment (no one told me beforehand that it was appropriate to dress casually in theological seminary). Some of the students knew me and they could talk with me. They asked me, "Jemimah, where are you going?" I sat down in the class and I scanned the room to see my other classmates. I noticed that nearly all the students had come in wearing t-shirts and jeans! My church had sent me all the way from Kenya to come and learn theological studies, and here I was in a room full of casual young people in t-shirts and jeans. Also, both women and men were wearing jeans. Sometimes, it was difficult for me to differentiate whether a person was a man or a woman until I looked much more closely. Before I came to USA, I had not even seen women wearing trousers – they only wore dresses and skirts. Occasionally, the teenagers might try out some trousers, but it was mostly the girls out in the city (never in the countryside where I was from). Certainly, the women did not where jeans where I was from – especially not Christian ones. This was nothing at all like what I imagined it would be. I was scared, wondering if this was the right seminary after all. Was this for me? It frustrated me. It really was not just the clothing. The clothing just symbolized the attitudes and the environment I saw (everything was casual. It did not feel sacred or special; just common and casual). They were so casual in clothing as well as in speech. From my perspective, it seemed like they were not taking it seriously or respecting the education they were there to receive. I was totally shocked.

You know, I had just come from Presbyterian Church East Africa (PCEA Kenya) and this was the starting point for me. I continued trying to understand western culture.

Let me say this, when the professor entered the classroom for my first class, I could not tell the difference between he and the students. The students used to call the professor by his first name (like "John" or "Peter"). This was hard for me because in Kenya, I had never heard of a pastor or a professor being called by his first name. If you wanted to call someone in a profession by their first name, in my culture it means that you did not have respect for that person. Calling older people by the first names sounded like you did not have respect for the elderly people in your community. I have come to understand that when you are in the United States, the meaning behind actions is different than it is in Kenya.

The time came when we were given a fifteen-minute break. Students went out the door, and I was left in the classroom alone. Then I said to myself, "let me also go outside." I went outside (and to my complete shock), I found some students smoking cigarettes - right there in the seminary! I also found them laughing and telling coarse jokes. Another shock was seeing *men* wearing earrings (some had one earing; others had two). In my country, only women wore earrings sometimes (again, church women did not), but never men. This confused me so much. My classmates were supposedly future pastors and church leaders, but they looked very different from what I thought church leaders were supposed to look like.

During orientation week at the seminary, we were told that the new students would be taken for a weekend retreat not too far from the seminary. The seminary had organized the retreat at a placed called Kendrick Catholic Seminary. This was another shocking moment for me. I found myself in a Catholic facility (we were *protestants!*). I asked myself, "are we really going to a retreat in a Catholic facility?" We went there, and we were welcomed. Where we were passing over, we saw priests studying the Catholic traditions, which I was not familiar with. I also remember seeing statues on the walls and seeing the pictures of Mary holding baby Jesus. There was a fountain and many other things I noticed for the first time in my life. Another surprising aspect for me at that time was that we planned to take Holy Communion after lunch and after break. It was announced that students were to have a free time. If someone wanted to walk outside or play games, we were told to make a choice. For me, I decided to walk around (to release the fear and worries over what might happen next). After break, we came back for Holy Communion. We were told to stand in a circle, and the professor came over. He was still dressed just the way he was, in his gym shorts and his t-shirt from the playground – it was summertime. He walked in and started the liturgy of Holy Communion. The elements were put in a small table where the silver cup and big round brown bread were placed. I had never seen this before. The professor began. The students all seemed to know what they were doing (each of them had cut a piece of brown bread, dipping it in the cup of grape juice and putting it in their mouths). I was observing them. Some students would cut big pieces which would not fit in their mouths, so they had to chew the bread (like eating a piece of meat). When the time came for me to cut a piece of bread, I did not do it. I passed it over to the next person. This was a big shock for me. In my church in Kenya, the Holy Communion day is a big day to celebrate the Lord's Table.

In my tradition, the minister who officiated the Communion had to wear a clergy gown (and clergy collar) and the church elders needed to be present to assist the minister in this holy time. The elders are normally dressed well (in suits and ties). We do not use grape juice (we usually use red sweet wine) and we also use pieces of fresh white bread (they are already in pieces). The officiating pastor reads the liturgy for Communion (the breaking of the bread). They usually do this saying, *"this is my body, broken for you. Do this in remembrance of me." (Luke 22:19)* Likewise, when we take the cup, the pastor says, *"this is my blood, shed for you…Every time you take this break and drink this cup, you proclaim the resurrection of Christ." (Luke 22:20)* This was the Presbyterian tradition for Holy Communion as I knew it. I did not know that some Americans practiced Holy Communion in such a different way. It was an experience to realize that other denominations (other than East African Presbyterians) could experience the same communion in so many different ways. I came to realize that it did not matter whether someone used brown bread or white bread (or grape juice or wine). What really mattered was remembering the sacrifice of Christ together during communion. The important thing was not HOW we do it, but WHY we do it. This was a learning process for me. Different cultures are not right or wrong, only different. Only what God says is set in stone. We only have to carry on what can be implemented or used to strengthen our culture in order to build the Kingdom of God.

14.   Reading the Menu in a Restaurant Experience

Another thing about American culture that shocks me (even today) is reading the menu in a restaurant. I have discovered that there is little food in restaurants I can relate to. Even understanding the language of what the food is called is different in America.

This reminded me of one day when I was watching the Oprah Winfrey show. I enjoyed watching the Oprah show. I liked it when she talked with people who needed hope. She gave hope to the hopeless and demonstrated the call of compassion (which Jesus calls every Christian to give – it is hope). Her shows have helped me so much to relate to my life in America for the first time. Oprah once said, "do not give your grandma the food she cannot relate to." I came to know that the food I could not recognize would make me sick and I would not be familiar with the taste of it. I agree with her! When you cannot relate with the food is very hand to and you cannot enjoy the food

One day, I was invited out to eat. Since I was the only student from Africa, the other students asked me whether I could join them for dinner. This was my very first time going out to eat at a restaurant with other students. It was terrifying because each student was given their *own* menu to choose the food they wanted to order. I came armed with the little English-Swahili dictionary with me to help translate (so when I got the menu and saw a word I did not recognize, I could easily look it up in the dictionary). I had never held a menu in my hands before. I was amazed at the size of the menu (it was very big with lots of different kinds of food. It reminded me of a newspaper). There was hardly any food from the menu that I could relate to. I scanned the menu for a word I recognized. Then I saw it! Chicken! I knew the spelling of "chicken" and I knew what it was. I liked chicken and I thought it would be a "safe" choice. One of the students asked "Jemimah, did you order your food?" I kept quiet not knowing what I was to expect. They asked me what I wanted, I just responded "chicken" (since that was the only word familiar to me). When the food came, it was a very thin piece of meat. The chicken that came was not at all what I thought it would be. It was brought to me boneless (I later came to know that this was called "boneless chicken breast"). It did not look like chicken at all to me. When the plate came, I asked the waitress to come over and clarified that I actually wanted chicken. I asked the waitress whether this was in fact the chicken I had ordered (or was this actually fish or maybe something else?). She said, "this *is* chicken". The waitress tried to explain to me that this was the type of the chicken I had ordered. I told the waitress, "yes, okay. This is the chicken I ordered." (I was afraid to say that it was not). I told her I wanted real chicken…with bones in it. I was supposed to eat it, but I did really not like it at all. When I tasted the chicken, it did not taste like any chicken that I had known. I pushed myself to try to eat it anyway, but I could not finish it. Finally, I ordered potatoes with tea. This was so hard because when the potatoes were brought over, they still had skin on them (it was apparently a baked potato). Also, once again, I was brought (American) iced tea. I really wanted hot tea, so I asked the waitress to heat up my tea. At that time, I was still struggling, but I kept quiet. The other students had already eaten their food, so I decided to let it go. I started to peel the skin off of my potato, so I could eat it. I told myself that is the first mistake. Next time, I will wait for other people to order first and I will see what they get. Then, I can order and say, "I want the food like the other person ordered".

The waitress asked me, "do you want to take this home with you?" I said "no, I am okay. Please bring me my ticket." At the time to pay, the students told the waitress "each person will pay for their own meal – give us separate tickets". This was new for me. From my culture, if someone is invited to a restaurant, the person who invites you is the one who pays for the food for you. I have come to understand that this is not the same in America. Fortunately, I had money and I paid for my dinner. On the ticket, I saw that my meal was very expensive! I compared that amount of money with what it would cost in Kenyan money (I converted the currencies with a calculator I had on me). This meal was SO much more in comparison! I still paid it (with a lot of pain).

I learned a lesson that day. If I get invited to go to a restaurant, I need be sure that have enough money to pay for my meal before going out (otherwise, I may be embarrassed). I also need to check the prices on the menu before I put in my order for the same reason. The food in this country is different from our food in Kenya. This experience reminded me of a time we received a missionary from America in our church in Kenya. He had difficulties in choosing what to eat (and now I understood why). In every country, people have food that they are familiar with. The missionary did not know what to do with the food he had never tasted. Sometimes, people fear eating something that they cannot relate to (and they fear getting sick or having food poisoning). I remember I met one pastor in Florida. His church had a mission trip to Uganda. When they arrived there, the food was prepared for the guests. He tasted the food and found that the popular food from Uganda (called Matoke that is green bananas cooked with spices) was delicious. The pastor told me that he loved that food and he ate it again and again for every meal he had. It had become familiar to him (and he could recognize it in the menu). After a while though, unfortunately he became sick and he was taken to the hospital (he had eaten far too much Matoke and his system was not used to it). It was not food poisoning; it was just different for his body. Of course, this does not mean that if you eat African food you have to be sick (it was because he had eaten the food excessively because he enjoyed of the taste of the food). The Pastor confessed to me he ate a whole lot of it. What helped in joining with students in America was that I wanted to try the food. I really enjoy trying buffets where I can relate with what I can see in front of me and take what I know. Buffets are good for me for the same reason that menus are hard (I did not like ordering off the menu because I did not know what I would be getting, even with some familiar words). This same experience has since happened in so many other occasions (when I order chicken, it will be brought without bones). It has been so hard to send it back and get something else. This has also been hard for my husband. He would always invite me with his friends, and many times he would ask me to join them to a restaurant (but I would always feel uncomfortable). Most times, I still prefer to cook at home (to avoid all the trouble). The bottom line is that if I have to go out to a restaurant, I prefer a buffet, rather than having to order off a menu.

No one ever taught me about these cultural differences in the United States (I was told nothing about the cultural practices of ordering food or how Americans ate food beforehand). I had to learn from being immersed in it and experiencing it first-hand. This was often exhausting! When I arrived in America, there was a lot for me to learn (all at the same time) since I had come from another culture and was also coming to learn theology in the American courses. It has been a blessing to understand how other cultures differ from where I came from the culture I was born and raised in.

Today, part of my calling is to receive refugees and immigrants to America. My own experiences have helped me to be able to prepare them in ways I was not prepared for in my community. I love answering any cross-cultural questions for newcomers into the United States. Additionally, any time I meet people who will be traveling to Kenya, I also try to prepare them for cultural practices of my home country (for example, to be prepared that if you invite someone to eat, you are expected to pay). I am also happy to equip people with basic Swahili phrases and words to be able to order food. I am so grateful that I had these experiences. It has opened my eyes to differences in cultures and helped me to prepare others for the differences they may experience.

As you continue reading this book, through this experience and what I went through, I want to encourage students in different fields to take heart and to not be discouraged by the American culture. Americans are who they are. Just as I am who I am. I grew up in Kenya and I carried my culture with me to America. I hope you will discover it is possible to remove barriers and start living in the community you have never been to before. I want to encourage all of us that we are called to journey (no matter what cultures we come from). I was asking myself "How can I sing a new song in a foreign land?" My brothers and sisters, you can make it, because our God is the Alpha and Omega. *"I am the Alpha and the Omega, the first and the last, the beginning and the end." (Revelation 22:13) "Jesus replied, 'what is impossible with man is possible with God'" (Luke 18:27)* There is nothing impossible for Him!!

15. Pastoral Care and Theological Studies

I was busy at Eden Theological seminary taking four classes, one of which was Pastoral Care. One day, my professor of pastoral care (Dr. Peggy Way) brought in a guest speaker. She invited Chaplain Nancy Deitch (who was the Chaplain supervisor from Deaconess Hospital in St. Louis) to speak to our class about hospital visitation. I asked her so many questions about the hospital chaplaincy ministry. She answered all of them and at the end of the class she wanted to talk with me (outside of class, out in the campus). She wanted to know more about my life and my ministry in Kenya. When we met up, I shared my story with her about working as the hospital chaplain at Kenyatta National Hospital in Nairobi. She was touched by my story (the way I loved the patients and the ministry in the hospital). She gave me another appointment to visit her office and to see her hospital. She wanted me to see the work of a hospital chaplain there firsthand. You know, I could not wait for that appointment to come and visit with Chaplain Nancy.

When I went there, she shared with me that she wanted to give me a scholarship to complete four units of Clinical Pastoral Education (CPE) with her. My desire was to finish those four units and to take that training back to Kenya to train other chaplains there with the training I had received. The fourth unit of CPE was a train the trainer unit that I could use to train other chaplains in Kenya. Since I was in the United States with a Student (F-1) Visa and this was a practical course, she needed to apply for a J-1 Visa on my behalf. This meant that I was to finish the courses and return to Kenya (the visa I had was very sensitive and specific). I was to complete the four units of CPE after graduation from Eden. I applied for and was accepted to start the program that year (this was in the Fall of 1994). Then she applied for and helped me secure my necessary visa. I shared with her that I would like to introduce CPE program in Kenya to empower the other chaplains how to visit the patients. Chaplain Nancy introduced me to the other chaplains in St. Louis and they also encouraged me to carry the program to Kenya. At this time, my husband came to visit me in St. Louis (later, in 1995, my daughter was also given a scholarship to study at Missouri Baptist University). In December of that same year, I was able to bring my daughter Joy and grandson Ben to join us together to live in the United States.

After I graduated from Eden (having completed one year of theological studies), I joined Deaconess Hospital in the

Chaplaincy Department, where I started my CPE training. It was a great challenge through the first unit of Clinical Pastoral Education. During this time, I remember crying and protesting. At my training, the Clinical Pastoral Education students were a challenge to me when it came to the confrontation discussions between the student peers and the supervisor. Sometimes, I was sick and tired of siting among the students, learning how I could do such confrontation. It was hard for me because I never learned confrontation when I was growing up. Confrontation was not something I had ever encountered before, especially as a Christian (I have my own dynamics I can use if someone needs to change). Discussion was better than confrontation, in my view. Confrontation seemed harsher to me (coming from my culture of clarifying and helping others to understand where we are coming from in a polite and friendly way). If someone needed to change, there were dynamics or many ways we could educate someone politely rather harshly confronting the other person. I learned that confrontation is a very American way of handling conflict and disagreements. Even children are taught this growing up in the United States. I think confrontation here is seen as a way of education (for one to understand what is going on inside that person where he or she cannot see). Yes, we as the church leaders still need to understand where the other person is coming from and the root of the issues. This job required lots of confrontation, and it was not something I was comfortable with. My peer group was entirely American. They were all very good at confrontation (and even enjoyed it) already and I was not yet. I could see that the spirit of confrontation was in their blood. I was also told not to carry my Bible around with me, and we were instructed not to tell patients to repent or to confess Jesus as their personal savior. I was instructed not to share my personal testimony (trusting Christ as my personal savior). I learned in their training that this was not the approach they took. During the group discussions, I protested that I could not understand what they were talking about in the CPE training. It was so hard. I felt like they wanted to change my faith to something else, which I could not understand. I felt very out of place, so I decided to talk with Chaplain Nancy and share that could not take it anymore. I wanted to discontinue the program. I had even agreed to use the training to train others, and this concerned me. I did not want to teach this to others. This was a hard, difficult moment for me. I cried everyday.

Chaplain Nancy called me into her office and she tried to communicate the reality to me. I met with her and I shared with her that in Kenya I had been working in our hospital as a chaplain. I could not understand how I was not allowed to carry the Bible to read to the patients during my visitation if I was going bed to bed. If I was not reading the Bible to the patients, praying with them and asking them to give their lives to Jesus, then how would the patients come to be supported spirituality? I used to share John 14:1 (which says *"Do not let your hearts be troubled. You believe in God, believe also in me")* with the patients, encouraging them not worry about anything, as the bible says.

It was a tradition for all chaplains working in the hospital to read the bible and ask the patient to give their life to Jesus. After they were discharged, they could go back and be active in their churches to continue their faith journey. Or, if they died, at least they would be assured of going to heaven because they had confessed their sins to God and had accepted Jesus as their Lord and savior. I used to also share Roman's 10:10 with patients (which says, *"for it is with your heart that you believe and are justified, and it is with your mouth that you profess your faith and are saved"*). This was my introduction – it was the first thing I had asked patients when I visited them. I always asked how they were doing and if they wanted to trust Jesus as their savior. If they wanted to, they could pray together with me right then. I used to share with them that they could repeat after me in a prayer (although, some of them were very sick were not able to repeat after me).

After I shared all of this, Chaplain Nancy looked at me and she had mercy on me. She knew that after a while I would become accustomed to the American hospital chaplaincy traditions and that I would understand the methodology and dynamics of what the CPE program meant (to me and to the patients). CPE trains the chaplains about what is important to share with the patients and what is not. She explained to me how the CPE program works. She shared that after two or three weeks, I would understand much more about what other students were discussing in the group. She emphasized that the training was not about sharing our own stories, but about listening to the patients' stories. She told me "Jemimah, stay where you are in your faith with God and wait for a short time. Then I will need to meet with you next week.".

After she talked to me, I prayed and asked God to help me. I sacrificed myself and I chose to continue. After three weeks I was challenged in understanding the process of what was involved in CPE training, and I was much more confident in group discussions. After three weeks, I came to learn that I did not need to carry any agenda (or even my own story) to the patients. This training was intense, and I felt overwhelmed at times by the weight of it – I felt as if I had been soaked in it. I came to reflect on how the ministry of hospital visitation in Kenya had previously been difficult to me. It was refreshing to realize I only needed to be present with the patients and listen to what they were feeling. The training helped me understand that "a patient is a book". I did not have to carry an agenda into each encounter – the patient was the document and each one was different. As a chaplain, I needed to deal with each individual story that was shared and treat is as special. Each person is individual and unique, and it is our job to read each one and listen to what they are saying. They each have their own stories and it is our privilege to listen to them and hear them. I learned very many listening skills. In fact, listening was truly the main part of CPE training. I cried, remembering how much I used to push the patients to confess their sins so they could be saved. Sometimes when I asked the patients whether wanted to confess their sins, they would tell me yes (quickly so I would just leave them alone). Patients truly wanted someone to listen to their pain and hear what they are struggling with. Often there is no one listening to their inner feelings. I learned a lot, asking God how I could use what I was learning to bring other chaplains from Kenya to be challenged the way I was challenged by this training. Through this CPE program, I was transformed. I become much more effective as a Chaplain.

After I completed my third unit, my supervisor asked me to meet with her and share my experience through my training in the CPE program. I met with her and I shared my confession with her that I was not the same person I was when I started. CPE had transformed me in my life as a hospital chaplain. She said to me that she was going to introduce me to the Association of Clinical Pastoral Education (ACPE) head office. She introduced me and shared that it was now time for her to train me as a CPE trainer. For the fourth unit, she trained me in leading the training for others. I practiced this by teaching students coming in to Deaconess hospital for one unit of CPE. I would teach the students in the presence of my supervisor, so that she could give me feedback, Nancy prepared me very well by doing presentations to the seminary students who were coming for one unit of CPE training. She required that I do presentations to her in the office before I presented my trainings to the group of students

At that time, I graduated with four units of CPE and I was ready to take the program to Kenya. In 1995, I was ready to return to Kenya and the Association of Clinical Pastoral Education (ACPE) gave me a $4,000.00 grant to help me start the CPE program in Kenya. When I returned to Kenya, my family had already come to live in the United States, so I went back to Kenya alone. I brought my training there, sharing it with the hospital administration. Because Chaplain Nancy had applied for the grant, I shared my vision with the hospital staff at Kenyatta National Hospital to start teaching CPE there. I was given permission and support. The Rev. Dr. Grishon

Karika had been trained in CPE in the United States. He was a church minister at St. Andrew's Presbyterian Church in Nairobi. We joined hands together in Kenya because of his previous experience. He became involved in implementing CPE in Kenya and was one of the trainers with me. I remember starting my first class with twelve students. Although we began with twelve students initially, there were three students who could not handle the challenges of seeing patients with pain and suffering in the hospital beds, so only 9 finished. I started Kenya Clinical Pastoral Education Theory at St. Andrews Presbyterian Church in Nairobi Kenya. I completed my practical teaching at Kenyatta National Hospital which had 1200-1500 beds. I was the Director of the program, and I had two facilitators (Rev. Dr. Grison Kirika and Rev. Dr. Chege Kimani, both of whom had completed three units of CPE in America). We trained nine students for one year until they graduated. That was the first class to graduate. They became effective and empowered in various hospitals throughout the Nairobi area. The $4,000 grant helped to give support to the students coming to the training. This included needs such as transportation (to help them to travel to the center and to the hospital where there were doing their practicals) and stipends for the outside speakers. The hospital ministry at Kenyatta became much more effective and interesting as a direct result of this training. It became popular. Many students were coming from different theological seminaries to take one CPE unit. Many students from seminaries came inquiring about how they could apply for the CPE program training. The Presbyterian Church East Africa supported the founding of the Kenya Ecumenical Clinical Pastoral Education (KECPE) program in Nairobi. The seminary students wanted to be accredited after they completed one unit, but we could not give them accreditation because our program was not accredited by any of the accreditation organizations yet. I called the ACPE accreditation office, and they required that I come back to the United States to complete the supervisory program in order our program to become fully accredited.

At that time, I applied to take supervisory training so that my program could be accredited in Kenya. I applied to come and complete the supervisory training at Lutheran Senior Services in St. Louis, Missouri (this was a nursing home that had a CPE program). I was accepted. Chaplain Joel Humble was the supervisor there. Before I returned to America, the CPE program I started at Kenyatta continued to run through the Presbyterian Church East Africa (in fact, even today, this program is running strong. Chaplains are being trained at Kikuyu Theological Seminary with CPE as one of their subjects). When I returned to St. Louis, I completed three more units of CPE there in my pursuit of becoming a supervisor. I was told that it would take five years to become a CPE supervisor (the training was a five-year course).

I was discouraged, because I did not have that time. I decided to instead graduate with three units (altogether, I had already completed seven units of CPE by this time). I was tired, not knowing which direction to go in. I prayed and I remembered the prayer that Jonah prayed when he was in stomach of the large fish. God heard his prayers *"Then Jonah prayed to the Lord his God from the stomach of the fish and said, 'I called out of my trouble and distress to the Lord and He answered me; out of the belly of Sheol I cried for help, and you heard my voice'" (Jonah 2:1).* At this time, I needed not to seek the accreditation, but instead I needed to seek God's direction. I heard the voice of God saying to me "This is the Lord's Table. Our savior invites those who trust in him to come and share the feast which he has prepared for them" I felt the presence of God and started claiming the promises of God (that even before I mentioned my prayers from my heart, God already knew what was best for me).

Let me tell you what happened! I decided that I was not going to take any more units of CPE (because the ones I had were already far more than the single unit students were seeking to be accredited in). I started thanking God for having opened the doors for me to become the ambassador of the living word of God (going to different congregations, preaching and giving my personal testimony that Jesus can save and sustain, and God does not reject any one). I wanted to do whatever God had for me. It was like it says in Isaiah, *"Then I heard the voice of the Lord saying 'whom shall I send, and who will go for Us?' Then I said 'Here am I. Send me!'"(Isaiah 6:8).* My original intention of becoming a CPE supervisor had been changed. I waited upon the Lord. He spoke to me and I heard God's voice. He told me to be open. He would do big things. "Jemimah, just be patient. I am the Alpha and the Omega, and I have good plans for you". *"I know the plans I have for you, declares the Lord, plans to prosper you and not to harm you. Plans to give you a hope and a future." (Jeremiah 29:11)*

16. Clinical Pastoral Education Experiences: Hospital Chaplaincy

As I have mentioned earlier, my life has been filled with compassion and a heart for the people admitted to hospitals (as well as for those who are suffering in their homes). My life as a hospital chaplain has humbled me before God. Working as a care giver to the patients has been such a blessing in life. I believe these experiences have truly prepared me for the second coming of Christ. *"Who then is the faithful and wise servant, whom the master has put in charge of the servants in his household to give them their food at the proper time? It will be good for that servant whose master finds him doing so when he returns. Truly I tell you, he will put him in charge of many possessions." (24:42-47)*

The purpose of hospital ministry is to be compassionate and to communicate with the spirit of the patients in their hospital beds. The patients are always waiting for whoever would stop near their bed to share a word of a comfort. This comes at critical time, when the patient is suffering with pain (and some are in their last days of life).

There is a wonderful book on pastoral care that I love called Do Not Sing to a Heavy Heart by Rev. Dr. Kenneth C. Hauk. In it, Dr. Hauk shares, *"...when you offer care and comfort to another, you are stepping into a holy place, into the other person's unique universe of selfhood, need, and pain. It is holy because, when you enter in, you will find Jesus already there ahead of you in that unique person. What a privilege...."* (p.35) I agree with Rev. Dr. Kenneth C. Hauk. After reading that book, I learned that sometimes we visit patients and start singing songs. This is often not the most appropriate thing to do when the patients are grieving or have heavy hearts. Dr. Hauk's book taught me a lot. We (pastoral care givers) need to remember that when we go out to offer the care services to the needy, we are approaching holy ground where Jesus is standing with those who are struggling with pain and suffering.

In another pastoral care text that I read, one of the writers said that "death was an enemy to a human being" because no one knows who will be dying next. This reminds me of one day when I was on call as a Chaplain at the Deacons Hospital in St. Louis Missouri. I was told that one of the patients was in the Cardiac Intensive Unit. This patient had been on a machine for more than three weeks. The doctor reported that the patient's brain, kidney and lungs had not been functioning, and so the patient had been surviving on the machines (life support). I was called when the Intensive Care Unit (ICU) team were discussing whether to stop life support so that the patient could die peacefully. The family was called in to consent to the advice of the doctors. I was called to be there when the doctors were explaining the condition of the mother to the family, and to hear what they had decided. It was a hard moment for the family (it was a large family). The doctor asked the family whether they wanted to be there when they took the mother off life support. I remember the first son said that they did not want to be there. The family said, "we want our Chaplain, who has been supporting our mother and us through this difficult time, Jemimah Ngatia, to be there." So, they asked me to be with the mother during her last moments. I agreed to be there for her (and represent the family on her behalf) while they took the mother off life support.

This was a nightmare for me, because I had never experienced this before. The family left. I walked together with the doctor and the nurse into the room as they began removing the life support machines, one by one. I asked the doctor how soon the patient would pass away once the life support was removed. The doctor told me it could take as little as one minute, or it could be thirty minutes or even an hour or a day. It all depended on how strong the patient's heart was. I remained there with the nurse and she continued removing each machine. This was so difficult for me. It was now just the two of us in the room with the patient. After everything was removed, the patient ended up living for another six hours longer! I was standing there the whole time because I did not want to leave her alone. I had accepted the request of the family (that I would be with their mother at the last hour of her life) and I needed to honor that. I remember that I had been there since morning. I was standing there the whole time without breakfast or lunch. I had not eaten for the whole day, because I did not want to take a chance of going for lunch and risking that I might find the patient had died while I was away. I was so hungry and exhausted. The hunger got to be too much. I finally decided to quickly run down to the cafeteria to grab a small bite to eat. Thankfully, I had a pager on me. I told the nurses that I was going to get something to eat and asked them to alert me if they saw any changes. While I went down to eat, I was alerted by the nurse. She called me to come back up quickly, because she believed the patient was about to die. I left my food right there and I ran fast upstairs to her room a few minutes later. I did not use the elevator (which might have stopped and made me wait). I ran into the room! The nurse saw me, and I observed that the patient's heartbeat kept slowing down. Finally, mother's heart stopped. So, after six and half hours, she died while I was looking at her. I was so grateful that I made it back in time to be present for this moment. I was able to witness her last breath and I was a blessing to be there with her. I was exhausted, and the nurses were supporting me. I was sad to see her die because I had loved her. I had gotten to know she and her family during her stay in the hospital. I came to know that she was a believer in Jesus. I knew her death was not a loss, because God called her home. The nurse called the doctor in to confirm her death. After that, the nurse in charge called the family. They came in (all of them). They each came into the room to see her body and say goodbye. I asked the eldest son if I could take everyone into the chapel. He agreed, and I took them to the chapel where they all cried, shouted and screamed. I allowed them to grieve together and I did not say any words to them (I was just present there with them). I brought Kleenex for their tears. I remember praying and thanking God for their mother's life (in my heart). When we were in the chapel, I had no words to say to the family, but I was able to give them my shoulder to cry on. I did not have to read any scriptures or pray out loud. I supported them in that process silently. I was fearful that I did not have the right scripture or words to say to them. They were in deep sorrow. I realized then that I did not need to say anything. I learned the importance of just being with them in their time of need. I gave them the gift of my presence, to be with them in their difficult time. I hugged them all before they left the hospital.

Later, after they had held their mother's funeral service, they came back to the hospital looking for me. They were so grateful that I had supported them in their time of need. They even wrote a letter to the director of the hospital explaining my journey with them. The director of the hospital called me to the administration office to be recognized by them because of the letter the family had written.

My experiences as a hospital chaplain have been such a support in my personal spiritual journey - to know it is not only for my own good that God called me to this ministry of the sick, but to bring others closer to God. Some of the patients I visit with for just a short time before they pass away (and their life ends according to the time God puts on their lives). Sometimes, I have heard people giving testimony that I was there for a few minutes and just when I came, the patient died. I have often stood with and prayed with patients as they take their last breaths. This is a great honor. I have gotten to witness their faith in God as they go home to the Lord. These experiences have taught me that this life is short. Only God knows how much time on earth each person will have. *"Teach us to number our days, that we may gain a heart of wisdom" (Psalm 90:12)*

Of course, not all patients that I visit at their hospital beds end up passing away. It is a great joy that many of them recover and are released from the hospital. Many get to go back to their families and home churches and they get to give testimony of what happened to them through their sickness. They share their journeys. I am grateful to have journeyed with many of them. Some patients return to the hospital to say hello and to compliment me for being with them.

Interacting with patients who both get to go home to the Lord (dying physically) and patients who get to go home to their earthly families (physically recovering) is a great joy and an honor.

17. My Life at McCormick Theological Seminary

My journey continued. Instead of finishing the CPE Supervisor training, God called me to continue my theological education. I applied to earn my Masters of Divinity through Giddings-Lovejoy Presbytery in St. Louis, Missouri. They were excited, because I was already a candidate for ordination (I had previously begun my candidacy for ordination in Kenya). I brought my recommendations from the Presbyterian Church East Africa (PCEA). However, there were some barriers to my acceptance. I did have theological education under my belt, but I did not have a Bachelor's degree. Because of this, I did not have enough credits at that time to be accepted into the Master's program. It was nightmare.

The year was 1997. McCormick Theological Seminary had an open house and I attended because I had applied for a Master of Divinity. I was invited to visit the seminary and get more information about the program.

This was for the prospective students and we were to spend two days on the campus. Students could ask questions, and professors could meet face to face with potential students. This was also where financial aid for the scholarships was determined.

After the first day, we were to be given the outcome (acceptance or rejection) the following day in the morning. Then, we would have lunch with the professors and students, and the leave in the afternoon.

The professors had a meeting. They determined that I was not accepted due to my previous academic education (or lack thereof). I remember was called in first and I was told by the Dean that I was not qualified to be admitted for the Master of Divinity program. I was told that the faculty had discussed my case, and there was no way that I could be admitted. I can still remember that moment. I cried very much, because I had hope that I would be taken into the program anyway. I was disappointed. I cried all day. *"So, my heart began to despair over all my toilsome labor under the sun" (Ecclesiates 2:20)*

I went back to my room to prepare to leave. I was screaming! My heart was broken, and I had no one to speak to me at that time. There was no one there to comfort me for the pain and hurt I felt when I found out I was rejected. At that time, the faculty were still discussing my case (but I did not know that yet).

When I came back to pick up my stuff (still crying and feeling lonely that no one was there to listen to me at that time), I heard someone come down the stairs. I remember someone coming down to walk to where I was seated with my suit case. He was a very skinny man. I was waiting for my transportation to the airport. I noticed that it was one of the other prospective students who had come to sit where I was still crying. My heart was broken and there were heavy tears in my eyes (my eyes were red). This student held my hand and asked me "why are you crying?" I told him my pain, and he prayed for me and he shared with me his own personal story. He asked me "So, are you so hurt because you were not admitted for the program in this seminary?" I told him "yes." I remember telling him that this was my sorrow, especially because I had high hopes that I would be admitted. I thought that God had called me to this program and answered my prayers. I knew God could do those things which we see are impossible (it is possible with God). And yet, I felt let down.

He looked at me and said to me "Jemimah, let me tell you about me. I was diagnosed with HIV and I have been HIV positive since 1989. My name is James Hicks. I have lived as a gay man with a partner, but my partner is HIV negative. Now Jemimah, my body is weak. I can die anytime now. My doctor has already shared this with me and my partner. But I am still here. Therefore, there are so many seminaries in USA! If McCormick will not admit you, surely others will take you as one of their students. You can go to seminary in another place!" As soon as I heard his story, my tears dried up. He prayed for me. My heart was touched by his story. I started praying for him and encouraging him to keep on trusting God in his life, and I was ready to listen to more of his story. At that point, I shared with him that I was a hospital Chaplain before I came to the United States and that I used to comfort and hear the stories of patients who were HIV positive in my hospital. Some of them were in the stage of denial and they could not relate to the love of God, because they felt that God was punishing them. The truth is that God is love, and He loves us all. We all fall short of the glory of God (Romans 3:23). I shared with James that God is a loving God. There I reminded him of that same scripture. God is a loving God. He shared with me that he knew he was not going to make it, but that he was trusting God. Our relationship would continue past this time, in fact, later I saw him fall sick to the point of dying and he sent for me to pray for him (in Swahili) in the ICU. I still remember him.

After we shared our lives in the apartment that day, someone came and knocked on the door. It was a secretary of the Dean of Academics. She was sent to me by the faculty to summon me to meet with them again. I remember Professor Homer Ashby was the Academic Dean. He spoke to me with words of wisdom. He shared with me that the faculty had continued talking after their initial discussion. He had remembered that there was a chance to admit "International Special Students", and he wondered if the seminary could admit me on that basis (instead of through the traditional credit requirements). Apparently, the seminary was able to admit two Special International Students each year, but they had not done so. In fact, I would be the first ever student to be given this opportunity. Professor Homer Ashby was a pastoral care professor in the seminary, and he a gave good recommendation to the faculty for me to be accepted. I went to the office and at that time and I was refreshed (not crying anymore). The Dean told me, after a long discussion with the other faculty, they had decided to admit me as a "Special International Student" and I was then given all the materials! I was accepted!! Where God had opened the doors, no one could shut them. *"Humble yourselves before the Lord, and He will lift you up." (James 4:10)*

When I went back down to pick up my suitcase (to head to the airport), I found the James still waiting for me to hear what the faculty had said. I told him what happened and that I had been admitted after all! He saw a smile on my face and he gave me a hug. I told the man "you know, the God we worship is a living God who can see where a man cannot see." We held hands and we praised God together, knowing that our God is God in season and out of season. My heart was full of joy. I had seen the victory of God. I started singing the songs of praise in my language (Kikuyu), which was my mother's tongue. At that time, I felt humbled before God knowing, that the presence of God gave me the strength and the power. I belong to a mighty God.

18. My Experience as a Minority Student

My life as a minority student has been a different experience. In most of my classes, I have been the unique one. I have had experiences where students made fun of me (for example, anytime I would stand to speak, I would overhear other students saying to one another "she is from Africa! I like her accent and the way she talks - she always has something spiritual to share. It's always about her experience in Kenya"). Some of my peers did not even know which part of the continent of Africa (let alone, my actual country) I had come from. Whenever we had discussions, I saw that some of the students did not want to be in my group. This was because of my identity and of them not having interacted international students like me before in classes. They were afraid of offending me accidentally, so they would avoid me instead. Most of the time, I was the last one to speak. This was because the American students seemed to know it all (the truth is that they actually knew very little about Africa). In my culture, we wait to be called on before speaking, but I learned that in America you don't have to wait. I remember one day, we were having a small group discussion. One of the students said his group had "we have nine plus Jemimah." The professor asked him what he meant. This kind of thing happened over and over (because some of the students did not see me – even if I was sitting right next to him or her, I was still not seen). Also, I felt rejected. I especially felt this way in my Greek class (the professor was a retired Lutheran Evangelical minister who was over sixty-five years of age). Anytime I got ready to give a presentation in my class, he would call the next student instead of calling on me (I felt like he did this because he believed I was taking too long or wasting his time, so he tried to avoid having me speak). If I asked him a question, he would always say, "sit down. Next! I cannot understand what you are saying." Then he would proceed to call on the next student to continue with his question. I remember one day I was frustrated by being in a community that did not understand my culture (and they of course had never interacted with someone else like "Jemimah").

It was difficult to find a friend who I could visit with when we did not have class. I started to come to the realization that to get what I needed, I had to intentionally make extra efforts to reach out to the students around me (even if they were not taking those steps first). One thing I said to myself was "since I love to cook, I have an idea! What can I do to cook for and bless my community?" After my prayer, I felt I needed to start doing something for the students. So, I started cooking pancakes every Saturday morning and I would give them out to my neighbors in the dormitories. Over time, my pancakes became so popular! If I knocked at the door, I gave at least two pancakes to each student. If there was a student who did not get enough, he or she would come to my dorm and ask for more pancakes personally. Cooking pancakes went over very well! When students came over for pancakes, I had the chance to talk with them (and often, the discussion continued). Many of these students became my friends. Because of the tradition of pancake Saturdays, I got to build relationships with my classmates. Now, when we were in class or doing group discussions, my peers' attitudes toward me had also changed and gotten better. Most of the students in my dorm became my good friends. Because of these relationships, students started knocking on my door before class and we would walk together across campus (it was not like this before). Some of them also helped proof read my papers as the year went on.

After that, I felt like I needed to do something to reach out to those who were not living on campus (i.e. those who did not get the Saturday Pancakes). I talked to the Professor of the Languages Lab. I made an appointment and discussed with him whether I could start teaching basic Swahili language in the Language lab. He was excited. He supported the idea and he promised he was going to meet with the business office (to see if I could even be paid). After a week, I was called into the business office to fill out forms for me to start teaching Swahili language in the language lab. I was going to paid $10.00 per hour and I was given instructions on how to fill out the paperwork. You know what, I thanked God for that opportunity immediately! I started teaching the class on my first off day. The class information was posted in the Seminary's weekly community newspaper. The message went out that students who were interested in learning basic Swahili could register at Language lab.

After a week, I had nine students registered in my first class! I met together with those want to learn Swahili. We had coffee, tea and snacks provided. Together, we decided on the day to start officially.

In class, I started teaching basic Swahili words and phrases (for example: *greetings* in Swahili is *jambo,* water in Swahili is *maji,* food in Swahili is *chakula).* These were the first Swahili words that I taught to the class. I needed to complete my report for the language lab professor. My report was encouraging. Let me share this. This class was a time of God opening a dialogue between myself and students/professors. This was something that I believe could not have been achieved or reached in any other way.

My dear sisters and brothers, there is no mountain bigger than our God! When you continue to read this book, you will see that my story relates to the vision Ezekiel saw in Ezekiel 37. *"The Lord took hold of me, and I was carried away by the Spirit of the Lord to a valley filled with bones. He led me all around among the bones that covered the valley floor. They were scattered everywhere across the ground and were completely dried out. Then he asked me, 'son of man, can these bones become a living people again?' 'O Sovereign lord.,' I replied, 'you alone know the answer to that.' Then he said to me, 'speak a prophetic message to these bones and say, 'dry bones, listen to the word of the Lord! This is what the sovereign Lord says: 'look! I am going to put breath into you and make you live again. I will put flesh and muscles on you and cover you with skin. I will put breath into you, and you will come to life. Then you will know that I am the LORD'"* (Ezekiel 37:1-6) When I first came to seminary, I felt like there were dry bones all around me. The place felt lifeless and I was not connected to those around me. Later (as God heard my prayers and I stepped out in faith to start Pancake Saturdays and Swahili classes), I saw those dry bones come to life! I pray this will help you to understand more about the fact that God can use you anytime anywhere for His glory! I remember senior Students would come to preach in our Wednesday community worship service. When I myself became a senior, I had prepared my Swahili students to sing a chorus in Swahili and read scriptures in the Swahili language. It was amazing to hear American students reading the Bible and singing choruses in the Swahili language! Amen!

What I want to say about this story is that many international students have gone through difficult times when they try to engage with other students who are not part of their culture. Many have gone through difficulties being a minority in a majority culture (for some this has led to discouragement, frustration, depression and has been big reason many do not finish school. They just return to their home countries). It takes lots of patience, perseverance and God's power for international students to complete school abroad (and even more to continue their careers in America). God gave me the idea and initiative to begin those two efforts. It was truly a breakthrough!! Leading Pancakes Saturday and teaching Swahili on Wednesdays helped many American students and professors in the community get to know me better. Many friends who were my fellow students even organized a wonderful surprise birthday party for me (the woman who organized this was my roommate - her name was Beth Myers). Through what God did in these efforts, I saw that students wanted to learn more from me. Walking together in faith means we serve the same God. We can work together for justice. We cannot say that we love God and we serve God if we cannot show love to a stranger. Again, I love the African proverb that says "if you want to go fast, go alone. If you want to go far, go together". I want us to go far. After we shared prayers and meditation in the chapel, I started walking together with other students and working together with them (other students learned to make pancakes as well and expressed desires to visit Kenya). As we did these things together, we learned so much from one another. We saw that we were all the same in the eyes of God. All Christians are called to support one another as Jesus supported those who were far off. He opened the door and made a way for us to know Him and to come close to His presence. This brought a lot joy in my heart. I started counting the blessings in my life, particularly as an international student. Where there is no way, God can make the way! It says in Isaiah *"I am the Lord, who opened the way through the waters, making a dry path through the sea"* (Isaiah 43:16). After doing all that God called me to do, I found that these things also helped me earn good grades.

After I graduated, I left a good legacy at McCormick Theological Seminary in Chicago, Illinois! By the time I left, all the students had learned so much about me and where I was from. When I first came, they were uninformed about even the continent of Africa (and certainly knew nothing about me except that I had an accent). By the time I graduated, they knew about Kenya and East Africa and about my life. If we carry Jesus in our hearts, He will testify to many people through us. I had trusted God in my journey (whether on top of the mountain or deep in the valley; whether in the light or in the darkness), God has been there! I want to encourage everyone reading this book that my God is a living God! God is my personal savior - Jesus Christ! He is a miracle God! My story has been strengthened by the story of the Israelites. They were in the wilderness for 40 years until finally God allowed them to reach the promised land. During my time at Seminary, God walked with me until I finished my studies (it was not quite 40 years altogether, but it took a long time). Amen!

"So the people of Israel ate manna for forty years until they arrived at the land where they would settle. They ate manna until they came to the border of the land of Canaan" (Exodus 16:15)

"For the LORD your God has blessed you in everything you have done. He has watched your every step through this great wilderness. During these forty years, the LORD your God has been with you, and you have lacked nothing." (Deuteronomy 2:7)

19. Master of Divinity Degree and Doctor of Ministry Degree

Before I began Seminary, I remember I was escorted to the campus by my family. We had two cars (driving from St. Louis to Chicago). One car carried food and luggage, and the other had people. When we drove to Chicago, my daughter drove one car and our friend, Mr. Frances Wambogo, was driving the other car. My husband was in Frances's car. My children and I were in my daughter Jane's car. Mr. Frances pulled up to my daughter and complained that we were driving too slowly. Then he pulled away. You know what, after that we lost each other for over 8 hours. We struggled. All my paperwork (including a map and directions to the seminary) was in the other car. When we reached Chicago, we fortunately saw a road sign for McCormick (and we were able to stop near there for directions). We did not see the other car again until we finally arrived at the Seminary!

The first day at the seminary was hard for me because. I had brought $11,000 with me (in cash and check). The admissions office was open when we arrived. I had all the admissions paperwork as well as the money I needed in hand. My family and friends had brought me there so that they could also see my school. This was on a Friday. My family wanted to come and settle me in before they went back on Sunday. My husband and my children needed to return to St. Louis, Missouri at the end of the weekend.

We tried to get to McCormick before the business office closed. To do this, we left St. Louis very early in the morning, and we reached Chicago at about 11am. I had the welcome letter from the seminary and instructions that stated I was to report to the financial officer when I arrived at the seminary. The instructions said that once I paid my balance, they would give me the key to my dorm.

By the grace of God, we found the office open. The Financial Officer (Bursar) was there. We waited for her to call me in while my family was waiting (they were so excited. They want to see mom's doom and to help me settle in). We went in with my daughter Jane and my husband and I introduced myself to the financial officer. She said to me "I remember you, Jemimah" She said, "You had difficulties because the seminary was not able to admit you, but the Dean convinced the faculty and you were admitted." She was preparing some documents for me and sharing the code of conduct of the seminary ("Dos and Don'ts). Then she asked me for the money. I gave her the $11,000 I had in hand. She counted the money and then she said, "I need $17,000 total. Your balance is now $6,000." She asked me where the rest of the money was. I reminded her that I had the tuition fee scholarship, and if that was not enough, my family would bring the remaining balance of $6,000 later. She responded to me (right in front of my family), "I know you are from Africa and Africa is a poor country." My family was so sorrowful to hear this. I asked her, "have you ever even visited Africa? Which African country is poor? I am from Kenya and Kenya is not poor!" I prayed to God, "now is the time to come down here in this office of the financial director of money and let her know your power! You are only one who has the KEYS to open the kingdom of heaven! To open this apartment dormitory is a small thing for you. It is for the righteous who enter in the kingdom of heaven! Let this white lady know who carries the keys of Heaven! When God opens the door, no one can close it! When God says yes, it is yes! No one can say no!" At that time, I said to God "I want, my God, to continue feeling your presence, because you are the only one in whom I trust. I am humbled by you, my God. I am requesting these keys." I told her, "please give me the keys, and we will discuss the financial matter on Monday when the Dean is in his office." At this time, she had completely refused to give me the keys. It was getting late. We did not know anyone in Chicago. My luggage (and food) was still in the car. My children were hungry and frustrated (this happened over the lunch hour). She locked her office and just walked out. She just left us outside, wondering what to do. She never did give us the keys… She just left us stranded with nowhere to stay.

My husband was talking to the security guard outside, and my children went back to the car to wait to hear what the director of money would say. They were expecting that the next thing we would do would be to go to my apartment. The security man told my husband he knew one student from Kenya. We considered calling him. We could not go back to St. Louis. My family would not leave me outside, and my daughter Joy and my grandson

Benson, Jr were supposed to go back to school on Monday. My husband, his friend, and my daughter Jane also had to be at their jobs on Monday. My heart was broken. My family did not want to leave me outside. Immediately I remembered that I had a friend who lived in Chicago (Wajuku Boro from Kenya). She was a student at Northern Baptist Seminary. I happened to have her phone number. I called her up and I told her the story of what had happened. She told me "you and your family, Jemimah, are welcome to spend the night with me in my home". She gave us her address and we went to her house. She prepared dinner for us and gave us all a place to sleep. We spent the night there and we slept comfortably. We praised God, singing songs of praise and telling stories demonstrating that we were covered with the blood of Jesus. In fact, we spent the entire weekend giving God praises. After our last breakfast, my family left back to St. Louis, and I was left there with my friend. I spent another night there and I drove back to the seminary on Monday morning.

On Monday morning, I returned to the seminary office. I went to the Dean and explained what had happened on Friday. I explained everything that happened. The Dean was so angry! He walked over to the Bursar's office (who had heard what I was saying as I was telling the Dean my story). She did not have anything to say for herself! I was then given my key (right in front of her). *"You prepare a table before me in the presence of my enemies…" (Psalm 23:5a)* The Dean told her "you cannot do that to our new international student! Especially not in front of her family!" The Dean asked me, "do you want a roommate?" "Yes!" I agreed. I was then assigned with another international student - a roommate from Korea (we also had another American roommate). It was an international room!

I was directed to the apartment. I walked in the door and I began settling in. I was warmly greeted by my new roommates. Sometimes the devil comes our way, and we always wait for the victory. He wants to distract us from God's mission. The woman from the financial office tried to come to me before the end of the day to explain the rules of the seminary. I told her that that was fine, but my family went home broken hearted because of her actions (and her attitude). "I am a Christian." I shared. "I believe there is no mountain higher than God" I told her I wanted her to understand that although she truly hurt me, I wanted her to know that I forgave her, because Christ died to forgive me. *"If you do not forgive others their sins, your father will not forgive your sins" (Matthew 6:15)* As you continue reading this book, I pray that you see that there is great gain in trusting God.

I began the Master of Divinity program at McCormick theological Seminary. The school year went on. The struggle to earn my Master of Divinity degree at McCormick Theological Seminary was so hard for me. I was often tired, especially when I was studying Hebrew and Greek. It took me two and a half years to complete my degree. I used to take four classes each semester (and three classes over the summer). I was a full-time student (because I was awarded a full scholarship).

I wanted to finish my degree quickly, so that I could be free to go and help with the wedding of my daughter Joy Nyawira. This wedding was to be held in the summer 2001. My time at McCormick Theological Seminary came with a lot of challenges. One of the biggest challenges was that I did not have my family there with me. I had to drive from Chicago to St. Louis every other weekend (and my family drove up to visit me once a month). I remember it was winter, and I used to drive alone. It was very hard to find my way in Chicago day or night (especially in Hyde Park, where my apartment was for Seminary). Once, on my drive back to Chicago, I finally reached the city (after driving seven hours), only to miss my exit. There are many one-way streets in Chicago and it is so easy to get off course! I got lost for about three hours! It was too dark (it was difficult to make out the street signs) and I could not find my way Finally, I found myself at the Midway Chicago airport! I did not have any idea where I was! I remember singing a Kikuyu song (saying "Nii ningenda Ngai umenyage ningenaga muno niwe…") which means "I want God to know I will always be happy because you are God…" I sung this because I wanted to share with God that I was always happy, even if I was lost. I could still experience the presence of God in the darkness. The song comforted me. I was hungry and tired (and the next day I had class!). I prayed to God that He would give me peace of mind because I had chosen this life to follow Him (every day and night). Choosing this life meant not being led by my fears, worries, depression or frustration, but my life mission was to enjoy God. This life reminds me of the promises of God. *"Keep this book of the law always on your lips; meditate on it day and night, so that you may be careful to do everything written in it. Then you will be prosperous and successful." (Joshua 1:8)*

After two weeks at the seminary, I was walking to class one morning and I met one of the professors. There was a lot of snow on the ground that day. She asked me "Jemimah, where are you going? I think you are in my class this morning". I told her, "I am going to class" but at that time I was walking in the opposite direction (there was so much snow, it was hard to tell where to go). She told me to follow her, and we walked together to school.

After a while, I asked Rev. Dr. Homer Ashby (this was the same professor who advocated for me to be accepted and to get the international scholarship) whether I could sign up for him to be my advisory professor. He knew who I was, and I knew he would expect a lot from me. I knew that if he could be my advisor, I would be more successful in my studies. He agreed. He said to me "Jemimah, you have to work hard on your subjects, and you will need to prove that you can do it." I promised him that I would try my best to not let him down.

In my third year, I was called by the Executive Director of the Institute of Leadership (ISL) in Chicago. ISL was a program led by Religious sisters of BVM (Blood of Virgin Mary) congregation (from the Catholic Church). She told me they were given my name from the McCormick Seminary. They heard that I was from Africa. They said they had been seeking a woman from Africa who could be trained to go to Africa and introduce the program they taught. This program was the Institute for Spiritual Leadership (ISL) program. They wanted a woman with experience with women's leadership. I explained to them that I was a leader in many programs in Kenya before I came to the United States. I had led several programs, especially for women in ministry. ISL was seeking a woman candidate that already had a Ph.D.

The Executive Director, Sister Patricia Bombard, called me on the phone to tell me about the interview. Before I shared my story, I said to her "this is not my position, because I have no PhD." They still called me for an interview and they accepted me! It was then that they told me they would call me back. However, at this time, I started talking to myself saying "this is not what I wanted to do. I need to finish my ordination and go back to Kenya and continue training the chaplains in my hospital in Kenya."

After one week, Sister Patricia Bombard called me and told me she needed more information and she wanted to continue the discussion. I had a feeling that they had accepted me, but I still sensed doubt over whether it would be possible for me to earn my doctorate. I wanted to be where God was calling me. I went to meet with her. She told me they had considered my name (among others) to be given a scholarship toward a Doctor of Ministry program at Chicago Theological Seminary. I did not say any word to her. I started crying and praying out loud in my mother tongue calling "Jehovah, Jehovah, Jesus Son of our mighty God come down! You are alpha and omega. I need you God, now, not tomorrow! You are Jehovah, my savior the one I trust! You are here today and tomorrow and forever. Amen! Amen! Amen!"

I was talking to myself, "me? Becoming a doctor?" In the Catholic tradition of prayers, they are not used to loud calling, "Jehovah Jireh". She gave me Kleenex to wipe my tears. I kept quiet for a while, experiencing the presence of God, and looking at the love Sister Patricia Bombard was showing to me. She had confidence that I could meet her need in taking the Institute for Spiritual Leadership (ISL) to Kenya for the benefit of African countries. After a long discussion, she told me that my story impressed her. Hearing about my spiritual journey helped her to trust me. She said that I would meet her expectations of starting this program in Kenya for Africa and that she had confidence in me. As you continue to read this book, you will read about how the Values-Leadership program would eventually touched many souls through our churches in Kenya.

When I joined this program, it shaped me. The program became a great part of my personal and spiritual growth. Ultimately, I took the classes in church and Spiritual Leadership for two years. Meeting Sister Bombard completely changed my life for the better. At the end of the ISL course, I was commissioned as a Spiritual Director.

As I mentioned above, I was given a scholarship for my Doctor of Ministry degree from Chicago Theological Seminary. My time as a D.Min student was full of challenges. Obtaining a doctorate was a high degree. Professors are used to teaching many students from America as well as international students from different countries. One of the most encouraging aspects for me in the D.Min program was that we had so many students from other counties (I heard so many accents…it was not only me that the professors could not understand). I worked very hard not to be left behind. My course load included homework deadlines, a lot of reading and turning in papers to the professors. My biggest challenge in all of this was writing. Unfortunately, this program had a lot of writing and research! My professor advisor called me and told me she wanted to see me in her office. I went to meet with her and we had a good discussion. She wanted to help me in areas where I was not as strong (particularly in my research for the writing of my thesis).

I struggled to think through what to pursue and write about. I wondered whether the Board was going to understand my ideas when I put them on paper. I did not know what to do. I went back another day and met with my advisor again, asking her for help in what I was going to write about. One thing one about me is that I am not necessarily a good reader (and now, to research my thesis, I would have to read volumes and volumes of books on my own time). She took me to the library and showed me areas that I could start thinking about for thesis topic. She left me at the library. I just sat down, not knowing where to start (it was difficult even thinking about what to write about).

In that same library, there was a friend of mine working. Her name was Dr. Emma. She was my classmate (and she was from Madagascar, Africa). At the time, Dr. Emma had her Master's Degree in Library Sciences. With her background, she of all people, knew what I would need from the library to help me to write my thesis. I took her to the shelves my professor had shown me. She sat me down and she asked me, "Jemimah, what do you want to write about?" I told her, "Dr. Emma, I do not know" She laughed and said to me, "Jemimah, you have to write something, so that you can tell people about it. It has to be something that comes from your heart." I said to her "like what?" She shared that we had to find time to discuss and pray for God's direction. "I see even now you do not know what you are going to write. Already, other students are about to finish their theses." I asked her "what do you think I can start doing?" "You need to pray for God to show what to write. You need that before I show you the resources of what you can do. We need to come up with the idea first, and then finding the resources will not be hard." We set a day and time to meet again to discuss together what I could write about. I left Dr. Emma and went home to my apartment with a broken heart. This was a huge task for me. The problem I was facing was denial. How was I in this place? How could I write a dissertation? I had come so far. This type of education was not supposed to be for me (how could I, Jemimah, write a doctoral thesis?). I was not yet there, but I was reflecting on my life and where I had come from. My feelings whispered doubt into my ears, "you cannot do this. You are just wasting your time."

I felt led to call my professor and explain to her about what I was feeling (about reading all those volumes and writing a thesis of more than two hundred pages, not to mention citing the books I had read). I decided to just not do it now (and to meet with professor to tell her I would drop my classes and just return to where my family and ministry were). My friend Dr. Emma waited for me at the library and I did not go to meet with her. She came to my apartment and found me lonely, watching TV (not really watching TV because I am not a TV person – I was just staring at it). When she looked at me she said I sounded to her like I was sick or I had been crying.

Dr. Emma was a spiritual person. Her husband was a Lutheran Pastor (Rev. Norbert). She started encouraging to me that God could show us the way. I did not like hearing that because God had not yet shown me the way to write and to read all those volumes of books (I could not tell where to even start). There was a lot going on in my mind about what to do next. My friend Dr. Emma prayed for me that night. The following morning, I went looking for her. She took me into her office and talked to me, encouraging me that I could really do it. My heart was still heavy, but she admonished me, telling me "Jemimah, you have already graduated with an M.Div. at McCormick! Even this you can do with the help from our mighty God." *"I lift my eyes up to the mountains – where does my help come from? My help comes from the LORD, the maker of heaven and earth. He will not let your foot slip – he who watches over you will not slumber; indeed, he who watches over Israel will neither slumber nor sleep." (Psalm 121:1-4)* Dr. Emma and her husband Norbert were such an encouragement to me. They really loved God and trusted Him and saw what He could do when my vision faltered. They were like spiritual mentors for me.

I remembered calling my daughter Jane Ngatia about it. She told me, "Mom, you have achieved so many things in your life. Now, God has opened a door for you to pursue your Doctor of Ministry degree. This is unbelievable!

Trust God, whom you have trusted since you went there, and you will see the victory of God." She said again, "Mom, you can do it! I know you can do it! All your family members are counting on you! At this time, the devil is defeated as he was defeated on the cross! Take courage, Mom!" After listening to what my daughter shared with me, I sat down, and I lifted my eyes to God. I remembered my life had been empowered by the Spirit (the ISL program had changed my life and strengthened my spiritual journey, too). I had followed God's calling for me (not only when things were easy). I reminded myself that my God was God in season and out of season. I felt the presence of God and I was encouraged!

I went out looking for my friend and prayer partner, Dr. Emma (and her husband Rev. Norbert), and I remember that day she saw me entering her office. She jumped on me and told me, "Jemimah, sit here! I know you have good news to share with me" She closed the door of her office and she reminded me the love of God (that if we trust in him, everything would be okay). I told her what my daughter Jane had shared with me, and she told me, "Jemimah, you can do it! Let us pray." She prayed for me and I felt encouraged. I was ready to work with her. The first question she asked was, "Jemimah, tell me: before you came from Kenya, what were you doing in your church, and which ministry were you empowering?" I started sharing with her that I was a Stephen Ministry Trainer. I was training Stephen Ministers as care-givers in my congregation. Then she asked me, "can you tell me more about what you were doing?" Then I continued sharing how I started the Stephen Ministry with the materials prepared in Midwest America, and how I was passionate about that ministry because it was very powerful in our congregation. The ministry helped members of my congregation to grow spiritually and support those in need through visiting those who are sick at home and hospitals). After I shared my story with Dr. Emma, she told me, "now, this is what you are going to write! Your topic will be: Introducing the Stephen Ministry into a Kenyan Context Using Materials Prepared in Midwestern America." This was a breakthrough!!

Let me tell, you my body felt like the way it feels when you take a warm shower! The next stage for me was to find resources to research my topic. Before we went out from her office, we prayed, thanking God for the breakthrough. I was finally ready to start writing my thesis.

My friend Dr. Emma showed me where to get the books I needed for the research. I was now ready now to call my professor and let her know what I was going to write about! She was happy and told me what I needed to do in writing the introduction of my thesis. I started my writing by going back to Dr. Emma at the library and showing her how far I had come. It was easy for me to write on this topic. This was because I was trained as Stephen Minister and I had been trained as a Trainer (because my work in church in Kenya - before I came here - was as a Stephen Minister Trainer).

I started finding materials and looking for books from African Countries. I came across great writings from authors and theologians such as Dr. John Mbithi, Dr.

Misimbi Kanyoro and Rev. Dr. Nyambura Njoroge. Dr. Nyambura Njoroge was the first ordained woman in the Prebyterian Church East Africa (PCEA) and she has been my model in ministry. I found so many helpful books and articles in the library.

My final presentation and defense of my dissertation to the team of professors and D.Min students was a challenge, but God is good! Thankfully, after defending my thesis, they did not have very many questions for me. This was because my project was focused in the Kenyan context (the Board was not already familiar with my context, so they did not have many questions). During my final presentation, my professor was proud of me and she gave good comments on my thesis. She had helped me to organize everything in a way that people could read and understand. She also helped me write in the style that most American professors preferred. They all had something to learn from the Kenyan culture and context.

The next stage for me was to start thinking about my graduation day. This seemed like a dream! During the rehearsal for our graduation, the professors started calling my name, "Dr. Jemimah Ngatia". I looked behind me to see whether there was someone else in our class called Jemimah Ngatia (because I could not believe that I was finished, and that I was actually going to be called "Dr. Jemimah Ngatia." I started crying. I was understanding the love of God to me (and feeling that only God can move mountains).

When you feel like you are at the end of the road, that is the time God comes and shows the way. My family (and Dr. Emma's family, my professor and Sister Patrica Bombard and Sister Cathy) all came to praise God for the wonderful achievement. They all came to celebrate the victory! I had completed my doctoral degree! My daughter and my husband reminded me that there was nothing too hard for God. I learned to be patient and humble before God (even today, I know that waiting for God is the way to achieve my goals). I thank God for my husband, who was so helpful in supporting me while I was writing my thesis. He was supporting me through not giving me extra work when I was doing my homework (many times, my husband cooked for the family to give me more time to study). I gave God glory for such a gift of a committed husband and supportive family.

God is good! Finally, I graduated with good grades on my transcript. I had mostly As and Bs (and only one C). Pastoral care subjects came easy to me because of my previous experience. I had been a hospital chaplain in Kenya (and trained in the US), and I had lots of church experience. I did very well in pastoral care and this continued to be a great strength in the life of my ministry.

As you continue to read this book, you will understand that after I earned my Master of Divinity degree (at McCormick Theological Seminary) and my Doctor of Ministry degree (at Chicago Theological Seminary), I came to be ordained as the first new immigrant woman from Africa to be ordained by the Presbyterian Church USA (PCUSA).

During the time I was getting my doctorate, my husband Benson was able to move with me to Chicago. He was there living with me from that point on. My children stayed behind in St. Louis (by this time, they were already adults). I graduated from Chicago Theological Seminary (with my Doctor of Ministry degree) in 2003.

20. The Wedding of My Daughter Joy Nyawira

While I was busy at seminary (for my Master of Divinity at McCormick Theological Seminary), my daughter Joy told me she wanted to get married. As is our Kikuyu custom, the mother traditionally buys the gown for her daughter's wedding (my mother bought my dress for me). I was so excited! Joy told me the day and the time she would get married (unfortunately, during this time, I would be finishing my degree). I sat with Joy and I promised her I would be there (even though I was taking four classes, and then over the summer, I would take another three). It would be tight, but I would still be able to finish school and come out to pray and help her organize the wedding. Since we were in a foreign country, we would try our best! I wanted her to have her dream wedding, even in America. I really worked hard to finish in time! God is good! I finished my degree and graduated, and we were able to come together now to pray and organize the wedding.

While I was still a student, I called my daughter Joy and told her to go with her sister Jane and do some searching (window shopping) for her wedding gown. At the time, my family was living in St. Louis, Missouri (and I was at Chicago Theological Seminary studying for my Doctor of Ministry). They visited a few of the bridal stores there until she found the one she liked most. The two of them went into one of the bridal stores where they found a very nice gown. Joy liked it very much and her sister Jane recommended that she get that one.

Then she called me and told me "Mom, we have gone to many stores and we found the one that I want very much." Then I told her I would find time to come to St. Louis, so I could also see what it looked like. I arrived one Friday, and we went to the store on Saturday (where she tried it on before me). It was so nice and beautiful. I started crying, seeing now that my daughter was going to get married and go into another family. I told her it was beautiful. She told me, "You know, mom, this is called the 'Cathedral gown.'" I asked her "what does that mean?" She said, "it can only marry in a Cathedral church." We laughed together at that. Then, I looked at the price. It was $900.00! My immediate reaction was, "wow, this is expensive!". My daughter told me "you told me to look for the gown I wanted. This is the gown I like the most." We had not discussed the money beforehand and I had not given her a budget to spend. This was hard for me because I was still a student with no money, but God reminded me that I had asked her to look for her gown and to pick out the one she really liked. *"When a man makes a vow to the Lord or takes an oath to obligate himself by a pledge, he must not break his word but must do everything he said."* *(Numbers 30:2).* God, through His word, reminded me to keep a good example for what the bible is teaching us.

The Lord gently nudged my heart that I should not complain any more about the gown being expensive. What I needed to do was to pray for God to provide the money (for me to keep my word to her and buy my daughter's dream dress as a mother's gift). So, I said "Yes! I remembered that!" I said "it is okay. God will provide." I knew that God would provide, because He is a provider (I was reminded of Abraham's heavy sacrifice of Isaac and how God then provided a Ram). *"Abraham answered, 'God Himself will provide the lamb for the burnt offering, my son' and the two of them went together" (Genesis 22:8)*

The time came for me go out looking for the "cathedral" – the big Presbyterian Church in St. Louis Missouri. I called the First Presbyterian Church in Kirkwood and they offered me a place for my daughter's wedding. They reserved the date and we were blessed during the wedding and the afterwards.

During the ceremony, when the pastor was reading about the institution of Christian marriage, I started crying. At that time, we were standing in front (my husband Benson was holding Joy's hand to be ready to hand her over to the husband to be. I was holding her other hand, and Joe and Joy were waiting to be joined). I was next to Benson and I started crying. The tears were flowing. When Joy looked at me, she started crying. When Joe the bridegroom saw Joy crying, he also dropped his tears. The only person who I did not see crying was my husband Benson (he is a Kenyan man. Kenyan Men do not show their tears - this does not mean that they do not cry, but Kenyan men hide their crying. Many people say they don't cry, but they do; they just hide it. It is very rare thing to see a Kenyan man's tears). When my husband handed over our daughter Joy to Joe, Benson and I went back and sat on the pew where my family was seated. I was sitting next to my sister, Cecila Kamau, who had travelled all the way from Kenya to attend Joy's wedding.

After the vows, new the newly married couple walked to Chancellor to sign the wedding certificate (holding their hands very tightly). At that time, I was still seated by my husband and my sister Cecilia Kamau. As our daughter walked past us, the train of her gown was so beautiful and trailed over the steps. My sister Cecilia said to me, "she has now gone to a new family." Then I saw the way they walked and her cathedral gown flowing by step by step. My sister again said "Oh, she has now gone." Then, I broke down again into tears. My husband asked me quietly "were you not expecting this?" I answered that I had mixed feelings of both joy and sadness. I said to myself, "it is good that now Joy has a husband, but it also means that she and I will not be doing things the way we used to do anymore".

Today, this is my advice to those mothers with daughters about to get married. Be prepared for these feelings. I thought I had been strong when I helped prepare other mothers during their arrangements for their daughters weddings, but when it come to my own, the reality was very different than what I had imagined or expected.

When we got to the reception, there were so many people (350 were invited, but over 500 people come to celebrate

Joe and Joy's wedding!). The reason why we had so many people there to celebrate was because Joe and Joy's wedding was exactly like a wedding in Kenya. In the Kenyan community of St. Louis, Missouri (where the wedding was performed), it was not our tradition to return RSVP cards (saying that you would attend the wedding or not) like the American tradition. In our culture, you just needed to show up (and sometimes people also would bring their friends). In this wedding, we had lots of food and were well prepared for all the people. Food was to be served to those who came, even though many more people came than originally expected (which we say is a blessing to those who are getting married and to the people who were putting wedding together!). God blessed the food in the celebration – everyone who came had something to eat. The wedding cake was wonderful. It was called a "unity cake". In our tradition, first the bride and groom enjoy the cake, then the parents of the groom, next the parents of the bride, and finally, all of the guests get to enjoy the cake. We did not know what to prepare before the wedding, but it all worked out. As you read this book, it will give you an idea that sometimes things do not always go the way they are expected to.

My husband and I were blessed with two daughters, Joy and Jane. We were also of course blessed with a son-in-law (Joy's husband): Joe Njoju. We would eventually be blessed with four grandchildren: Benson Ngatia Jr, Zawadi Wangui Njogu, Zahra Wanjuru Njogu and Arman Muita Njogu. We also would go on to have a wonderful granddaughter-in -law (wife to our grandson Ben Ngatia, Jr.): Rochelle Ngatia. Additionally, we would become blessed with great-grandchildren: Hezekiah Ngatia, (the late) Hannah Jane Ngatia and Josiah Ngatia.

21.   Ordination Exams: God Can Move Mountains

I faced a significant challenge on the road to ordained ministry. The Presbyterian Church USA has a process in place. Before you are ordained as a minister of Word and Sacrament, you need to pass the ordination exams.

The ordination exams for the PCUSA denomination are difficult for an immigrant to pass. This is because they are set up in the American cultural context. They are designed for Americans (who have been raised in and are familiar with the American church tradition and context). The process was hard and complicated for someone who had just come to America from another culture like mine. I had only been in America for a short amount time. Because I was born and raised in Africa and newly arrived in the States, my cultural context was far more African than American. This brought extra challenges to the ordination exams.

During my second year at seminary, I began the process of my ordination exams. This was so hard, that on my first attempt, I passed none of them, and I failed five (there were five exams total). I took a class at the seminary to help me pass, but I still could not pass all five exams. I graduated from Seminary in two and a half years (with my Master of Divinity) because I wanted to graduate in time to go out to help prepare for my daughter's wedding.

I tried other times to the pass the ordination exams, but I still could not. Finally, my husband had a dream in which I tried my exams again. In his dream, I had passed. So, I tried again. Unfortunately, this dream did not come true the way he dreamed it. I did not pass in real life. The actual result was that I passed one and failed four (which I had experienced already). Over the course of many years, I promised my children that I would soon pass. I promised them that I would pay for their school and would meet their financial needs just as soon I become a pastor in a congregation.

I continued taking the exams, answering the questions based on my own cultural and theological framework and experience. I was thinking with an African vernacular language (which is Kikuyu language) and just translating that into English. By doing this, I continued not to pass the ordination exams. I came to learn that the secret of passing ordination exams was to answer the questions *as the readers expect you to answer* (not as you would personally answer yourself).

One day, one of the professors called me and read my answers. There were three test graders in place to evaluate exams. They would pass you based on a majority (i.e. if two out of three leaders agreed, you passed). Each time I took the tests, only one of the evaluators would pass me, and so I would fail.

On one of my exams. the reader's summary was written on my answer paper. One of the graders told the others "if this candidate's first language were English, she would easily pass." The grader wrote "language is not what we are looking for, but we are examining the content of the answers. It is the meaning of the responses, not the way that they are worded, that matters."

Here is an example of one of the questions:

A church member did not have time to have holy communion with the rest of the body because he needed to work to provide for his family. The question asked was what I would propose to do to solve this as his pastor.

I responded that he needed to find a way to take communion with the rest of the church because, it was so important to have holy communion together with the church as a key part of worship (as communal faith). Community is very important in my culture.

(The answer they graders were looking for was something along the lines of leaving the elements somewhere in the sanctuary for him to pick up at his convenience. They were looking for a very American answer - contextualized for that perspective. Americans worship individually; Africans worship communally).

It took me many years to pass my ordination exams. Let me say this: I stayed in the process! I tried to pass the exams many times until I was frustrated. I tried again (and again) and I kept not passing. I remember after the results came out the first time, I did not pass even one out of five different exams. However, the first one that I eventually passed (out of the five exams) was theology. Every time the result came out, I got sick right beforehand. One of the examiners said I would never pass the exams "even if I tried ten times, I would never pass." Ouch!

After trying many times, I went to the Committee of Preparation for Ministry to request a waiver. Unfortunately, the moderator of this committee said that the committee could not waive it. The only way to move forward to become a Minister of Word and Sacrament was to successfully pass all five exams. This was a requirement to be ordained as a minister of Word and Sacrament in the Presbyterian Church USA.

When the CPM moderator told me that no waiver was possible, I prayed to God with a lot of tears. My heart was broken. My husband had become frustrated. My family asked me, "Mom, must you go through all of this just be ordained? We are concerned about your health. We know God has called you to carry on the ministry where our grandma started the ministry because she was a missionary in her own community, but this is too much".

I remember one day I cried, I knew God could see that my heart was broken, that nobody could feel or understand my pain from my heart, except for God. I opened my Bible and I told myself, "Jemimah, *I can do everything through Christ who strengthens me." (Philippians 4:13).* My God is the God of the minority and the God of those who are rejected. I believed that God could work beyond the color, culture and language. God works beyond the boundaries! My God is not in the box!

One day, I made an appointment and I talked to my friend in Indiana who was a professor of New testament at Notre Dame University. She agreed to meet. I took my results to her and I shared my frustrations. I cried before her with a lot of tears, and I said to her "I think God did not really call me into the ministry". I continued to share my pain with her. At that time, I started feeling hurt and broken and had a lot of fear about who God was in this process.

I knew that she was a Presbyterian minister herself, so she had already passed her ordination exams. She told me "you know, Jemimah, if God didn't call you, He could have removed you from the system before now". She sat me down and listened as I wondered about and doubted God's call. She finally said, "We are going to work together. I want meet with you two days every week for one hour." She asked me to bring all my ordination papers. I answered the questions and she wanted to know why I did not pass. After one week, I brought my papers to her and she told me I had not been answering the questions well (because I had been answering questions through my own cultural understanding, which is different from the American culture). After she read my results, she told me, "Jemimah, read the questions according to their perspective, not according to your culture or your African theological understanding and ministry experiences. Answer their questions according to their American context and culture. That is what they are looking for". I took her advice to heart and resolved to answer the questions in the American way the next time. So, I changed my attitude and I answered the questions based on what test readers wanted to hear.

Reflecting on what my professor told me, I took the test one more time (and I took her advice). **Finally, I got the result that I passed ALL my exams!** I remembered what King David said in *Psalm 121:1 "my help will come from God"*. My God is more powerful than the readers of my exams because my God is more than any human being, power, authority and understanding. I trusted my God and he strengthened me.

My God is more than able to empower me to pass my ordination exams. My trust in God was bigger than exams. He helps us to overcome barriers! Our mighty God can pass us though many mountains or over deep valleys. I want to pass this message on to those of you who are going thought difficulties of any kind. I want to remind you that our God is able and can move us from any circumstances. I know that God works everything for good for those who love Him. I share this message to encourage men and women who go through struggles, who cry, or who feel rejected. Know that God can move any mountains. He moved this impossible mountain of exams from my life and He can do anything for you. The mountains may look unmovable and the valleys may look dark and lonely, but God can do the impossible.

God counts the drops of our tears and sees the pain in our hearts. We need to remind ourselves that God's hands carried the cross to Calvary. Our God is watching over us every step we take. Let us remember that when things are hard, and you have no one to turn, to we need to see God, who prepared the dinner table in front of our enemies. *"You prepare a feast for me in the presence of my enemies." (Ps.23:3)*

The Devil is not happy to see my blessings from our God which are flowing to us on the way. My sisters and brothers in Christ, it does not matter how long the journey is, do not forget Moses' forty years day and night in the wilderness. The same God is with us today holding our hands day by day.

Remember our God who raised Lazarus after three days and healed the blind. This is the same God today. I have nothing to say other than to say I was able to pass ordination exams to enable me to be ordained (which was an issue for me after the journey of the Presbyterian Church ordination process, which took me over twenty years since 1984).

I was not able to pass ordination exams, but now I know with help from God I passed. How I passed, I do not know. Only God knows. *Even the readers of my exams did not know how I passed because they did not mark or comment on my exams (but my God was the best reader of my exams!)*

Yes, God knew me before I was born and before I came to America. God ordained me and called me into His ministry before I was born ("*For we are God's workmanship, created in Christ Jesus to do good works which God has prepared in advance for us to do*" (*Ephesians 2:10*). In my process, I had never met the readers of my exams. Me and God we were meeting about the issue of my ordination through prayers and the meditation of my heart. The readers of my exams did not know that I was meeting with God before I sat for my exams. I was praying and fasting. My husband was also dearly praying for me and my family. This was because this ordination exam had become a big issue in my family and with my Christian friends.

I want to give God thanks because He is the one who has taught me theology. The death and resurrection of Jesus Christ as my personal savior is the best news in the world. God taught me this through the Spirit; not the readers who failed me in my exams many times, because of who I am. God gave them my personal testimony that "Jemimah is my beloved Child and I died at the cross for her". I said to myself, "next time, the readers will not grade me, because God has already confirmed me as a minister before I was born. With or without a passed ordination exam, I knew I was already ordained by God. I knew that the next time God would be the true reader of my exams." I was reminded that *"Man looks at outward appearance, but God looks at the heart" (1 Samuel 16:7)*

I cried when I read the email informing me that I had passed! I had no words to express my thanks to God. This caused great celebration for my family and friends.

I believe that if we surrender our burdens and pain to God, it will be easy for God to carry us (no matter how heavy, or how bad it is for us to carry, or painful, or frustrating). No matter how many years it takes, our God is with us in this journey day by day. This journey reminds me that God is always with us. I experienced God's presence every single minute and I know that God is able.

Finally, when I passed all five of my exams, the heavy burden was now gone! My next step was to wait to be called to a church to be ordained as a minister. Why was this still in my heart? I want everyone to know God that is able no matter what circumstances you are in. Your situation may be exams or something else. When we go through the battle, this is to remind us that we fight a good fight, and after we go through it, we will never be the same.

After this battle of my ordination, I am no longer the same. The journey has deepened my faith. This created a deeper foundation for me in my spiritual life. Nothing can separate me (or you) from the love of God and from what God has promised us. He suffered so that we can be who we are today in the ministry of God.

22. Waiting for the Call

Even though I had passed my ordination exams, the journey was not yet over. I had not yet reached to the level of the promise of God (that I was ordained for my life before I was born). Now, the second hardest experience in this journey began. *"Wait for the Lord; be strong and take heart and wait for the Lord" (Psalm 27:14)*

After I passed all my exams, the next step was to wait for a call. In the Presbyterian denomination USA, you cannot be called unless you have graduated with Master of Divinity <u>and</u> passed the ordination exams. Once these steps are completed, you must then wait for a church to call you (to become a church minister for their congregation).

I waited for my call, and it was so hard. This was because all the churches that were interested in me could not understand my accent. That was another problem for me to be hired by any church in America.

After I passed my ordination exams, I waited for about a year trying to wait for a call from any church. None of the churches called me. I started taking note of most of my former classmates from McCormick Theological

Seminary. Most of them had already received their calls (but none of them were from Kenya).

At that time, I used to receive invitation cards to celebrate their ordinations. I started asking God questions about it. "God, you empowered me to pass my exams and now no church is calling me. What is going on here, my God? God, you are never late. I don't understand." I believed and trusted God. I knew that my call was on the way coming. Through this process, I learned so much about being patient. *"Be joyful in hope, patient in affliction, faithful in prayer.' (Romans 12:12)*

Waiting to be called by a church was an entirely different challenge from passing my exams. This proved harder than passing the ordination exams, because most of the Presbyterian Church is made up of white people (and some of these church members are also elderly, so they are stuck in their old ways). In church tradition, members are used to short sermons (15 minutes or so). In my country, the preaching in Presbyterian churches there last at least thirty minutes or more. Many church members in America had never visited another country or traveled much. I was invited to preach in different churches to perhaps receive a call from one of them. The members of the church would give the report to the senior pastor. They did appreciate my message and most of them said they loved my accent. They said they were happy to hear that I was from Kenya, Africa. Unsurprisingly, some of the congregations (with elderly members) also complained because they could not understand my accent. In fact, the biggest barrier I experienced in waiting for my call had to do with my accent.

When I was invited to preach, I spent a lot of time praying (asking God to give me the message for that specific congregation). God knew them specifically and what they would need to hear). I was also preparing my sermon (studying different commentaries and bible versions, and I never forgot to read my vernacular bible first to correctly interpret what the English bible was saying). I would have 3 bibles in front of me: English NIV, Swahili and Kikuyu (my vernacular language). I would preach the main message as well as the children's message. I remember there was a child there that was 7 years old. He asked me "Pastor, are you speaking Spanish?" I told him "no, honey I am speaking English, but my English is not an American English. I speak English with an accent. I am from Kenya, East Africa, and we were taught English by the missionaries from Scotland." I then gave him a hug. After a few minutes, the mother of the child came and wanted to know more about me. She came to me and shared with me that she had a friend who visited Kenya five years ago. Teaching children was a blessing. Once, I sang a chorus for the kids in Swahili 'Asante Sana Yesu' (which means, 'thank you, Jesus'). When American adults listened, my sermon was difficult for many members who could not understand my accent. What I remember most was that the members of the congregations were saying, "pastor, your sermon blessed me when I heard your personal story related to the message. Your accent is great". Then, I asked myself, "Did they really understand my sermon? Introduction? Interpretation of scripture and illustration? Did they understand my conclusion? They like my accent, but they might not understand my words." After preaching in some of these churches, I went home with mixed feelings. This was difficult for me, after having prepared and prayed for my sermon for an entire week. When I would ask myself if they really understood me, I was comforted knowing that the Holy Spirit was able to interpret for me.

I often felt broken, but I encouraged myself saying, "if these members were in Kenya, would they be able to speak even one word in Swahili?" I comforted myself, reminding myself that English was not my first (or my second) language, but that it was my third language! Since that was the case, I truly was doing well in preaching and sharing my personal testimony that "Jesus Christ is my personal savior" in English! I had graduated with my Masters of Divinity (from McCormick Theological Seminary) and went on to earn my Doctor of Ministry (from Chicago Theological Seminary) *all in my third language!* All in English, I have earned my doctorate (not to mention other courses on top of that, like 7 units of clinical pastoral education (CPE) as well as Spiritual Leadership courses. All of my professors were enjoying calling me to testify about my faith in God, even in English as my third language. I found that in seminary, I was able to engage well in my classes and with my professors (all in English). And yet still, I would feel like I was nothing, because a few members of some Presbyterian churches told me they "like my accent" (rather than sharing about the content of what I was preaching). I reminded myself of the truth of God's word. There is nothing impossible to endure with God! *"I can do all things through Christ who gives me strength" (Philippians 4:13).* At the end of the day, I chose to believe God rather than to be discouraged by people.

I began to wonder whether it was a good idea to go back to Kenya and serve Kenyans there before my ordination (in my home country, no one would worry about my "accent").

At this time, I needed to give myself credit and be proud of being a black woman born in Kenya East, Africa and studying and living in America. Having an accent was part of my identity. This was certainly true when I was studying in America. In the United States, I was part of a diverse group of students who ranged in age, all studying together with me. Is this not part of the American Dream?

One night, I called on God and asked him to let me know if I really had the call for ordination into ministry or not? "Am I really going to receive my call to be ordained, God?" I asked. "Please answer me!" I talked to God and cried out again to Him, saying, "I want to re-examine my call again." I wanted to make sure that I was hearing Him clearly.

I shared this with my professor friend (she was a New Testament Professor at Notre Dame University in Indiana. She was the very same professor who had counseled me when I had doubts about the exams, before I finally passed). I told her, "maybe I didn't hear right when I thought God had called me. …Or if He called me, why I am suffering like this?" She told me "Jemimah, I know you! I know you love God. Don't go there! Sit back and pray. If you were not called by God, God could have removed you from the process before this point as well." I remembered that she gave me similar advice when I wanted to give up on my examinations. She reminded me that it had been a while since I started the process, but now we needed to thank God that I was still in God's plans. *"For God's gifts and His call can never be withdrawn" (Romans 11:29)*

She called me twice, "Jemimah! Jemimah! Remember what God has done in your life. You have passed all exams and you have completed your ordination requirements! Let us wait upon God and you will see God show up in a special way."

As you continue to read this book, you will understand how God works for his people in the deepest and the highest. He knows us when we sit down and when we walk. He knows our hearts and He walks with us. *"Oh Lord, you have searched me, and you know me. You know when I sit and when I lie. You have perceived my thoughts from afar. You discern my going and my laying down. You are familiar with all my ways. Before a word is on my tongue you know it completely oh Lord." (Psalm 139:1-2)*

I was reminded that when God says yes, it is yes! When God open the doors, no one can close them. At this time, my husband and my children started asking me questions, "Mom, you have been telling us that you will get a job after you finish ordination exams. It has now been over two years waiting. You need to help dad pay for the apartment." They continued, "You need to help us." I did not have any answer for my children. I did not have any word to explain what was happening or to justify the wait (even I did not understand completely). It was true. I had high hopes. I had promised my children that after seminary, I was going to be ordained and that I would help them until they finished college. But, they had already finished college. They had graduated. They were working in professional jobs. And yet still mom continued saying "I am about to get a church call and support you."

When my husband would hear what my kids were saying, he always encouraged me and my children saying, "Mom is going to get ordained. Let us keep supporting her. Let us keep praying for her. This has been a difficult time for her. We need to stand with her as a family!"

My grandson, Ben Ngatia Jr., reminded me, saying, "Grandma, remember, you are the one God called. Your husband and your children were not there when God called you into vocational ministry. He called you." He meant that God had called me personally and directly. Ben continued, "you have been a model of ministry, for me and many others, Chu Chu (Grandma)! We have learned a lot from you." He continued to admonish me, "Don't listen to what we are pressuring you to do! Focus on *your* vision of your future ministry and on your call to serve in the ministry of God." After this conversation, my family stood with me and I called them to partner with me in my journey. This reminds me of the story of Joshua. "...*But as for me and my household, we will serve the Lord." (Joshua 24:15b)*

To my sisters in Christ reading this: What does my journey remind you of as you continue to serve in your ministry?

I have learned that waiting upon the Lord in faith is the beginning of renewed hope every single minute. This is despite barriers! We can have hope for tomorrow! When I happen to feel like God is far from me, I just open the inner feeling of the love of God and start seeing that God is within me. He is struggling with me on the way. This is the invisible Kingdom of Heaven. Sister Patricia Bombard (from ISL – International Spiritual Leadership program) said that throughout the process of our call, God is in the midst. She often repeated this again and again during my program. She understood my frustrations and she encouraged my willingness to answer God's call in my life. She has been such an encourager to me.

Our suffering and struggling does not mean that our God is not hearing our cries. In fact, He suffers together with us, in every kind of suffering. *"For he has not ignored or belittled the suffering of the needy. He has not turned his back on him, but has listened to their cries for help"* -Psalm 22:24

I have learned that when I am in deep pain and loneliness, I can cry out to the Lord alone. Other people may not be able to understand where I am coming from or where I am going. Maybe they are also suffering and might be in more critical condition than me. God understands us individually and collectively and He knows us completely. God hears our cries and understands our pain!

23.   Life in South-Bend, Indiana

After I graduated from Chicago Theological Seminary, I sensed God's leading to move to South-Bend, Indiana. God wanted me and my family to move to South-Bend, Indiana and start a ministry there. We did not know anyone in South-Bend, Indiana. So, we obeyed God and moved to the Wabash Valley Presbytery there. This reminds me of the story of when God told Abram *"…Go away from your country, and from your relatives and from your father's house to the land which I will show you" (Genesis 12:1).* The reason why I went to Indiana was because the manager of the Memorial Hospital in South Bend, Indiana called me for a job there. She had promised me a job as a hospital chaplain. I had previously met her in person, and she told me that she would offer me a job. She said she just needed to consult the other staff at the hospital. When she called me for an interview, I met her and the other chaplains on her staff. I told them all about my chaplaincy experiences. I shared about the hospitals I had worked in previously (including Kenyatta Hospital in Kenya for ten years, in Bains Hospital in St. Louis, Missouri for 1 year, and in Chicago Hospital in Chicago, Illinois where I served as an on-call Chaplain for 1 year).

My husband and I started looking for a Presbyterian Church in the community where we could worship. I told my husband to hand over the phone book. We quickly looked in the yellow pages to see if there was a Presbyterian Church in the neighborhood. We went through many Presbyterian churches in the neighborhood. However, I saw that there was only one church near our apartment.

I picked up the phone and I called the church to speak to the pastor. The church secretary answered the phone. I introduced myself and told her that I wanted to speak to the pastor. She sounded so nice over the phone and she put me right through to the pastor.

I introduced myself to the Reverend Ron Miller. I shared with him that my husband and I had relocated here in this community, and we were looking for a Presbyterian church to join (since we were members of Presbyterian Church USA).

I shared some of my background and story with him.

"I was a student and I graduated from McCormick Theological Seminary. But originally, we came from Kenya, East Africa. I came to this country to study Theology." I went on to tell him the story of my interview with the chaplaincy manager at the Memorial Hospital here. *"During my interview, one of the staff chaplains asked me how many units I had done in Clinical Pastoral Education (CPE). I answered that I had seven units of CPE. Right there, the manager said "oh, you have more than me and I am the CPE manager of this hospital. I have only 4 units".*

I could not get any job, even a chaplain job, since I was apparently overqualified. I did one interview for a hospital chaplain position, but the manager said I was qualified more than she was (and that the other chaplains might not be comfortable to work with me, because I had more experience - by many years than they did - in hospital chaplaincy).

After my interview, I walked out of the conference room and went home. Within a few days, the manager called me and told me to come back. I thought for sure this meant I got the job (my first interview was positive). I was well qualified. I also sensed the presence of God in the staff. Even one of the staff said she wanted me there because she wanted an African female. I was also told by a woman that she loved my accent). I went to meet with her again and she said to me that the chaplain staff decided that they were not going to hire me. She said the reason was because I had too many CPE units and too much chaplaincy experience and it would be a challenge for them. Even though I was more than qualified, she did not offer me the job (despite my extensive hospital chaplaincy experience and 7 units of CPE). The manager feared that my experience would intimidate the other staff and be a challenge to them. I lost the job opportunity because I would have done it too well! In that moment, she prayed for me and she started calling other hospitals and institutions where I could be used a Chaplain. She remarked that I should be somewhere teaching instead of serving as a chaplain They talked about my theological studies and my other educational credentials. The manager told me she loved me so much and she would try to see whether she could introduce me to another hospital. Perhaps I could be given a part-time chaplaincy job at night. I decided to go and look directly into her eyes as my tears streamed down. One reason I felt compelled to cry was because the chaplaincy staff were all white mostly men (only the manager was a woman, and since I was black from Africa with accents I felt more ostracized). Yes, I am a woman and from Africa and at that time (because of who I was) I lost that position because I told the truth about my credentials and hospital chaplaincy experiences. It felt so unfair. I cried, and she gave me all the time I needed to cry. Then I asked her whether she could introduce me to the hospital kitchen or anywhere else because my heart was to work in that hospital. Working at that hospital was the primary reason why I moved from Chicago. The reason I was asking for even a menial job was because my husband was not working at the time. We did not have steady income yet. It would become increasingly difficult to find money to pay for our apartment. Losing the job (which was our reason for moving to Indiana to begin with) greatly impacted our life and caused hardship. I wondered if I was out of will of the Lord. I could not see the light at the end of the tunnel. My husband still did not have a job. We had moved to Indiana because of this promised chaplaincy position that had fallen through. The hospital chaplain again called me back to come to her office and share what else we could do.

I lost that position, but still I went out seeking what I could do. Someone called and told me there was a daycare that needed help. I asked for the telephone number and I called the owner of that daycare (who called me back for an interview). I went in and she gave me the job (it was for eight hours a day at eight dollars per hour). I began working at the daycare, and we got money for food. I continued working there until I was ultimately called to start United African Presbyterian Church.

The chaplain manager set up another appointment with me and I went to meet with she and her church's leaders (she was part of the United Church of Christ). One of the first questions I was asked was whether I could accept an ordination by their denomination (UCC) and be taught their doctrines. I had high hopes for this job. I loved the job description that the pastor shared with me. They wanted someone to be effective in pastoral care. With my background and experience, they thought I would be effective with shut-ins and hospital visitations.

One of the UCC church members told the pastor that I was waiting for a call. She called me, and I met with the UCC pastor. She introduced me to a United Church of Christ pastor. Their church had an opening position for a part-time pastor (which I qualified for). The pastor called me for an interview, and she loved me so much. She said to me "you can help her visit the members who are shut-ins and those who are in the hospitals. You can also preach some Sundays, do pastoral care (which was the focus of my Master's program), and lead children's Bible Study." She said they did have an opening for someone to preach two Sundays each month and other times to visit elderly members in their homes and do hospital visitations for the members. They offered a good salary that would meet my financial needs. At that time, I was in Indiana (South Bend) with my husband who did not have a job. We often did not have food and depended on others at the time (on one occasion during this season, my daughter opened our refrigerator and she found only two bottles of water).

The pastor invited me to preach one Sunday. Their congregation was very young, and I preached about Joshua chapter 1 (one of my favorite scriptures).

After the sermon, the pastor called me into her office. She shared with me that I had done a good job, and that my message was received well. She was going to talk to the leaders of the church on the following Tuesday and she would get back to me.

I remember my husband was seated in another room waiting for me to come out with good news. I come out from her office smiling then *my husband said to me "congratulations!". After I got in the car my husband was driving and I told him "I think I got that job."*

The Pastor called me and told me she had talked with the church leaders and they were more than happy to meet with me.

After a week, I had a meeting with her. The leaders recommended that the church hire me as an Assistant Pastor to do the work. We also negotiated my salary (it was a good salary with benefits!). When they called me back, I found out one of the biggest requirements they had was for me to be received by the United Church of Christ to become a UCC pastor. I had to go through the training and to learn the practices, procedures and doctrines of their church. This was very difficult for me. You see, I was born in a Presbyterian family and I grew up as a Presbyterian. I studied at Presbyterian seminaries. I was a candidate to become a Presbyterian minister. Now here I was offered a job as a Pastor, but I needed to totally change my denomination and become affiliated with the United Church of Christ instead. I had to study the doctrines and practices of this different denomination. It became very hard for me. Still, I started crying, not wanting to abandon my Presbyterianism. I said to them "this might be hard for me because I am a Presbyterian from birth and I my parents were the founders of our Local Presbyterian Church in Kenya. I was raised as Presbyterian member. I wonder if it might be too late for me to study another denomination and to be taught new doctrines". She told me "Jemimah, I will try to speak to some of the leaders because now I am planning to take my vacation. I do not have anyone to help me with some of the duties that you could carry with us." She continued, "Jemimah, you can help me so much in this, but the church leaders would also like you to serve the communion and other licensed sacraments of our church (that required ordination as a UCC Pastor)." The continued to have doubts.

I called the pastor and I told him was not possible for me start learning about another doctrine. For the reasons I shared, I ultimately declined the offer to be hired as a UCC Pastor. I prayed. I felt strongly that this was not where God was calling me. This was disappointing because it seemed like a good job with a good salary and benefits, it was something I qualified to do, and my husband was still not working. The pastor prayed that I would find the right job. I was flustered.

As I recounted this story to the Reverend Ron Miller, he was interested to get to know us and he asked me for our address. He wanted to come over and visit with us. After three days, he indeed came and visited with us. It was such blessing to meet Reverend Ron Miller, who was the pastor of Mishawaka Presbyterian Church in South-Bend. It was a special moment when we welcomed Rev. Ron Miller to our apartment. He was so excited to meet with us as well. We shared more of our story with him. During that moment of sharing, he shared with us that he was happy to meet people from Kenya (because at one time he and other pastors had previously visited Kenya for a mission trip). He already had a special connection to my country.

It touched our hearts to know that we had now met someone who had visited our country. Rev. Ron Miller told us about his church, where he was the senior pastor. He asked us whether we had any questions. We felt loved. We felt we had found a good pastor who could take on our spiritual care. He welcomed us to worship with him at his church.

He offered prayers for us. He touched our hearts with his love to us. The following Sunday, we went to his church for the first time. Rev. Ron Miller introduced us to the congregation. After the worship service, we went to the fellowship hall and many members greeted us with a lot of joy. Some were telling me "Jemimah, I love your accent!".

Thereafter, we found a home and we became active members involved with the church activities. We came to know there were many great people in the community. We also discovered that there were others from Africa in the community.

After a while, we started gathering a few people from Africa to come to our apartment for prayers and Bible study once a week. I shared with Pastor Ron Miller about the group from Africa who were meeting in our apartment. Finally, I invited the pastor to come and meet the group in our apartment. The pastor was overwhelmed by the chorus of our praise and worship in different African languages. He loved that we ate African food together.

Rev. Miller was amazed at how quickly I had formed the group (and even where I had found them). I told him these people were from Africa. I found them in different African food stores in the community. He asked me, "Jemimah, how do you find them from the stores"? I told him I met them where they were shopping for African food in the local area. While they were shopping, they talked to one another in their vernacular African languages and I could tell that they were from Africa. I intentionally joined their conversations. I introduced myself and let them know that I had just re-located into the neighborhood. I gave them my telephone number as well as our address.

People Started coming to visit us. They did not even call to find out if we were home - they just knocked on the door. That is our culture. We do not have to make an appointment to come to visit.

I told Rev. Miller that was basically how I formed the group. After that, Rev. Miller's church put out a message that there was a Presbyterian couple who had moved into the community. Some of the Presbyterians in the community started looking for us. I invited them to come and see my new church. Then the pastor introduced us to the members of the church and we were given an opportunity to sing songs in our vernacular languages, such as Swahili (it was wonderful!).

The group continued to grow bigger and bigger. Our apartment became too small to hold everyone (it was a large group). At this point, I asked the minister (Rev. Ron, my new friend) whether we could be given a place where my husband and I could host this group and move into it.

Rev. Ron Miller and the session of Mishawaka Presbyterian Church Wabash Valley Presbytery, met and welcomed the group. After that, I was called to the session meeting and was interviewed by the leaders of the church (and the pastor). I was given permission to bring the group from our apartment and start worshiping together at the church building. The group would be given a space inside the building to hold our traditional African worship services each Sunday. We were given a place to Fellowship by the Session of Mishawaka Presbyterian Church under the supervision of Rev. Ron Miller, who was a minister of Mishawaka Presbyterian Church in Wabash Valley Presbytery. Once we started meeting at the church building, people from Africa started coming one by one and the group continued to get bigger.

After few months, the group elected African church leaders. The group appointed me to officially continue being their spiritual leader. Rev. Miller and the leaders of the church continued supporting the group. The African leaders who were elected were to pray and seek God for the name of the group.

The African leaders came up with the name "Neema", which means "Grace" in the Swahili language. In August of 2004, I started Neema African Refugee Fellowship for people from Africa under Reverend Ronald Miller. We continued with the fellowship, and many women in the group supported the church by leading women, children, and youth ministries. The men also started a fellowship group for men.

Neema continued growing and becoming known in the community (and the Presbyterian Churches in the area). We were often invited to go out and sing African songs. The people in our group were from African counties worshipping with their African traditions.

Rev. Miller introduced us to the Office of New Immigrants of the General Assembly (PCUSA). Once the Office of New Immigrants of the General Assembly was informed about our group, Reverend Angel from their office came and visited us. He found that our group was growing and had people from many different countries in Africa. He met with the leaders and we shared food together with him. He advised our leaders and gave us direction to continue with the design of Neema African Fellowship. After this visit, the Office of New Immigrants of the General Assembly also started financially and resourcefully supporting us. This was such a busy time of sowing seeds and gathering people together.

It was so meaningful to lead worship, singing in African traditions and eating African food together. It was also a milestone to preach in three languages (Swahili, English and Kikuyu). This transformed each of us. The Neema Fellowship group still exists even today! It is still being supported by the New Immigrant Groups Ministries, from General Assembly office of PCUSA.

As this church continued to flourish, God confirmed my call to serve and support new immigrants and refugees living in my community. I was able to meet the needs of the African immigrant and refugee community who had lived there. I was called to serve those who did not have a home church in that community. They could relate together with their African cultural worship tradition. I saw the hand of God at work. I started attending international meetings to represent our group (meeting other African pastors with groups like ours). My heart was full of joy to see how God had lifted me up from grass roots to the high passion of being the leader of a new group for the people from Africa.

Through the training, with the help from God, I offered to oversee the group leaders that the church had commissioned (two lay pastors) to continue the ministry of God in that community.

The Neema Fellowship was formed with women, men and children to reflect African tradition of worship. The group was known by singing African songs and eating together the food our people could relate to. They also began visiting the sick (among the African refugee community).

24. Sensing God's Leading for A New Assignment

Back when I was still serving with the Neema ministry (when I was still living in Indiana), I was invited to attend a Conference of New Immigrant Ministries held in Atlanta, Georgia. While attending the conference, I received a call from my daughter, Jane Ngatia. I picked up the phone and listened as Jane told me, "the Rev. Dr. Linda Shugert is looking for you. Give her a call as soon as possible. She has good news and a dream for your future ministry." First off, I wanted to know what this call was about because she had never mentioned anything to me before about being hired. I was curious. When my daughter, Jane, told me that Rev. Dr. Linda was looking for me, I called her back. She shared with me about her dream for my future Ministry. Linda shared with me that she wanted me to move back to St. Louis, Missouri under her care at Giddings Love-joy Presbytery. Since I was an active member with my family and other Kenyans, we had previously been worshiping at that same church (Rockhill/South Webster). She wanted me to come and start the Church of people from Africa. That message touched my heart (I had previously lived in St. Louis, Missouri, and I of course had recently started a similar ministry in Indiana in South-Bend). I as shared earlier, my previous ministry in Indiana was to minister to immigrant and refugee families.

25.   Difficult Trials

A year before I got Rev. Dr. Linda Shugert's call, I had become very sick. I remember one day, my husband wanted to take me to the hospital, but I told him, "I can't go because we do not have the money or health insurance." I was so sick. I told my husband "if you take me to the hospital at this time" it was two in the morning then, "the doctors will admit me to the hospital, and we would not be able to pay the hospital bills." I got so sick that night. Against my wishes, he decided to rush me to the hospital anyway. The doctors admitted me into the hospital (just as I thought they would), and my husband left me there for the night. In the morning, I requested permission to go home and the doctor agreed to discharge me home with treatment. We did not have money to buy the medicine. My husband collected loose coins he had been saving in a box (pennies and other change). He took the coins somewhere to change them, and he returned with a twenty-dollar bill. With this bit of money, he managed to buy one of the prescriptions I needed (he could not afford to get all of them). I continued to feel ill. After a few days, we received the hospital bill (of $800.00) in the mail from the accountant's office. When the medical bills arrived, I reminded my husband, saying "See! What we are going to do now?" My husband at that time was feeling like he had lost everything (no job, loss of wife's job, wife was sick and now we were saddled with more bills). He identified with Job in the Bible, who also lost everything (from the least to the greatest of his possessions, starting with oxen and donkeys and camels). Job lost everything, except for his wife. *"Why is life given to a man whose way is hidden, whom God has hedged in? For sighing has become my daily food; my groans pour out like water. What I dreaded has happened to me. I have no peace; no quietness; I have no rest, but only turmoil." (Job 2:24-26)* Benson was feeling the same way.

Benson said to me, "you know, I could not have kept you in the house to die!" I answered, "I told you, I knew I would not die then. God is not finished with me." I shared with him again that it would be very hard for me to die in this country. I knew then that God still had good plans for us and that they had not yet been completed. I thought of God's word for his people when they were about to go into captivity. God had a plan for them, even knowing the suffering they would endure, *"for I know the plans I have for you, declares the Lord. Plans to prosper you and not to harm you, plans to give you a hope and a future"* (Jeremiah 29:11)

26. God Heard Our Cries

"Then you will call, and the Lord will answer; you will cry for help, and He will say: Here am I'..." (Isaiah 58:9a) What a privilege and a joy we have to able to call on the Lord for help. We are not doing life alone because He is with us. Today, He says to us, 'Here I am!' He is the one who hears our prayers and cries and He helps us.

We continued to live in that condition until a lady finally came to visit us. At that time, she asked whether I had all the medicine I needed. I told her "no". She was so kind! She asked me to give her my prescriptions so that she could purchase my medicine for me. She went and bought the remaining medicine for me! After she I started taking all the medicine I was prescribed, I got better quickly! I continued praising our mighty God (and continued looking for a job).

In my heart, I had joys of the Lord regardless of circumstance. This was because I had trusted him, having hope that our mighty God was everlasting. He is God for every step we are going though. I reminded my husband to keep trusting God and we read scriptures together. *"I*

lift my eyes up to the heavens; where does my help come from?"
(Psalm 121:1)

We still were not able to pay the hospital bill. The hospital had to take our name and our debt into collections. We went to the hospital and my husband and I talked to the business office. We told them our story (including why we moved to Indiana and that our jobs fell through). They felt compassion for us. They asked us whether we had enough food to eat (this was a tough time and we did not). They directed us to go and get food from the community food pantry. The administrator at the office gave us the address. We went there later and were able to get some food. The following day, the hospital administrator called us back into her office. When we arrived, she inquired about whether we had gotten food the previous day. We told her that we were indeed able to get the food from the pantry. The administrator looked at my husband Ben and asked him, "do you want a job?"

From that time on, Benson was hired at the hospital (in a housekeeping position). Immediately after our meeting, he was directed to the HR department. Benson walked in armed with a recommendation from the hospital Administrator. Almost instantly, after filling out the forms, Benson was given a uniform and he was put on the schedule to begin his job. The Administrator helped Benson get a job and she allowed us to pay back the hospital bill on a payment plan.

Because of my pride, I did not want my children to know what Benson and I were going through during this time (although that one time my daughter opened my fridge and only saw bottles of water gave it away). I also did not want to ask for money from anyone. I am one of those people who does not want people to know how much I am suffering. My husband and I tried to keep it private. We kept quiet because we thought it would look very bad for us to ask for help from people, especially since we had just moved to that community. After two weeks, Benson received his first paycheck from the hospital. He brought his check home to me and told me "let's go to the bank and cash this check!" We deposited the money (and we were finally able to go to the store to buy some necessities).

After Benson received his check, I got a call from the same Chaplain who had previously interviewed me. She introduced me to a director of one of the skilled nursing homes in the area. I called the director, and he asked me to come in. He told me he had heard about my story and he believed there were jobs at the nursing home I could serve in (mediator, bible study leader, and leading the chapel each Sunday). The residents of the nursing were from diverse backgrounds (Anglos, African Americans, and several from various African countries). There had apparently been some conflicts amongst residents from different cultural backgrounds. They had communication problems and had been arguing. The director knew about my education and experience. He said there was an opening for a conflict mediator. The director thought that I could help the residents all work together. He hired me at $35.00/hour for 20 hours per week!

The first thing I did was to have a meeting with each of the different cultural groups (separately at first) to listen to each of their perspectives. The complaints I heard most often were that the African residents were speaking in ways the others could not understand (the other groups could not understand any languages outside of English, and they felt excluded). The Anglos complained that the Africans ate separately (and the African Americans ate separately). The Anglos were frustrated that they could not enter into the groups. There were also bias issues (where if anything was missing or something went wrong, the first people to be blamed were those from Africa). I also heard complaints about the schedule. There was once a misunderstanding where a woman gave a male African resident deodorant because she said he smelled bad. He was so offended. He came to me to discuss the issue. I spoke with the lady and shared with her that in African cultures, to tell a man such a thing (the way she did) was inappropriate. I shared with her ideas for better ways to share this that would not be offensive. She was so grateful that I shared what I had with her (she did not know there could be other ways to communicate that). Afterward, I called the gentleman and explained to him that she did not mean to embarrass him. It was just a miscommunication. They both came to greater understanding of one another. I enjoyed bringing all the residents together to help them learn to communicate and respect one another's culture.

I began holding Bible Studies each Tuesday. I had friends from Africa in the community and I would invite them to come and sing for the residents. They all enjoyed hearing the African choruses being sung.

When I got my first check from this job, I took it to my husband. We held that check together (it was a big check). We thanked God and we committed to tithe back to God out of both of our *checks "Bring all the tithes into the storehouse, so there will be enough food in my temple...If you do, I will open the windows of heaven for you. I will pour out a blessing so great you will not have enough room to take it all in. Try it! Put me to the test"* (Malachi 3:10)

I can remember talking with my husband. I said, "It was good for us not to burden people with our problems. God came through! Only God needed to know what we were going through at that time". With God, we are more than conquerors because our help comes from God. God renewed our faith *"But those who hope in the Lord will renew their strength. They will soar on wings like eagles. They will run and not grow weary. They will walk and not be faint"* (Isaiah 40:31)

27. Rev. Dr. Linda's Dream for Me: Moving Back to St. Louis

I asked God questions about why we had been suffering like that. I felt like we were trees in the wilderness.

After I got better, that was the same time that my daughter called me and told me to call Rev. Dr. Linda Shugert in St. Louis Missouri. As I mentioned above, Rev. Dr. Shugert was then the minister of Rock-Hill/South-

Webster Church in St. Louis, Missouri. She was the moderator of Giddings-Lovejoy Presbytery.

I called her up. She asked me to come back to St. Louis because she had found a job for me. She told me that her Church was going to be closed very soon because there was not enough money to carry on the church programs. This was because the church membership had declined. After I listened to her, I did not have any words to respond with at first. What I remember telling her was that before I could say yes, or give her any word, I needed to pray and share her invitation with my husband and my family. I told her I would call her back (after seeking God and hearing Him). I would wait upon direction from God. After she explained these things, I prayed, and I talked it over with my family. My next step was to go to visit St. Louis to visit her church.

When I got that phone call from Rev. Linda, I had already passed my ordination exams and I was waiting for a call to be ordained. I had completed all my ordination exams and all other requirements for me to be ordained. Rev. Dr. Linda did not promise to come and ordain me because I was already in the process of waiting for my official call. God blessed me! After our conversation, I knew that she understood my call. I was excited because my vision was to be ordained as a minister of Word and Sacrament, and to continue the ministry for African immigrants and refugee families who were here (and those who were newly arriving to the United States).

As I shared above, I was not able to get a call from a church up until that point. I decided to accept what Rev. Linda was sharing with me. I chose to move from South Bend, Indiana to St. Louis, Missouri, even without a firm call from a church. I already had connections to some of the refugees and immigrants in her congregation.

As I was preparing to come, I also carried with me my ordination papers. I introduced myself to South Minster church, where they processed my papers into the Presbytery of Giddings-Lovejoy. I had already been accepted as an Enquirer (one qualified to seek ordination). After one year, I was accepted as a Candidate of the Ministry by the same Presbytery (I was not new to their Presbytery, since I had already been "on their books").

At that time, my daughter Jane Ngatia who lived in St. Louis, Missouri, had already found a place for me and my husband to move into. We moved into an apartment (where we lived for a while without jobs) before I started working in the ministry. Sister Patricia Bombard continued paying for our apartment after moving to St. Louis. I remember one day, we went to church, and I could not hear the sermon because the time was so hard for both of us (my husband and I) after again moving. I started asking myself again why we moved from Indiana. I was a spiritual leader for a group of people from Africa. I was busy doing something at church where I tried to organize a group. Now it felt like we were starting over again.

I was commissioned as a church elder in that church (not the same as being ordained as a pastor). In 1998, I became a Candidate of Word and Sacrament (unpaid). Although she was a white woman, The Rev. Dr. Linda Shugert was my minister and a friend. She was my mentor who understood the culture of people from Africa. Rev. Dr. Linda always wanted to learn about our culture. She worked beyond her boundaries to bring the Gospel of Jesus Christ to the different cultures from Africa.

I wanted to keep myself busy, so that I could take my mind off not having a job yet. This helped me so much, because I met other people going through similar difficulties then. It was healing (at that time of sickness and suffering). My strength was coming from reading the Bible and remembering that God was in the midst of what I was going though. Once I started ministry work, I discovered how hard it was. It was so hard. The group did not have money, so I was working 45 hours per week and preaching every Sunday at 3.00 p.m. (all with no salary!) Still, I was happy serving the Lord in the ministry of Refugees and Immigrants from African countries.

When Rev. Dr. Linda called me from Indiana, I had a little hope of getting a job right away (because in St. Louis, I knew more people than I knew in Indiana). Even with this hope, I still found myself with no job. I stayed in God's plans without getting a job for a while. I was so lonely. I started thinking about going out everywhere - to different hospitals. However, one chaplain told me that it would be hard for me to get an open position. They said that chaplaincy positions in this country did not come easily. This was because, in general, most patients wanted white chaplains. I asked her "what about the black patients, and patients from other countries?" She responded, "I do not know about that. All I know is that we do not have many chaplains from Africa."

It was difficult to get a job, even with my credentials and experience. Since I could not get a job, I started thinking about how to go back to Kenya. I remembered the love of my parents and the words my mom told me at the airport. I discussed the matter with my husband, and he told me we could not do that, even if we did not have enough money to pay for our apartment. He encouraged, "God will still show us the way." I realized I could not go back to Kenya because I was already older. In Kenya, I could not be ordained in the Presbyterian Church East Africa (PCEA) if I was over a certain age. I felt it might be very difficult for me to go back before I finished my ordination process in America.

My husband always spoke words of wisdom. We discussed this matter and we agreed to stay in the United States. I discussed this with my husband, and we felt it was better if we did not go back at that time. My ordination process was one of the biggest reasons. I had completed all the requirements for the United States – now I just had to wait in America to be ordained. We said, "let us put this prayer before God and, we will get the answer".

After a while, I went out looking for anything I could do for work. Our God is faithful! I started looking for a job in a nursing home as Nurse's Aide. I got one agency who told me to fill out the application forms. I filled out the forms, but I forgot not to write all my education and former experiences (I have learned that sometimes being overqualified is worse than not being qualified when it comes to working in America).

I finally got a job! I was sent to the home of a client where I worked for a time. The client was a wheel bound patient using oxygen. It was so hard for me, but I really wanted something to do. I was tired of not working. The client's husband oriented me in what I was to do there each day. I carried on my daily duties, and I loved that job so much. It was enjoyable mainly because I was supporting the couple, and we were sharing prayers together. This was a Christian couple. For me, it was healing for my spirit to get to be helping those who needed my care.

The woman from the agency called me told and me told me she had been given a good report by my clients. They wanted to assign me even more hours. The senior office called me again and told me to come back and do higher-level orientation. I went to take a class for three days (paid hours). These courses taught me how to make beds, how to remind clients about the time to take their medication, and how to help prepare meals for those with special diets. I liked to cook, and this was a great time to learn how to prepare American food. Throughout all of this, I was reminded by God that He saw me. He wanted to encourage me in whatever job I was performing.
"Whatever you do, work at it with all your heart, as working for the Lord, not for human masters." (Colossians 3:23). "Whoever can be trusted with very little can also be trusted with much, and whoever is

dishonest with very little will also be dishonest with much." (Luke 16:10) In this job, God did not let me forget who I was. I humbled myself to do that job and I worked hard at it for the glory of God. It was a blessing to (actually) get paid for my work. I was able to bring a check home twice per month to contribute to our bills.

Since I had worked in hospitals as a hospital chaplain, it was no big deal to listen to the feeling of my clients. When we were sharing our stories in the home, the couple got interested in me (they also loved my accent). Once, the wife asked me why I came to this country. I did not want to tell her the whole story (because I did not want to lose my job at that time if I revealed my pastoral background). I did tell her that I came to study theology. She asked me, "did you say 'theology'?" I said to her "yes, yes, and I have already done it". I did not want that discussion to continue, so immediately I asked her if she wanted something to drink. She nodded, and I went to her refrigerator and brought her cold water. That was the end of our discussion on theology.

I was driving 25 miles per day (one way) from my apartment to the home where I was taking care of the couple. I was being paid $8.00 per hour, and I used to work twenty-five hours per week. One day, I was feeding my clients, and something came to my mind. "Is this the job I came to do in America? After all the education I have gotten?!" My tears were flowing down my face. I was asking God, "is this the work you have given me now, after being in the Seminary for over ten years?! How much longer am I going to do this?"

My frustrations continued. Finally, I decided to resign from this job. I called the office and told the supervisor that I needed to stop working there "as soon as possible." She asked me, "why, Jemimah, do you want to stop working with us? Can we change you to another client? The company doesn't want to lose you. You are a good worker". I told her this did not have anything to do with their offices or my clients. I wanted to discontinue because of what I was going through with my denomination. I did not want to do this job anymore. I could not continue with what I was doing. If my church was not going to say anything about my process, I would continue waiting for the will of God. If God told me I was to go back to Kenya, that would be okay. If it was God's will to open the doors for me to be ordained, that was okay, too. This lady could not understand what I was talking about, but she accepted my resignation and I left the job immediately. I continued to pray for God's leading and His call.

It was like a surreal dream. All my classmates from McCormick were being ordained and hired as ministers. My heart had been broken because of my many barriers along the way. Sometimes, I would feel that I could not bear to witness the ordinations of so many others when I was left behind. Whenever I would attend these celebrations, I would always hear well-meaning (but painful) questions from people about when my own time was coming. I did not know, so I could not give an answer. I thought after the completion of my Master of Divinity, the ordination would be soon on the way, but it was taking so long. The issue of ordination exams (which was a big issue) hindered my process for a time. After I passed my ordination exams, I made a covenant with God that I wanted to continue being humble before God until His will was done. I was asking myself many questions about whether God was really standing with me in my time of suffering. By this time, *I had waited more than twenty years for my ordination.* I had made a covenant with God that no matter what I was going though, I wanted to continue to experience God's presence. I continued to be reminded of God's promises in His word. *"Hear me as I pray, O Lord. Be merciful and answer me! My heart has heard you say, 'come walk with me' and my heart responds 'Lord, I am coming'"* (Psalm 27:7)

After I resigned as a Nurse's Aide, I called Rev. Dr. Linda Shugert for an appointment. She told me to see her the next day. When we met, she asked me whether we could go for lunch. I told her "I'm not hungry. I do not need any food right now. Food is not my priority now. To be ordained is the most important issue right now. What I need to know about is how my process of my ordination is coming." So, we decided to stay in her office (which would later become my office). I asked her "what do I do?" I started crying and calling out to my mother (who had been dead more than ten years at that time). I shared my story and continued crying in her presence. I was also crying out to God, because I had pain in my heart. I said again to her, "Rev. Linda, I have passed all my ordination exams and I have met all the Presbytery requirements, so at this time, I need to be ordained." I said again "Yes! I want to be ordained!" I continued crying. She was so worried and was wondering what to do with me.

Rev. Linda was a good listener. I said to her "you know, Rev. Linda, my vision is to minister to the immigrants from Africa. I feel that right now, this is what God is calling me to do. I feel led to start a group with the people from Africa." I continued "God wants me to do this, and I feel God has confirmed this call in my heart to minister to immigrants. I feel this is my vision for my future ministry." She listened to me and she said to me, "Jemimah, if this is what God wants you to do, the doors will be opened for us." At that time, God reminded me that my role in the church was to bring Jesus' ministry to the people. I remembered I came to this country for one reason: to know Him more and to witness the power of the cross. If not for the death and resurrection of Jesus Christ, I could not have come to America. I believed God when He promised, "nothing in all of creation can separate us from the love of God" (

After I shared with her, she told me that she was going to call for a meeting and discuss with the other leaders the possibility of waiving some of the requirements that were in place to receive a call to a Presbyterian church for ordination (specifically, the requirement that a church needed to call me to be their pastor). Then she told me, "I have an idea! Let's pray." She continued, "This is what we are going to do. Gather a few people from Africa and bring them to the church you are already working with. Come every Sunday. Come to Bible study and keep on bringing these African people. Since I am a moderator of this Presbytery, I am going to suggest that the Presbytery can hire you as a Presbytery Evangelist as African Organizing Pastor. You never know, Jemimah, this office could someday be your office". (Her words would later turn out to be prophetic, because that is what eventually happened). She then took that request to the Presbytery and I followed her instructions.

When I realized that God renewed the joy of my salvation through prayers and meditation, God answered my prayers in a mighty way. Let me tell you! My life changed from this point on! It did not take too much time before I started a group for African people to fellowship together. God's miracles began at that time through direction from the Presbytery. I believe the process of my ordination started from that time forward. I started inviting people to come to my apartment for fellowship, and then invited them to come to church and worship together with others. I began with my husband and my children and two of my old friends (and the church started from that moment on). We were permitted by the Rock-Hill/South Webster Session to fellowship in the Sanctuary at 12:30 p.m. (because the members of Rock hill/South Webster with Pastor Linda Shugert worshipped there in the morning).

Rev. Linda asked that I prepare something (give the structure of my ministry) so that she could present it to her meeting to discuss my ordination. Here is what I shared:

#1. Why do we exist?

Neema Mission: Neema exists to serve the refugee population in Denver, building a community of faith through initially focusing on the following needs & services according to the Great Commission (Matt 28:16-20):

Services	Felt Need Met
Welcome Center/Home	Welcome Center for Refugees
Rescue and Resettlement resettlement	Identify families in need of and community
Educational/Leadership Training	Develop programs, offer Classes that serve, nurture and empower the whole family (i.e. ESL, Youth Empowerment)
Spiritual Empowerment	Establish place of worship where Africans can grow in their Christian faith through Bible Study, discipleship and Worship
Spiritual Counseling	Restore individuals and family To community to address sociological, psychological, and theological traumas
Cultural Revitalization	Create opportunities for the African community to Experience fellowship and Connection specific to refugee cultures using the arts
Food Bank	Create accessible local food Bank for refugees in the community

Vision:

vision is three-fold:

- Becoming and belonging to a family of faith and a caring community from Africa.
- To empower one another so as to reach out to nurture others according to our cultural heritage.

- To become a one stop umbrella center with the ability to train and reach the needs of men, women, youth, children, elderly, and the poor.

#2. How do I fit in?

- The worship & spiritual practices will be in accordance with the policies, practices, & procedures of the PCUSA church.
- Neema will be a family, reflecting dynamics of Gods' image
- There will be periodic consultation with Denver Presbytery staff

#3. How Do We Know We Are succeeding?

Qualitative Measures: When Christians come together and are cemented by our central unifying commitment to Christ; giving their lives in the direction of evangelizing and/or economic development relieving human suffering or injustice to make a difference in the refugee community.

Quantitative Measures:

- will keep records of all activities while coordinating and managing the center of refugees
- By the growing number of people receiving assistance
- By the number of people who are empowered by the gospel to go make disciples
- By the number of people who grow in their English-speaking skills

- By the number of people acquiring employment in their trade
- By the community & Presbytery volunteering in activities and services to help refugees
- By increasing our territory to include colleges and university students in meeting their needs.
- By refugees finding homes

28. My Prayers Were Answered!

After I submitted my proposal, I traveled to Kenya for a conference. I was out of the country in Kenya. I was there attending the conference for Values Spiritual Leadership that was held at a Presbyterian Guest House. This was sponsored by Sister Patricia Bombard, who traveled with me and was there with me at the conference. She was the religious sister who had been praying and supporting me in my studies since I began at Chicago Theological Seminary. At our conference, there were 60 people in attendance from different denominations and I was one of the speakers. I spoke at the conference about how to prevent burnout amongst pastors and church leaders. It was a wonderful training.

Sister Bombard had been my long time spiritual friend and sister. She had been praying for my ordination and was so committed to me. She had been encouraging me throughout the whole process (crying with me when I did not pass my exams on multiple occasions). She also reminded me that I was still in God's plans for my future ministry.

While in Kenya at the conference, the Committee of Preparation (CPM) had been meeting and reviewing my proposal. They had met and voted that I would be (finally) ordained! I received their email stating that I had been qualified to be ordained! When I got this information, Sister Bombard and I held hands and thanked God together while we were still attending the conference. She kept saying "I'm so glad for you, Jemimah!"

Here is what the email said:

"Congratulations! You have successfully passed all 5 of your ordination exams and met our requirements in receiving a call to be ordained. You are now invited to meet with CPM for a final consultation. You will be ordained on Saturday the 12th of November 2005, at 10am in the Giddings-Lovejoy Presbytery gathering in Ferguson, Missouri at the First Presbyterian Church"

When I got back to the United States, I met with the CPM. I was nervous because I had met with many committees for my ordination preparation and they were not always good experiences. In my statement of my faith, I had misspelled the word "Holy" (as in Holy Spirit). Instead of writing "holy", I inadvertently wrote "holly". One of the members (perhaps jokingly) asked me whether "that is another faith". I responded politely, "please remove one 'L' and read it as 'holy'. That is what I believe." Afterwards, I was told to go outside so they could discuss and vote. They determined that my ordination would indeed take place on Saturday during the presbytery meeting.

On this day (the Thursday before by my ordination Saturday) my heart wondered, "is this true? Will this really happen soon?"

The Lord is so faithful to fulfill His promises! *"Therefore, say to them 'this is what the sovereign Lord says: none of my words will be delayed any longer; whatever I say will be fulfilled, declares the sovereign lord"* (Ezekiel 12:28).

29.   My Ordination

After waiting for decades for the vision to come to fruition, **I would be finally ordained on November 12, 2005!**

The time came for my ordination! The long wait was finally over!!

Saturday finally arrived, and I was ready with my family and friends who had been waiting for my ordination. I was called to declare my statement of Faith before the members of our presbytery. The church was full (you could not get a seat because so many people from different denomination came to witness my ordination, even many people from different countries in Africa!). After I presented my Statement of Faith, I waited for any question about my statement of faith or my story, but no one asked me any questions. I was then escorted outside for the official and final answer of whether I would be ordained or not. During my time outside (which was minutes but felt so much longer), I lifted my eyes to God and I remembered Psalm 91:1-2 *"God, it is you whom I trust at this time."* After that prayer, I was called back inside. Everyone shouted my name (then I knew there was a victory!). I particularly heard my African friends yelling out in celebration "ayeee ayyeee". Everyone was standing up when I walked back in. Just before I was told that I was to be ordained, the crowd shouting and clapping told me my answer. I started crying!

I was given a mandate ("Charge of Charge") by a Presbyterian Minister from Kenya (serving in Dallas, Texas) named Rev. Dr. Cyprian Kimathi. He had known me for many years. I remember his words, he said "Ministry will not be smooth or easy. Humble yourself before God and know that He will never leave you or forsake you. Keep on meditating. Read the bible. Continue to commit yourself to the Call God has given you." He reminded me of what God says in Joshua. *"Be strong and very courageous. Be careful to obey all the law my servant Moses gave you; do not turn from it to the right or to the left, that you may be successful wherever you go."* (Joshua 1:7-9)

I was ordained by Rev. Dr. Linda Shugert (who was the moderator of the presbytery at that time). *I was ordained as the first new immigrant woman ordained by the Presbytery of Giddings-Love joy PCUSA!*

The time surrounding my ordination was emotional and deeply joyous. This was especially true because I had my family, friends and the members of United African Presbyterian church (because many people have waited for my ordination for many years here in US and in Kenya) by my side. After I was ordained, the Rev. Terry Empling (who was the Stated Clerk of Giddings-Lovejoy Presbytery) announced my name as "*Reverend* Dr. Jemimah Ngatia." I remember that day and the sound of his voice at that time. There was a joy in the whole place and everyone was ready to celebrate the victory. They came to witness the victory of God through my ordination.

I remember after my ordination, I received many hugs from many people who wanted to share my joy. One of the ladies who was a church elder (and my Raising Officer since 1997). Her name was Jean Snyder. She gave me a huge hug and she started crying, saying that she feared she might die before my ordination (there were times in my process when I visited her in the hospital when she was sick). She was so happy she got to live to see this day (Jean would live on, well into her elderly years, and she would always talk about how hard it had been during on my ordination process). I remember earlier in my process I was with her (at the consultation meeting for the Committee of Ordination). We were seeking permission from committee to waive the exams (which of course they did not, but God worked it out). Jean had been with me at the very same meeting where the Chairman said, "even if Jemimah fails the exams fourteen times, the committee cannot waive the exam for her." (That was very hard for me and I prayed for him because I knew that one day I would be ordained no matter how long it would take). Jean had been with me throughout that entire process and her rejoicing was deep.

My ordination was like a dream. It felt like I imagined it must have felt like when the Angel told Sarah she would have a baby after so many years. *"Abraham fell face down; he laughed and said to himself 'will a son be born to a man who is one hundred years old? Will Sarah bear a child at the age of 90?"* *(Genesis 17:17)* *"So Sarah laughed to herself as she thought 'after my lord is worn out and my lord is old, will I now have this pleasure?"* *(Genesis 18:12)* I had waited many years for the process of my ordination, just as Sarah and Abraham waited so many years for their child. When Sarah found out that she was going to have a child at such an old age, she laughed. In my case, when the promise was finally fulfilled for me, it was my tears that flowed. I cried, praising the Lord because my dream had finally come true!!

As you read this, I would like you to consider my story. Have you been waiting a long time for a promise? Do not give up! Just as Sarah was under God's promise, so was I. It does not matter how long it takes to happen, but the promise of God will be fulfilled for you. If it could happen for Sarah and it happened for me, it can happen for you. Keep being faithful to God! As Moses told Joshua, *"be careful to obey all the instructions Moses gave you. Do not deviate from them, turning either to the left or to the right. Then you will be successful in everything you do. Study this book of instruction continually. Meditate on it day and night so that you will be sure to obey everything written in it. Only then will you prosper and succeed in all you do"* *(Joshua 1:7-8).*

The process of my ordination taught me to continue seeking the face of God (the process certainly humbled me before God). I remember sharing with some of the committee members that my ordination would come in God's timing. I remember after my ordination, I experienced so much peace and became more committed to my ministry more than ever before.

30. The Story Continues

On June 31, 2005, the Rock-Hill/South Webster Presbyterian Church closed their ministry. The building was only left open because our fellowship was still meeting there at 12:30pm. We were given the building to continue worshiping there. The power of God continued working day and night. The Presbytery upgraded my position (in which I had been part-time). I was officially hired by the as Presbytery on staff for the position of Presbytery Evangelist (and to do the work as an Organizing Pastor of the United African Presbyterian community, with my ordination to follow).

As I shared, I was hired for one year and offered a part-time salary. I was hired as a staff of the Presbytery and as an Organizing Pastor. I did not ask the Presbytery what would happen after that one year. I had put all my faith and hope in God's hands (that there would be something else coming for me after that year). Let me tell you, just before the year's end, the New Church Development Committee (NCD) met and they voted and confirmed my salary as an ordained Minister of Word and Sacrament.

My prayer in this journey is to glorify the name of our mighty God in every way. Today, God, I celebrate the victory, remembering Rev. Dr. Linda Shugert and Rev. Paul Reiter who brought my case before the presbytery. I also recall Rev. Dr. Terry Empling.

The Rev. Dr. Empling really supported me and applied for my visa (from a student visa to a religious worker's visa, to Green Card and eventually to citizenship). I am now I US Citizen – glory be to God! My citizenship came right before I could have been deported. Rev. Empling worked hard with my lawyer. We have seen the Glory of God in my suffering. I have gone through valleys and mountains, but the hand of our mighty God has been over me. The Presbytery asked me whether the salary they offered was too little. I told them that it was okay with me, because I had been working without any salary for many years before that point.

There is a book called *Suffering is a Gift*. In it, suffering is described as a gift rather than a curse. I came to understand that after you suffer, you become a different person. In a deep painful experience of suffering, God is still there. When you come out of that place, you have been spiritually nurtured. After suffering, you will never be the same. This is the reason why it should be a gift. *"Dear brothers and sisters, when troubles of any kind come your way, consider it an opportunity for great joy. For you know that when your faith is tested, your endurance has a chance to grow. So, let it grow. For when your endurance is fully developed, you will be perfect and complete, needing nothing"* (James 1:2-4).

I waited upon God. I have seen what Lord has done in my life and in my ministry. I am sure God is going to do great things if we wait and allow the Lord to work in His own way and time. Through my personal experience, I have come to understand clearly that there is nothing truly hard or impossible with God. We can be okay in any circumstance. *"I can do all things through Christ who gives me strength" (Philippians 4:13).*

The people around you may encourage you or discourage you. They do this because some of them might not understand what God has in store for your future, but we need to wait upon God because God moves the mountains. I have witnessed the victory! People can close the doors for us, BUT GOD opens the windows (and doors) and nobody can shut them. God will make a way for us to pass through if it is His will. My help has been coming from God who created Heaven and Earth and all things in it. The doors God opens nobody can shut because our God is the Alpha and the Omega!

After my ordination, one of the members of the ordination committee (CPM) talked to me. He told me "Jemimah, when you appeared to the committee where I was a member, we did not know what to do. We had not interviewed any other candidates like you before. You are unique in many ways". Then I told him "Yes, I know the committee had difficulties to consider me for ordination, because they didn't know me. But God knew me before I was born. He was IN the process of my ordination." So, the man hugged me and told me "congratulations!" I had made history in that Presbytery. I was the first immigrant woman from Africa to ever be ordained by the Presbyterian Church USA.

God knew what I was going through! God held my hand until the end of the journey (and after I had completed the journey). I took the flame high and shouted to everyone that "God is the finisher of unfinished business!" My God is the beginner and the finisher of my process because God created me in His own image. *"Fixing our eyes on Jesus, the pioneer and perfector of faith. For the joy set before Him, He endured the cross, scorning its shame, and sat down at the right hand of the throne of God." (Hebrews 12:2).* I am wonderfully and beautifully made with full understanding of my creator (who created heaven and the earth and everything in it*). "…God saw all that he had made, and it was very good" (Gen. 1:31a).* Yes, God did a very good job in creating us and God said it was very good. Some people stereotype people who come from Africa. They believe our brains are not complete. This is so sad (and SO untrue)! Now that I had become ordained, who could come after that and say I did not have a complete brain? I know my loving God and I acknowledge the power of the death and resurrection of our Lord and savior Jesus Christ! I came to this country knowing Jesus Christ as my personal savior. Because I know Him, I know that there is nothing better than that in all the world. I am a born-again Christian (BA)! If I had nothing else, I already had everything. This surpasses any achievement (including ordination). I have Christ and therefore I have everything.

It is my joy to share with you my happiness on the day of my ordination. It was an answer to prayer and a fulfillment of God's promises to me!

As I shared, God already knew what would happen with my position after that one year. The Presbytery again met (through the emphasis of Rev. Linda), and we were given permission to continue worshiping in the building. I continued offering my services to the St. Louis community, especially those who were from Africa (I had been visiting them and evangelizing in the African community for some time).

I continued to visit international stores where people from other countries came to buy food from their home countries. I also visited universities and colleges and reached out to the international students (so they would know about our fellowship). I visited Missouri Baptist College and met with their International Director. She organized a meeting for all international students from Africa at the campus. I remember at the end of the meeting one student came forward and asked me "can I call you 'Mom'?" I gave him a hug and he told me it was his first time to come out from his family's home in Kenya. Now, he felt lonely and he was missing his family (as well as the taste of the food his mother used to cook). I gave him another hug and I invited him to my house for dinner. He continued coming to my house and he became an active member in our fellowship. Eventually, he started conducting the choir and leading choruses for our worship service. I reached out not only students, but also other people from Africa who were newly arriving (and other immigrants who were already in St. Louis). I welcomed them to our fellowship (alongside the other African people) and we worshipped at United African Presbyterian Church. The Presbytery voted for us to continue worshiping inside that building. Additionally, the Presbytery would support us by covering all the building expenses (such as utilities). Also, at that time, I was hired part-time (paid!) as an organizing pastor for one year.

The Word of God reminded me that when we obey God's word, we are demonstrating where our faith rests (and how strong it is), but sometimes we may not always understand God's ways. We must always walk in God's steps.

If I thought the LORD was telling me to jump through a stone wall, I would jump! I trusted Him. Jumping over the stone wall would be God's business to make the path for me to pass through. All that time, I continued experiencing the presence of God in every step and lifting my eyes to God because I knew only God could make the ways possible. *"I look up to the mountains – does my help come from there? My help comes from the Lord, who made the heavens and the earth" (Psalm 121:1-2).*

31.   What Did This Process Teach Me?

One thing I have learned is not to give up until God finishes his process. This is because people can walk away from us, but God never walks away. He always completes His promises and His processes (in His own perfect timing). It is now the time for women today to not give up! This is because God is at work and He is moving in our lives. He works with us personally and collectively!

My journey strengthened me and taught me how much God cares for me. The same God cares for you, too, and He is the same God *yesterday, today and forever* (Hebrews13:8). I know this is true, especially when I was about to lose my hope in God (because my process took more time that I ever expected). In every step, I experienced the presence of our mighty God. I believed God called me with a purpose even though I came from different culture. I still knew God had a purpose for my future ministry. I kept asking myself, "how can I sing a new song in foreign land?"

"…and we know that in all things God works for the good of those who love him, who have been called according to his purpose" (Romans 8:28). This journey strengthened me. I grew to realize that God was in the midst - even in my struggles. At every step, I was encountering His love, His grace and His mercy.

I want to encourage especially women in the ministry not to give up because what God says, He does. His yes is yes (no one can change the plans of God). Women in the ministry need to continue serving their God who has called them (and speak up with words of wisdom). The day will come for them to celebrate their victory!

32. Experiences as an Ordained African Woman Minister of Word and Sacrament

As I mentioned above, my experience during my ordination was a nightmare. I remember how long my journey took throughout my ordination process. Before and after my ordination, I had already been working amongst the African communities.

Sometimes, when I was in a group of African minsters who were men, I was the only woman minister. I saw that the men from Africa would view me as a woman "that surely does not understand the values of her own community in Africa" (i.e. the traditional African roles of males and females, where the husband works outside the home and leads, while the wife serves the family by raising children, cooking and taking care of the domestic responsibilities). While I sometimes was aware of being viewed this way by some men, I overall felt truly welcomed by many in the African community.

Many of us know that it is difficult for women to rise to leadership anywhere. This is even more true in my culture. Women from most African countries are often seen only in the domestic roles (house cooking for the family and bearing and raising children). Traditionally in the past, a man would marry a wife and they would have a few children (this has been the case in situations even where the man is not known as a wealthy man in the community). Traditionally, the woman is not to work outside the home. She is to stay at home and perform her home duties.

There is a saying in my community that goes, "a woman should not speak when the men are speaking". In other words, the woman is not supposed to comment in the discussions of men or ask questions. Also, she is supposed to jump when a man asks the woman of the house to do something. If any woman or a child dares to ask a question or comment, this is frowned upon. I was often hearing "this is not a women's discussion - this is only for the men!" This kind of thinking is not right. It sets up women to feel inferior to men. This is what I grew up hearing from my father and other men in my community. Coming from this culture, you can imagine what a big deal it was when I not only earned my Doctorate degree, but when I became the very first immigrant woman from Africa to be ordained as a Minister of Word and Sacrament in the Presbyterian Church USA.

I remember when I was a little girl, my father would ask my mother to do something. It did not matter if mum was doing something else at the time. She had to stop whatever it was and start doing what my father asked her to do. There were no questions. She was to go and do it and ask questions later.

When I first planted the church (and the session members were elected), sometimes it was difficult for me to moderate in the church session meetings. This was because church session was formed by men (the church was made up of people from the same traditional cultural practices I had grown up with). They, too, were born and raised in Africa. At the first meetings, the men wanted to tell me what to do and how I should do things. They related to me as inferior to themselves. I was a "woman like their wives" and they tried to treat me as "less than". They could not see past their viewpoint of women being only for the home. I would tell them I was the pastor of this church (and therefore the moderator of the meetings), and here was the agenda for this meeting, but that did not matter. It was so hard at the beginning, but my Presbytery supported me so much through the process. I needed to train them not to look at me as a traditional woman from Africa, but rather to see me as their minister of the congregation.

I have encountered some resistance to my leadership, mostly from the men from the African community. Not all of them, of course (just those few who viewed women as if they could not be called by God). I explained to them that if they visited me in my house, I would gladly cook tea (chai) and chicken and rice for them in our proper traditions. When I am at home, I am a mother and a wife, and I keep a great home. However, we were not in my home! We were at church. When we were in church business, I was the minister of the church and they were to view me and treat me as such (not to look at me in the way they normally saw women). My husband was a church elder. He did not look at me as just his wife or as just a woman in the house in that context, but he honored and respected me as a minister of the church. He really modeled and demonstrated what it could look like in front of the other men to treat me with respect as a pastor. When we were at church doing church business, my husband addressed me publicly as "our pastor". Privately in our home, he would address me as "Mama Jane" (a nickname he called me, referring to my oldest daughter).

The ordination for a woman from Kenya was difficult. I first learned how difficult this was when the Presbyterian Church East Africa denomination ordained Rev. Dr. Jane Nyambura Njoroge in 1984 (she was the first woman to ever be ordained in that Presbyterian denomination). I remember at the time, there was big talk and controversy among the community, especially when the question came up about ministering the Holy Communion. People viewed her as if (because she was a woman), she would somehow drop the communion cups when serving the members. She was even in the Kenyan news. People looked suspiciously at her when she answered the media's questions. The ironic thing was that the very work that "traditional" women's roles filled was the same work that prepared her wonderfully for the physicality of that particular sacrament. "Could she not hold heavy dishes of food and take them from the kitchen to the dining table?! The Holy Communion Cup is not even as heavy as a dish of food from the kitchen to the dining table!" The naysayers continued. People questioned whether a woman would be able to baptize a baby. They criticized, "won't she drop the baby when she holds it?" Of course, Rev. Dr. Jane Nyambura Njoroge proved that she could do it all well! Fortunately, following her legacy, the PCEA denomination would go on to ordain many women after her. She demonstrated and modeled great leadership. She eventually held a senior position at the office of the World

Council of Churches Switzerland. (WCC). Rev. Dr. Jane Nyambura was a great role model for me in my ministry. Just as she was the first woman to be ordained in the Presbyterian Church East Africa, I, too, was the first new immigrant woman from Africa to be ordained by the Presbyterian Church USA!

After working through difficulties and hardship of being a female church leader, I still encountered resistance from a few in the community. Some of the men who struggled with my leadership tried to use the bible to back up their concerns. They referenced Jesus' twelve disciples (who were men) to make their case. They failed to see the many women who ministered to and with Jesus during his entire ministry. The women may not have been as highlighted, but they were instrumental to what He did. The Bible tells us Jesus was supported by women and he showed us all that women were important in his ministry. The most notable example of the value Jesus placed on women was when they were the first witnesses to the resurrection at Jesus' tomb. *"Early on the first day of the week, when it was still dark, Mary Magdalene went to the tomb and saw that the stone had been removed from the entrance. So, she came running to Simon Peter and the other disciple…and said, 'they have taken the Lord out of the tomb and we do not know where they have put him!' So, Peter and the other disciple started for the tomb"* *(John 20:1-3)*

Men who did not agree with women in ministry would often cherry pick and use their selected passages to make their case. This is a strategy known as "proof texting". They would refer to specific early worship instructions to burgeoning churches in the New Testament, or to Paul's letter to Titus about elders. The tricky thing about proof texting is that it goes both ways. Like them, I, too, could use scriptures to share about women in leadership and in ministry.

To counter what they would choose to share in the Bible, I shared about how important women were to Jesus, even in leadership (Mary Magdalene and her sister Martha were some of his closest friends, and of course women were first to discover and report the resurrection). In fact, God valued and raised up women and used them greatly in his narrative since the very beginning. Eve was made from Adam's rib (not his feet, but his side). Moses' wife Zipporah saved her husband Moses' life by obeying God and circumcising their son herself in obedience *"At a lodging place on the way, the Lord met Moses and was about to kill him. But Zipporah took a flint knife, cut off her son's foreskin and touched Moses' feet with it 'surely you are a bridegroom of blood to me' she said" (Exodus 4:24-25)* God used the prostitute Rahab to hide and help the Hebrew spies, helping God's people lay claim to the promised land. Later she would become part of Jesus' blood line and family tree by marrying and having children with one of the spies *"Before the spies lay down for the night, she went up on the roof and said to them, 'I know that the Lord has given you this land and that a great fear of you has fallen on us, so that all who live in this country are melting in fear because of you. We have heard how the Lord dried up the water of the Red Sea for you when you came out of Egypt, and what you did to Sihon and Og, the two kinds of the Ammorites east of the Jordan, whom you completely destroyed. When we heard it, our hearts melted in fear and everyone's courage failed because of you, for the Lord your God is God in heaven and on the earth below" (Joshua 2:8-11).* Later, God raised up Deborah as a woman judge over His entire kingdom. *"Because he* [Sisera, the commander of King Jabin of Canaan] *had nine hundred chariots fitted with iron and had cruelly oppressed the Israelites for twenty years, they cried to the Lord for help. Now Deborah, a prophet, the wife of Lappidoth, was leading Israel at that time. She held court under the palm of Deborah between Ramah and Bethel in the hill country of Ephraim, and the Israelites went up to her to have their disputes decided" (Judges 4:3-5).* In that very same story in scripture (where a woman, Deborah the Judge, leads her army to defeat the oppressor Sisera), God raises up another women (Jael) to be the one to physically slay him. *"Most blessed of women be Jael, the wife of Heber the Kenite, most blessed of tent-dwelling women. He asked for water, and she gave him milk; in a bowl fit for nobles she brought him curdled milk; Her hand reached for the tent peg, her right hand for the workman's hammer. She struck Sisera, she crushed his head, she shattered and pierced his temple. At her feet, he sank, there he fell- dead." (Judges 5:24-27).* Queen Esther of course served as courageous leader who stood up for (and saved) the Jews at the risk of her own life. *"Then Esther sent this reply to Mordecai: 'Go, gather all the Jews who are at Susa, and fast for me. Do not eat or drink for three days, night or day. I and my attendants will fast as you do. When this is done, I will go to the king, even though it is against the law. And if I perish, I perish.'" (Esther 4:15-16).* In the "hall of faith" in Hebrews, two women (Rahab and Sarah) are mentioned in the cloud of witnesses. *"It was by faith that even Sarah was able to have a child, though she was barren and was too old. She believed." (Hebrews 11:10) "By faith, the prostitute Rahab, because she welcomed the spies, was not killed with those who were disobedient" (Hebrews 11:31)* Honestly, I could go on and on. There are so many women leaders throughout scripture that God called and used to lead and serve mightily.

My point was that we need to take the whole counsel of God's word (not just pick out the verses that back up our own case and proof text our way through it). Just as those men needed to wrestle with all those examples in the Bible where God called women to lead, I must also wrestle with the passages the men loved to share. It's ALL in God's word and we must deal with all of it. We need to contend with all what is found in scripture and to ask God for help in understanding it.

It has been a blessing for me to serve in the ministry among the other ministers of Word and Sacrament in PCUSA. Many of the ministers have been supportive (helping me to reach where I cannot reach on my own as an immigrant minister). I have seen the power of God working among many pastors, directing me to the right paths of the ministry of God. Whenever I hit a wall in ministry, I can call on other pastors. They have been standing with me and holding my hand so that I can succeed in the ministry to refugees and immigrants God has put on my heart.

While I shared some of the barriers I have had to overcome with some African men, I have also encountered difficulties and roadblocks having to do with American culture. For example, I have been left behind in some meetings and interactions. Sometimes I feel I am taking more time than others to understand what is expected from me (there are many unspoken American cultural customs). Additionally, my African theological framework is at times different than the American cultural theology. Sometimes, I have experienced frustration when I have dealt with other ministers and colleagues (especially those who had money, power and authority). Unfortunately, politics and power struggles happen in the church just as much as they do in the secular world. It has been a struggle to deal with such ministers. In comparison to them, I would feel less affluent and powerless. It is worth noting that my salary was significantly less than my American male counterparts with similar credentials (like many of the male ministers, I also had my doctorate and years and years of ministry experience, but my paycheck said that the church valued my services less). My church had many needs and we were in a minority context. Because I came from Africa (and the mission of my church ministry is to help settle immigrants and refugees who are newly arriving to our community), I often felt needier than they appeared to be. This does not feel good. I also at times felt like nobody was ready to listen to me (because people were too busy – another marker of American culture). If you wanted to talk with someone, you had to make an appointment, and you had to tell the secretary what you want to tell the boss. Many times, I just wanted someone to talk to, but there were so many hoops to jump through in order to do that. Most of my colleagues could not relate to my stories. I was known as someone who would boldly share about the needs of my community. Many times, I was hearing that the other ministers had no time to listen and sometimes (many times) my heart was broken. This was because my way of doing things and my understanding was very different than theirs (of course, this was understandable because I had been raised in a different culture, but it was still hard for me).

Many ministers enjoyed visiting our worship services. Sadly, I would hear that they would complain afterwards. I would hear complaints that we "take many hours in our worship" (it is true that we sing a lot, pray a lot and talk a lot using different African languages as well as English). Sometimes, the American visitors (who were ministers) did not come back again. The ones who did not return often said it was because we "took too long." They wanted to impose their cultural norms onto our cultural context. The truth is, it takes a long time to have different choruses sung in different languages. It is a value to us to give time for members of the church to share their testimonies of what God has done in their lives and to share the blessings and miracles which came to them during the week. We also take time to lift up our needs to the Lord. After the service, we also have lunch together. Of course, all of this takes much longer than most American services (which are sometimes barely an hour long). In Africa, we have a saying, "a day of seeking firewood and fetching water is like a day of worshipping". Fetching firewood and water usually takes up a whole day (and it prepares us for the future). This is a fitting analogy for our time worshipping together as a church. We believe it is time well spent and it prepares us for the rest of the week!

In my church, we follow the African tradition of worship. If one has not visited in Africa and experienced worship there (and if they have been accustomed to the shorter American service), it might be difficult to get used to.

My interaction with other pastors in our denomination has been a blessing to me. I have gotten to see how different it can be in a western culture. Most of my colleagues have wanted to learn about my culture. We are so happy to let them know how we do things in Kenya. We welcome them! The pastors wanted to learn more about the ways we worship and do ministry in Africa. Many have invited me to speak to their congregations and to share my experiences in ministering to immigrant refugees.

My time in my ministry has been a blessing to many (I am happy to support people arriving here from Africa). Today, I thank God for my life as a minister. I am proud of being ordained as a Presbyterian minister for Word and Sacrament. I have proved to many men and women that I am a minister, because I have lived for many years singing a new song in a foreign land. I have carried the church duties in my heart just like any other church minister in our denomination would. I count daily my blessings from God, who has enabled me to accomplish God's call on my life of being a minister of the Word and Sacrament (in a different culture from my own).

I want to encourage the women from other countries who God has called into ministry. The same God we served in our own countries is very same God in America! I want to encourage women not only in the Presbyterian churches, but all women in ministry who God has called to minister the Word. To the women of God from Africa and other countries, I want to empower and encourage you, letting you know that you can do it with the help that comes from God. Yes, the joy of the Lord has been my strength in my ministry day by day. *"I can do all things through Christ who gives me strength" (Philippians 4:13)*

Throughout the entire story of my ordination and my ministry, God has continually lifted me by His hope. I pray that that He continues to strengthen and lift you by His hope as well. Continue serving the Lord!

33. My Relationships with Other Ministers and Church Leaders

One of the gifts my mother gave me was the time that she blessed me with. She asked me to continue the ministry within her family and in the world. My mother prepared me to do ministry both inside and outside her community. She taught me to work outside of the box (or boundaries), so that I could go out and meet other people in the name of Jesus Christ. When I remember those words from my mom, it has given me strength to trust myself (it lifts me knowing I can work with both men and women in ministry). During my childhood, I did not like to do anything with men (because I could see that many men were like my dad who was not always the best model when I was growing up).

When God called into full-time ministry, my worry was how I was going to interact with my male colleagues within ministry leadership. However, it has overall been wonderful working together with both females and males in this way. It has been a blessing to meet different pastors supporting me and walking together with me in difficulties and in happiness.

I cannot forget the time I lost my daughter Jane (She passed away on October 12, 2009). Everyone came over to support me during that sad time, both spiritually and financially. In particular, I was blessed by other ministers and colleagues. The Rev. Terry Empling (and his wife Annie) and the Rev. Dr. Linda Shugert really came forward to give me support throughout everything. My relationships have been such a blessing! Walking in relationships with others has empowered me to see myself deeper than I ever thought. We carry the ministry of God together. I have learned so much from other ministers when we have worked together (whether in Africa or America).

My goal was for the different programs we developed to be continued and furthered. This certainly involved other pastors in the process. We need all of them to touch the hearts of the people that we were all being called to usher into the Kingdom of God. What I came to understand clearly was that when God was holding me in His hands, there was nothing that was ever truly difficult. There are no mountains bigger than God!! It has been beautiful to see so many ministers working together for God's glory. There is an African proverb that says, "if you want to go fast, go alone; if you want to go far, go together." I have discovered firsthand that this is a true saying.

There are many women in ministry who are my heroes and an example to me in my own ministry. Sometimes it is hard, but when I remember the women who have gone before me, I get energized (remembering what they have gone through to keep their ministry going). My colleagues have touched many people all over the world. At this moment, I can say that my relationships with other leaders in ministry have been powerful and effective. However, not everyone has been able to understand my accent or where I come from. Also, there have been some who have not liked the way I did my ministry (my identity is very much in the Kenyan way of doing things). There have been difficulties for some of my colleagues (who had not been open to having female pastors from other cultures, especially a "typical woman" pastor from Africa). I realized that when I obeyed God to do different activities in ministry, I am pleasing God and not man.

Therefore, I encourage pastors to continue to have good relationships and partnerships with whoever God calls into His ministry (whether from abroad or from within). The people that God has called into His ministry from other countries can always offer something – and there is always something we can learn from them. We should accept one another as one in the ministry of God (not focus on skin color or where someone comes from). It is more important that we have all been called by God. God has given His favor to those involved in the HOLY MINISTRY of God. *"All authority in heaven and earth has been given to me. Therefore, make disciples of all nations, teaching to obey everything I have commanded you and baptizing in the name of the Father, the Son and the Holy Spirit. And know that I am with you to the end"* (Matthew 28:18-20)

34.   Sicknesses in my Life and Experience of Being Hospitalized

I want to share about my sickness. But first, I want to share about a time when my husband, Mr. Benson Ngatia, lifted me up through the stairs (from the third floor of the apartment we lived in) in 1972. I was very sick at the time. I remember I was so weak and sick that I was not able to walk. There was no one there to help Benson take me down the stairs and help me get into the car to go to the hospital. Since I could not walk, my husband had to carry me. This reminds me of the story in the Bible where the paralytic's friends lower him through the roof so that he can see Jesus. *"Soon the house where Jesus was staying was so packed with visitors that there was no more room, even outside the door. While He was preaching God's word to them, four men arrived carrying a paralyzed man on a mat. They could not bring him to Jesus because of the crowd, so they dug a hole in the roof above his head. They lowered the man down on the mat, right in front of Jesus"* (Mark 12:2-4) This scripture encourages me. I relate to this story in scripture because it is the way Benson carried me to the car. Benson prayed as he was carrying me down the stairs and he prayed all the way to the hospital. He prayed that angels would minister to me and give me the help I needed. Once Benson managed to take me to the hospital, I was admitted. I had a recurring problem. I stayed in the hospital for a long time and the doctors had trouble finding the cause of my symptoms.

One day, in 1976, I was driving home with my Sister Louis Muthoni Kabuga. I drove through traffic on a busy road. There was a funeral home on the road, and just before we reached it, I had a great pain in my abdomen. It was a sharp pain which impaired my vision and made me unable to concentrate on my driving. My sister became very worried because she thought I was dying (in fact, my sister thought I *had* died). But after a short time, I recovered. We called my husband and he came with a friend and drove me home. My sister had a good sense of humor. She told the story of how it all started. She said she said she was just about ready to call the funeral home staff (through the fence) to pick me up and put me there because she thought I had. Praise God, it was not yet time for me to go to heaven.

That problem continued. I was hospitalized on and off for several years. One day, a doctor came and read my hospital chart and he requested that the doctors investigate whether I had gall bladder stones. The doctors gathered around my bed and discussed whether I should undergo the gall bladder tests. They hesitated because I was under 40 years-old and not at all overweight – gall bladder disease was often referred to then as "the fat 40." The doctor who was ordered to do the tests reluctantly performed the lab rotary test and x-rays on me. The result came out positive for gallbladder stones. I indeed had that disease called "fat forty" (even though I was not yet forty and I was skinny).

I had to undergo major surgery (which took eight hours) in 1977. They removed several small stones and one big stone from my body. They kept those stones until I was able to see what had given me problems for all those years. One of the church elders, Rueben Mwendia, came and visited me in the hospital. I was crying, asking God, "why is this happening to me?" The elder prayed for me and assured me that God has taking care of me. He said, "when you were in surgery, God was holding your heart". Then I came to praise the Lord. After the surgery, the disease was completely gone! I was discharged from the hospital after ten long days. I came back from the hospital saying, "I have seen the hand of the Lord". My husband and my family rejoiced. I praised God for what I went through. At the time, I saw the mighty hand of God taking care of me when I was on the operation table for eight hours. God truly was holding my heart. I felt the presence of God. When the doctors were busy, my God was holding my heart and keeping it beating because He knew the future ministry He had in store for me. I thank God for keeping me alive for those eight hours, not knowing where I was or where my children and my husband were. I remember one of the church members coming and praying for me before I went into the surgery. When I came out, he prayed again and praised God. He knew that God took care of my heart even when I was unconscious. I remember when I was trying to wake up, there were so many people surrounding my bed. I heard the voice of God saying, "you are beloved, daughter of mine". The second voice I heard was from my oldest sister Phillies Wamuyu Kabuga. She said, "let us go". In my drugged state, I felt like she had really said "she has already passed away and God has taken her home. Let's go". That's the time that I woke up and became conscious (after the eight-hour surgery).

When I returned home, my family and friends were there to celebrate the successful surgery. So many people came there to thank God with me. I was able to testify before my church (Bahati Presbyterian Church in Nairobi).

This whole experience was a wake-up call to take my health seriously. I came out testifying even more that the Lord is my savior!

My dear sisters and brothers in Christ, reading this book, can you reflect on any times that you have experienced the presence of God holding you in a special way?

Some people feel they are walking with heavy burdens in their lives. Sometimes we forget that God holds us (whether we are conscious or unconscious). This reminds me that there is no mountain bigger than the power of God. "*...My heard rejoices in the Lord! The LORD has made me strong. Now I have an answer for my enemies; I rejoice because you have rescued me*" (1 Samuel 2:1)

The other major sickness I had was when I was in Chicago working on my Master of Divinity. This was during the winter. I remember it was so cold, I cannot forget (it was the year 1999). I was a first-year student at McCormick Theological Seminary. I had just started the semester. I started feeling sick. I was in too much pain and I remember trying to wake up for class and not being able to. Instead, I spent the whole day in my apartment, and ended up sleeping for two days after that. I did not eat anything, even though my roommate tried to give me some food. Even so, I was not able eat or to drink anything. My roommate was busy with homework and classwork, but she still came into the apartment and kept asking me, "Jemimah, are you okay? I missed seeing you in class today." I told her, "I do not know how I am feeling. I do not know how to describe the pain I have." I requested that the international director come and take me to the hospital. My roommate called her. We were told she was not in the office at the time My roommate again came back to the apartment to check on me. She told me she was so busy with her exams. I sent her to call Rev. Cathrine Kageni (she was a student from Kenya and another one of my classmates). Rev. Kageni came immediately. She took me to the emergency room at Chicago Hospital. I was so weak (not even able to walk) and she wanted to carry me on her back (but she was shorter than me). She carried me dragging my legs two steps and putting me down like that until we got to the emergency room at the hospital. She helped me to do all the registration paperwork. I was admitted to the hospital, given a bed, and hooked up immediately to two IVs. The doctors were unable to find the cause of my pain at first. During this time, my family was back in St. Louis (while I was in Chicago).

The doctor ordered the following tests: blood, urine, x-rays, laboratory tests, blood pressure, diabetes test, temperature and many others. Every test was done immediately. I was sent for a chest x-ray and the nurse took me to the Radiology Department. I remember I was in a wheelchair because I was not able to walk or to stand up at the time. When the nurse took me to the department, she left me there. I was still attached to the two IVs (that were administering medicine and fluids even after the tech left me). I remember hearing the Radiologist saying, "next patients." I was pushed outside through a different door (I think it was a back door because no one was passing through there). I stayed there in that same spot from ten o'clock in the morning until three o'clock in the afternoon! No one came through where I was and the nurses from the emergency room never came back to get me. Apparently, they were looking for me all over the hospital. The nurse who originally took me there had already ended her shift, and I was left behind. I felt so cold! I shivered in my wheelchair. If I saw someone passing by, I would try to waive them down with my hands (in America, this is taken not as an emergency, but as a greeting, so people just waived back as if to say hello and just kept on walking). No one could find me. No one knew where I was. I did not know where I was either. The IVs had long finished dripping their fluids into me. I had become so cold my fingers got numb. I kept trying to call anyone who was passing by to help me. Over and over, when I did the sign of calling someone (in my culture), it was like I was saluting them or waving to them. They just waived back. My throat was so dry - I was so weak. I could not easily talk (and my arm and hand waving had no effect). I was not until I mustered everything I had and began shouting and screaming that my voice was heard. By that time, the door had been shut again and no one could answer my cry. When I was sitting in the wheelchair for all those hours, I looked down and I remembered my beloved husband (and my children and my professors and my students' friends). They were not with me. I felt alone. No one was there with me. I started calling God and I remembered again in Psalm 121:1 when King David said, *"I will lift my eyes to you God where will my help will come from at this time."* I remember I said that prayer in my Language (Kikuyu). I knew at that time the hand of our mighty God was over me and He knew right where I was. Immediately, after the prayer, I finally saw the janitor (who was cleaning that hallway). She heard my voice and she came over and asked me, "can I help you?" She came to ask me what she could do for me. I told her to check on my file (that was with me in the back of my wheel chair). She looked at the notes on the side of my wheelchair and then she called the emergency room. Once she called them, they came quickly to take me back to the unit. I was shivering, the IV fluids had been leaking out of the tubing. It was very dangerous that I had been unattended for so long when I was so sick. Because I was left for so long, my condition had worsened. I had a very high fever and my lipped developed fever blisters. I tried to cry, but there were no tears. When I finally arrived back in the ER, I was cold, miserable, hungry and lonely. I remember the nurse in charge brought me warm linens and was put on a warm bed and covered with warm blankets.

Apparently, people from the seminary had come to check in on me and no one had been able to find me. In fact, during the time I "went missing", many people had been looking for me. The nurses did not remember that I had been dropped off in the x-ray department (and my records and paperwork were with me, attached to my wheel chair, so no one could trace me).

The Rev. Margaret Asabia was my classmate from Ghana. She came and visited me (once I was "found") and she discovered that I very cold and very hungry. When she saw me, I started crying and I said "I'm so hungry! I would love something warm to eat." She went out of the hospital and came back with some food from Burger King (including French Fries). I ate all the food she brought with her and I cried. At that time, she called my family. The following day, my daughter Jane Ngatia got on the earliest flight out to Chicago and she came to visit me in the hospital. When I saw her by my bed, I started crying again. She saw the condition I was in and felt so bad for me. I was still so hungry and dehydrated (and still had the fever blisters on my lips). I told her my story of what happened, and she said she was going to "sue the hospital" (she never actually did). Everyone who heard my story was so sympathetic to me.

The doctor came and asked me what had happened. My story spread to everyone in the department. The following morning, the senior doctor came to my room. He asked me to share my story again. When he asked me my name, I said, "my name is Jemimah Ngatia from Kenya and I love Jesus Christ as my personal savior." He said to me, "what happened yesterday?" I told him my story. That is the time he consulted the social worker. My case was so serious that the social worker had to be called in. I shared my story with her as well and she consulted the Department of Peace and Justice as well as the hospital chaplain. So many people were involved. One of the medical students from Africa told me that we needed to file a case against the hospital (for mishandling my care as a patient). The nurse who had dropped me off (and forgotten me) at the x-ray department was a white woman (some people were viewing this incident as racial discrimination). I tried to calm down because I was still very sick. My first priority was to get better (I did not know if I would die or if I would be healed and go back to my family). We never filed a case against the hospital, but I was glad that people realized how serious my situation had been and that they were angry about it and cared about me. What happened was wrong. I could have died.

My test results finally come back. A doctor came into my room to share the results. "From the labs" he shared "we found that you have a kidney infection, high blood pressure and high blood sugar. You also have a fever." It was so hard for me to hear all of what was found happening inside of my body. The doctor was so kind to me (I remember he was a Jewish doctor). I told him, "you know what, doctor, I love Jesus so much! Even at this time, I am experiencing the presence of God because the stripes of Jesus on the cross healed all our diseases! Even now, my God is the same yesterday, today and tomorrow!" I quoted Hebrews 13:8 (*"God is the same yesterday, today and forever"*) to him and I told him, "I know you do what you are supposed to do, but my hope is in God who is my helper." The doctor kept quiet for a while. I think he was trying to observe my behavior. He asked me "how are you feeling now?" I told him, "I am doing well because Jesus went to prepare a place for me! When my place is finished, I will go and live there in heaven with Him for years and years." Then I told the doctor "if you get a test result coming out with another problem, please treat me. But know that I am waiting for the healing from above. I am expecting a miracle from God because God knows me! I came here to Chicago not to be sick but to study the living word of God as a true messenger. After I finish my studies, I will go back to my own country." He left my room and he told me he would come back in the afternoon. While my doctor was gone, he had consulted the Psychiatrist doctor. The Psych doctor came to my room and he also asked me my name. I told him, "my name is Jemimah Ngatia. I love Jesus as my personal savior. I am married. I have a husband. I am also a mother of two daughters and one grandson (who is studying to become a church minister like me). My family is now living in St. Louis, Missouri. I came to Chicago for theological studies." After I said all of that to him, he told me to count from one to ten. Then he asked me to count from ten to one. Then he asked me how many days were in a week. I said, "seven days in a week." Then he asked me, "how many months in year?" I said, "twelve months in a year." "How many days in a year?" I answered, "three hundred and sixty-five." He kept asking questions like that. He also asked me other questions. He held cards up with colors and he asked me to tell him which colors were in his hands. I did so. Then he told me "I will tell you a story. I want you to repeat the same story back to me." So, he told his story and I repeated the same story back to him. He finally finished with his psychological exam and said, "I will see you in the afternoon."

When he came back to my room, he asked me what I was doing in Kenya before coming to USA for studies. I told him I had worked as a hospital chaplain in our National hospital (a big hospital which included a medical school). I also shared that before I joined the Department of Hospital Chaplains, I had worked as a Health Educator (educating mothers with children suffering from Kwashiorkor and Marasmus diseases). It was then that the doctor asked me if I would be willing to speak to his fourth-year medical students about those two diseases. I told him we could do that just as soon I got better and regained my strength.

After few days in the hospital, I finally got better. The tests were repeated, and lab results eventually came back normal. I was in the hospital for five days altogether. The day I was discharged from the hospital, I remember it was on a Friday morning. My doctor brought his medical students to me and I shared with them the causes of the two diseases I knew well from my time at Nairobi Hospital (Kwashiorkor and Marasmus). The fourth-year medical students asked me so many questions and I was able to share with the whole group about my work in the hospital. When I came out of the hospital, I was praising God for His divine power of healing. Since that time, I have not suffered like that (at least physically) again. Praise God! I do not even remember that pain and suffering I went through at that time because know it was an attack from devil. My daughter Jane came for me and took me back to St. Louis, Missouri to join my husband and my family. I did not return to seminary until after Christmas in 1999.

There are many people right now who are in dark places. They believe they are stuck. They look around and don't see anyone to help them. BUT GOD is always with us when we are in the deepest pits! He never leaves us! I call upon everyone who is reading this book to be encouraged in any situation or trial that you may be in. Remember that even if no one else sees you, God sees you. God can see into the dark and bring the light at the end of the tunnel. *"If I say 'surely the darkness will hide me and the light become night around me,' even the darkness will not be dark to you; the night will shine like the day, for darkness is as light to you"* *(Psalm 139:11-12)* Just stay tuned into His presence! Remember the Holy Spirit is in you. *"Greater is He that is in you than he who is in the world"* (1 John 4:4)

My sisters and brothers in Christ, I continue feeling presence of God always because my God is a God in season and out of season. *"Preach the word; be prepared in season and out of season; correct, rebuke and encourage – with great patience and careful instruction." (2 Timothy 4:2)* What did this experience teach me and others about the ministry of God? Being a minister of the Word and Sacrament (or being in God's ministry) does not mean that we cannot be attacked and oppressed by the devil (God allowed his servant Job to be attacked by Satan). We want to remember that all of us in the ministry of God (and those God has called to build His kingdom) we are the enemy of devil. I learned through my suffering and trials that I am a target for the devil.

I reminded myself that when I mention the name of Jesus Christ as my personal savior, the atmosphere changes! God uses everything and will change even the worst things to better. Yes, when we call upon the Name of God, we will overcome all trials and tribulations. This is because there is power in the Name of Jesus Christ! I walk in the presence of God because I know God walks with me (and he talks with me and he hears me when I cry out to him). I said to myself, "I need continue experiencing the presence of God each and every moment." I want to be close with him in both times of good health and in times of pain and suffering. I need to experience the presence of my God, because only God has the power of healing. God alone has the power to overcome barriers and bring hope to the hopeless to sustain our faith in God. Paul and Silas sang songs of praise in prison and God heard their prayer while they were in a deep prison. *"About midnight Paul and Silas were praying and singing hymns to God, and the other prisoners were listening to them" (Acts 16:25)* Jonah also cried to God and God heard his cry. *"From inside the fish Jonah prayed to the lord his God. He said, 'in my distress I called to the Lord, and he answered me. From deep in the realm of the dead I called for help, and you listened to my cry. You hurled me into the depths, into the very heart of the seas, and the currents swirled about me; all your waves and breakers swept over me. I said I have been banished from your sight; yet I will look again toward your holy temple. The engulfing waters threatened me. The deep surrounded me; seaweed was wrapped around my head. To the roots of the mountains I sank down; the earth beneath me barred me in forever. But you, Lord my God, brought my life up from the pit. When my life was ebbing away I remembered you, Lord, and my prayer rose to you, to your holy temple. Those who cling to worthless idols turn away from God's love for them. But I, with shouts of grateful praise, will sacrifice to you. What I have vowed I will make good. I will say 'salvation comes from the Lord'" (Jonah 2:1-8)* Jonah got a "free ride" (in the stomach of the fish) and was taken to Ninevah to fulfill God's plans for his life. Anytime we cry out to God and call upon His name, God answers our prayers!

35.   The Death and Funeral of My Mother

As I mentioned above, I grew up being the momma's girl until she passed away (while I was out of the country). For all the years she lived, I do not remember her ever being admitted to the hospital her whole life. She would only go to the hospital to deliver babies, but not for any kind of sickness. My mother gave birth to eleven children (two died before I was born).

Growing up, my work was to be home with my mother helping with her daily work. I was raised and loved by my other siblings (and I was a "momma's girl"). Africans say that "it takes a village to raise a child." Sometimes, my brothers and sisters would send me to Mom if they need something - it was an easy way to pass messages to Mom. They knew that their baby sister Jemimah had favor with Mom. My mother was such an encourager for me in many ways (and she paid a price for me). She is one of the biggest reasons why I am who I am today. My mother raised me well. She taught me how to be humble, how to have compassion and how to be a servant to the older people in our community. My mother was a missionary in her own community and she left a great legacy in so many peoples' lives.

My mother raised us in the Presbyterian church tradition. She was the first woman from our community to ever be married in the church. She practiced well what she was taught by the missionaries and would go on to lead others. *"And the things you have heard me say in the presence of many witnesses entrust to reliable people who will also be qualified to teach others." (2 Timothy 2:2)*

After I did my theological studies and pastoral care (during my schooling for my Master of Divinity), I truly realized and recognized that my mother was practicing theology and pastoral care in our community extremely well (not even knowing that she was practicing theology). Just knowing the truth intellectually is called Orthodoxy. Living those truths out is called Orthopraxy. My mother was amazing at orthopraxy! She lived out her faith in very practical ways such as visiting the sick, caring for the women who had babies in their homes and reaching out to non-Christian women in the community. My mother spoke out against the marriage enforcement for the young girls and she fought against female ritual circumcision. She also educated and encouraged women to deliver their babies in hospitals rather than at home (many women who delivered at home died due to prolonged bleeding). My mom was also a strong advocate of parents putting ALL their children into school – both boys and girls! My mother was a great and strong example to me.

My mother died when she was one hundred and three (103) years old (she lived on for another twenty-three years after the death of my father).

My mother lived a happy life. She was strong until the end (still going out and visiting her children and grandchildren). Altogether, she had raised nine children (and more than fifty grandchildren and twenty-five great grandchildren).

My mother taught me how to treat both the children and the elders in our community. During my marriage, she taught me so much about what it looks like to be a Godly, loving and honoring wife. She taught me how to respect my husband, to honor the elderly and to love my husband's family. I remember one day, she told me, "if you want your marriage to succeed, never ask your husband whether he wants to eat." she leaned in, "one thing I want you to remember is that when your husband walks into the house and sits down, just bring the food out to the table. Never make the mistake of asking him if he wants to eat. He will always want to eat! Just put the food on the table for him. If by some chance he is not hungry, you can always bring your food back to the kitchen, but it's easier to put it back than to prepare it" Even more important than food, the best thing my mother taught me about marriage was to forgive often, read the bible together, pray together and go to church together (and do church activities together). These became very healthy practices for Benson and I in our marriage. I practiced what my mother taught me…and I had a very happy marriage! Benson and I would go on to celebrate even our fiftieth anniversary before he later would pass away! I have never regretted following the teachings my mom imparted to me. Throughout my marriage, I would remember all that was taught to me by my mother. I would remember and follow her wisdom (what she modeled to me and taught me) and I would often see joy and happiness result.

During her old age, my mom lived with Benson and I and we cared for her as one of our children. She was fun! She loved singing and reading the bible, and she prayed often.

One thing I loved about my mother was that when she prayed, she would pray by name for each of her children (and grandchildren and even great grandchildren). Every day, she would begin her prayers at five in the morning. She was a prayer warrior. Our family really sensed my mother's prayers in our spirits. My mother's prayers supported our family so much. When I came home, tired from work and feeling like I wanted to sleep, she would wake me up and say, "let us give God thanks, for He has brought us together this evening." When mother said, "time for prayer" it was time for prayer! She taught us this discipline since we were children – we were to honor the time of prayer as sacred.

It is very difficult to remember the death of my mother. Her death shocked me. Before I left for America, my mother had been living with me and my husband. My family escorted me to the airport to come to America (for Theological studies at Eden theological Seminary in St. Louis, Missouri). As you may remember, I was leaving Kenya to come to the United States for the first time (on August 22, 1992). My mother (and my family, relatives, pastors, and Bahati Presbyterian church members all) escorted me to the airport. It was a joyous and tearful moment for me to leave my family and my job to come to the United States for theological studies. My children were crying to see me leaving them. I think even my husband cried (but of course, Kenyan men do not show their tears). I remember, it was so hard for me seeing my children crying (and my husband asking me "are you really leaving me? When will I be seeing you again?"). My husband and my children hugged me as a sign of letting me go. Everyone gave me a big hug…But my mother, she was the last to give me a hug. She hugged me and told me "I want to let you go since I have never been to the United States of America. Go and study that Good News I first started sharing in our community. And if you come back and find me dead, I will go before you to heaven and I will wait for you. Remain faithful to God, whom I have served for many years." At that time, I felt something in my stomach and I started crying loudly. She called my name and said, "make sure the word of God will remain in my house and remain faithful to God." Let me tell you, I did not like to hear what my mother was telling me. I was telling everyone to come and listen to what my mother was telling me, and she repeated the same again to them "I am telling my sister to go and share the Good News, and if she comes back and finds me dead, I will go and wait for her in heaven. I want her to remain faithful to God and serve His ministry as I have done all my life." The reason why my mother said that to me was because my parents had been the founders of Karindundu Presbyterian Church in our community. My mother started the ministry in our community. It was not easy back then, especially because of the transformation from the cultural traditions to Christianity. My parents were taught by the Scottish missionaries. Mom and Dad got baptized and theirs had been the very first Christian wedding in the community. My mother would not release me from her embrace. She was looking up and wiping my tears with her hands…she would not let me go. She called me again "my sister" (that meant her sister in Christ and it was also what she called me because she had named me after her late sister). She held me tightly like that for a long time. She did not want me to leave her until I absolutely had to. She held me tighter and she could not let me go until she was told by my brother that it was time for my flight. I continued crying and everyone started crying at the airport until I boarded the airplane. I had to run to the gate quickly because it was time to board. I was still crying. I remember when I got to my seat, the flight attendant came to me and asked me "can I help you?" When she asked me that, I did not talk to her. I continued crying. She thought that I had lost my travel documents. It was a long journey which I will never forget. **That was my last time I saw my mother alive.**

After I reached the seminary, I requested to call back home so that I could let my family know that I had arrived safely (and was ready to start my studies). Because my mother lived in my home in Kenya, she was like one of my children to me at the time. I talked with Benson, my mom, and my children. I felt very good.

The day my mother finally passed away was on May 5, 1993. I was doing my final exam (in preaching class) and we went to a church where the professor had organized the preaching exams. I was the second student to present my sermon. I remember I preached about Zacchaeus the tax collector.

"Jesus entered Jericho and was passing through. A man was there by the name of Zacchaeus; he was a chief tax collector and was wealthy. He wanted to see who Jesus was, but because he was too short, he could not see over the crowd. So, he ran ahead and climbed a sycamore-fig tree to see him, since Jesus was coming that way. When Jesus reached the spot, he looked up and said to him, 'Zacchaeus, come down immediately. I must stay at your house today' So he came down at once and welcomed him gladly. All the

people saw this and began to mutter 'He has gone to be the guest of a sinner' But Zacchaeus stood up and said to the Lord 'Look, Lord! Here and now I give half of my possessions to the poor and if I have cheated anybody out of anything, I will pay back four times the amount' Jesus said to him, 'today salvation has come to this house, because this man, too, is a son of Abraham. For the son of man came to seek and to save the lost'" (Luke 19:1-9).

After I finished my sermon, just before I concluded with short prayers, I fell face down at the pulpit and I became unconscious. No other students preached after I fell. After a little while, when I was laying on the pulpit, those around me tried to call 911 to take me to the hospital. While they were waiting for the ambulance, I started regaining consciousness and I heard my professor calling my name "Jemimah! Jemimah!" I recognized the voice of my professor, Martha, but it was just like she was far away, and she was calling my name. Then I started calling to her "Martha, Martha, I came to preach. I know that today is our exam for preaching". She responded, "Jemimah, you have already preached. You did a good job and your sermon blessed us." After that, I was escorted to my room. I slept, but not very well, because I was thinking about what happened. It did not make sense. I was not sick, and my health was good at the time. After a while, one of the students brought me a fax that had been sent from my husband. The student was trying to read the fax in my vernacular language. All I heard was "Cucu had rested in peace." I understood that this meant my mother had died. It was such a shocking moment to me that I could have had a heart attack right then and there. I flashed back to remembering what my mother told me at the airport before I took the flight to come to

America. I came to learn later that the exact moment when I fell at the pulpit (and lost consciousness) was the very moment that my mother had died (thousands and thousands of miles away).

After I heard the message that she had passed away, I started screaming, shouting, and crying loudly while calling my mother all her names. I could remember at that time I saw darkness during the day. Soon after that, I visibly saw the Holy Spirit ascending to the sky. When the students heard me shouting and rolling on the floor, they came to see why I was crying (some of the students did not know what had happened). At that time, I did not have the energy even to cry. There were no more tears flowing out from my eyes. My eyes and my mouth were dry. I was so thirsty. One student brought me a glass of water. I took the water, and then I vomited all the water out and I became very sick. After few minutes, I decided to go into my bedroom and have a quiet time alone with God. I said to God "the way you talked with Moses at the mountain, I want you, God, to talk and speak to me and for you to answer my questions. *The Lord would speak to Moses face to face, as one speaks to a friend…*" (Exodus 33:11). "God, why did you call my mother when I am away in a foreign country?" God kept on telling me "Jemimah, I am who I am." I also asked God, "why did you do this to me?" I said to God "speak, I am listening. In the Holy Bible, your word says, and it is written, that you know and number of our days of life. Is that not what is written? *"Your eyes saw my unformed body; all the days ordained for me were written in your book before one of them came to be"* (Psalm 139:16) You wrote that! You knew when to call my mother home to come to you. You made possible for me to come to America for studies. God, why did you do this to me?"

This was the time I was in the dark place. I had a hard time remembering my peers (not one I can call even my family). I forgot their names. I stayed in the room alone and after a while I became calm and started listening to the people who were in my apartment praying. When I was in my room alone, I heard a voice like my mother's calling me. It said, "Jemimah, I love you. I have left you just for a short time. Soon and soon we will be together." I started sweating and I opened my eyes. It was dark in the room, but it was open. I thought the students came into my room and they were watching over me.

Very much later, I come to know that God wanted me to understand that we are in this life for a short time. That time was my mother's time to go. Everyone has their own appointed time to go, this one was hers. I remembered that there was some work my mother wanted me to accomplish for the Kingdom of God.

My classmates had never seen someone grieving like this before. There were no Kenyans around or anyone who could call me and minister to me in my culture. I felt like I was in the wilderness. I was speaking my vernacular language, speaking to my mother and asking her why she had left me behind (she had never done that before). None of the students were able to understand my language (Kikuyu). Only my mother's spirit could understand the language I was speaking to her (and of course, God knew).

My roommate decided to call Professor Hale. He was the Dean of Common Life at the seminary (and my very own professor advisor). He came to my room and he started comforting me. He read the fax which was sent by husband. In it, my husband had quoted our family bible verse, Philippians 4:4 (*"Rejoice in the Lord always. And I again I say rejoice"*). The professor told me to repeat after him, but I did not understand what I could rejoice about as I was grieving the loss of my beloved mother.

At this time my heart was broken. Very broken. Feeling bad about what God had done to me. The students were so kind to me. They would come to my room bringing me a card and flowers (but they were just able to drop off the card and the flowers). They did not know what to do with me as they had never encountered Kenyan grief before. They wanted to help, but they did not know what to do or how to help. I missed having people around me, but I was crying. It was clear that the students did not know how to handle the grief of someone from another culture. At that time, my professor was looking at me, wondering whether I was normal, or if something had gone wrong in my head. His conclusion was that I was now depressed due to the death of my mother.

Professor Hale asked me "what can I or the Seminary do for you? I see that this is a very painful time for you. We know that you don't have your family here. We want to be your family here at Seminary. What can we do for you?" I replied to him "Professor Hale, the help I need is that I want to go home to be there for my mother's funeral". He told me "I'm sorry, but there is no money in the seminary that can pay for your air ticket". I looked at him and started crying again. I remember replying to him "whether I walk to Kenya, or use a bicycle, or a boat or a flight, I need to be with my family during the funeral of my mom". Hale replied to me "you know, your husband and your children can represent you at the funeral". I responded "this is *my* mother's funeral; not my husband's or my children. I need to be there personally." After our conversation, he left my room.

People at the seminary began to talk about me. They spoke about how I was wailing and rolling on the floor. They knew I was deeply impacted by the death of my mom. This is one of the things I missed about home and my culture. In my home country, when someone dies, people stay in the home of the grieving family until the funeral is done (and even after the funeral is done people will still be coming to the home to see how loved ones are dealing with the grief). In western culture, what I have learned is that when someone is grieving you need to give them space to be alone to grieve. This is quite different from my culture. When I was crying, I did not get any one to give me a shoulder to cry on or to lay my head on them (so my tears could flow). I missed that moment so much (the shoulder to lay on, missed hugs, someone to hold my hand). I also wanted someone to ask me about the life of my mother or to know more about my family in Kenya.

When the word spread, there were two students (husband and wife) who were my classmates. They came to me, gave me a hug and told me "you remember our own mother died three weeks ago. I know what you are feeling, and it must be even more bitter for you since she died in Kenya. I want to let you know that my wife and I are going to pay for your air ticket to go home for the funeral." They had worked for TWA Airlines. They knew how to get tickets quickly. They told me "get ready. You are going to fly out this Friday and you can be there for the funeral of your mother". The couple escorted me to the airport that Friday.

I got onto the airplane. My flight was routed through London. I was so lonely on the flight. On my final leg, I discovered that the woman on the seat next to me was my good friend Matron Rosemary. She had been my co-worker at Kenyatta Hospital. She knew my mom, and she had heard that she had passed away. This woman was like an angel. We sat next to one another and we went on talking. She could feel my pain in my voice. She comforted me, and she helped me so much because she knew my family. She talked with me and consoled me until we touched down in Nairobi International Airport. I reached Kenya on Saturday.

When we came into the airport in Nairobi, Ms. Rosemary was still holding my hand and helping me to carry some of luggage. We came outside and there so many people who came to meet me at the airport. I saw my children and my husband (and the entire family) as well as church members from where I used to serve before I we went to USA. The pastor of my church and church leaders were also there. There were so many people! When I saw all those people, I asked my husband "are all these people coming to meet me at the airport because my mother died?" He nodded. I started crying once more. It was so heavy to everyone who come to meet me at the airport – my mother had impacted the lives of so many people. I was so overwhelmed. I was not able to stand up. I had to be supported to get back on my feet. I was so touched by the love of everyone, especially my husband and children (Jane, joy and Ben Jr.). They came to the airport with a big welcome and many hugs! I remember their prayers. My mother's funeral had been arranged for the Tuesday of the following week.

I was on the program to speak at my mother's funeral, but I was unable to speak when the time. Instead, my daughter Jane Ngatia spoke on my behalf. During the funeral, so many people gathered to celebrate my mom's life. It was so painful for me to hear the stories about my mom – I missed her so much! The stories shared were a confirmation and an affirmation of the way I grew up (seeing my mother in the community serving the Lord, using her talents, raising her children and raising up the community spiritually).

My personal challenge today in the ministry is to remember my mom's legacy! My mother told me to continue doing the ministry of God and to be faithful. When I experience challenges and difficulties in the ministry, I sometimes still go to the corner of my house and I talk to my mom as if she is there. I remember telling her, "Mom, this is difficult, but I know you told me to be faithful. How can I sing I song of praise in a foreign land? I lift my eyes to God, my mother. I want to keep on being faithful."

Today, it is still difficult fighting a good fight for the glory of God. My prayer is to keep on knowing that my faith is rooted in the word of God. What God planted in my heart - through my mother's life - will live on for the rest of my life.

36. The Death of my Beloved Daughter Jane

My daughter Jane had been diagnosed with epilepsy in 1990. She fought with that disease even before she ever came to America. Jane was hospitalized on and off throughout her life. Whenever she was admitted, I would always sleep in the hospital room with her. When she would get discharged, I would take her home.

I remember once asking our parish minister in Kenya, Rev. Dr. Julius Nikonge, to bring Holy Communion to the hospital (M. P. Shah Hospital in Nairobi) for Jane. When he came (with other church leaders), he found that Jane was very sick. He offered prayers, but he did not know whether she could hear him or not. I remember that my mom (Jane's grandmother) had come even earlier. When she came, Jane kept on telling my mother "I want to eat meat". My mother looked at me and she told me, "you know, Jemimah, if you hear anybody asking for meat, it is a sign they are dying" (this was a cultural belief – to say that if someone wanted meat when they were sick meant they were dying). After this, my mother held me and cried. By this point, Jane had been given sleeping pills to help her rest (she had been convulsing with seizures when she was awake). She was only able to open her eyes and say one word. At that time, Jane was in a critical condition. She was taken to an Intensive Care Unit. At this hospital, Jane went into a coma. She would be in that coma for thirty days!

For all those days, my family and friends would wait outside the hospital the entire time (day and night, taking shifts). This was a very difficult time. Benson would often bring me food when I stayed with Jane in the hospital. One day, when Benson and Joy and Ben Jr. were bringing me food and coming to visit Jane, they got into a serious car accident on the way. The car was totally crushed (but praise God, they only suffered minor injuries)! It was a difficult moment for the whole family. I had so many sleepless nights during the time when Jane was in her coma. I would get very cold and I did not have enough blankets – the cold got to me so much that I contracted Pneumonia (and had to be put on treatments until I could go back to the hospital again to stay with Jane). After treatment, I recovered and was able to go back to the hospital to visit my daughter. There, she was still in her coma. I continued supporting her, day and night. I would go to the side of her bed and pray by her side as she lay next to me.

After those thirty days, the nurse from the ICU came outside (where we were all seated as a family). She told us, "Jane is calling you!" I could not believe what I was hearing, but we went to see her! When I went into the room, I saw her on the bed. She said, "mommy, mommy! When I was in the coma, I was not here. God had taken me to heaven. Mom, this is what I saw in heaven…" She began telling me about her experiences. She was so excited. She was smiling as she shared that when she was in heaven, she saw green grass and trees. She saw lots of people under the trees wearing white gowns or robes. She saw a gate with a narrow door and a shepherd with his shepherd's crook. She wanted to go through the gate and put on a white robe, too. As she was getting closer to the entry, she saw the shepherd point his crook at her. He told her "go back". That was when she came out of the coma.

After that, she recovered very quickly and was released to go home from the hospital. It gave us such joy to see her come home. She shared the story of her experience with many people (she had opportunities to share with different churches). She would often share *"Rejoice in the Lord always, and again I say rejoice" (Philippians 4:4)* She would often admonish others with the truth no one knows the time that they will die, so we need to be right with God now. She became so strong spiritually and powerful in the Lord after coming out of her coma.

After she was healed and got back onto her feet, Jane applied to attend Missouri Baptist University (in St. Louis, Missouri). She came to the United States in 1995. She was given a scholarship and granted a visa to come. She was studying to become a social worker. Jane was a very good student! She also got involved in a Baptist church near the campus (where she taught Sunday school). This also enabled her to get more scholarship funding.

I once reminded my husband of the many times that Jane was so sick. When I would come to see her, she was always on her same bed in her home (where we would one day find her dead body). Once, Jane had called me and said to me "mom, sometimes I feel you might someday find me dead on this bed." On that occasion, I had taken her to the ER at Burnes Hospital (in St. Louis, Missouri) were she had to be admitted again.

One Sunday, the week before we found out Jane died, we had a worship service. I was preaching that Sunday, and Jane asked me if she could sing a song to support my sermon. She slipped me a note that read, "Please Mom. Let me sing only the chorus. Please? To support the sermon" So Jane sang a beautiful Swahili chorus in front of the church that day. The song that she sang went, "nimetebia kwote kwote…hakuna na haitakue koo" (it means "I have walked everywhere, searched everywhere and gone around everywhere and I have never found someone like Jesus"). She sang the song with such passion! That was the last song she ever sang in our church before she died.

We had a choir meeting after worship service at our church that day. Jane had been the Director of Music. There had been a misunderstanding during the meeting and it was filled with tension. Jane felt so bad about it. She came out from that meeting crying and her heart was so broken. It was our tradition that every Sunday after worship we had lunch together as a congregation afterwards. Before Jane went down to eat, she came looking for me (as a pastor and as her mom). She came to find me in my office getting ready to go down. When she walked into the room, I could tell that she was not happy because she was crying. I asked her what happened in the meeting. She did not respond right away (I could tell she did not want to talk about it) and we walked down to lunch together.

She looked at me and told me, "mom, today is my last day to lead worship in this church". I did not believe her. I said, "this is your church. Where else will you go?" Jane truly believed that this day would be her last Sunday to lead worship there. She had a sense of it. She did not know at the time how prophetic her words would come to be. She was so peaceful and loving. She had been faithful to sing choruses after my sermons.

So, she came down to where all the people were eating, and she was telling people "goodbye. You will not see me here again". My heart was so touched. We had no idea that would be the last time we would see her alive. That day, she did not eat. After she said her goodbyes, she simply pulled her car out of the parking lot. I went up to my office and from my office window, I could see her car. Although she had pulled her car away, she stopped. She was waiting for a long time before really driving away (there were no cars coming. It was clear. She was pausing intentionally). God may have let her in on something that He knew, but we did not yet. Seeing Jane hesitate before driving away from the church was my last sight of my daughter alive (although I got to talk with her once more over the phone). She drove that day to her cousin's apartment. When I later talked to her cousin, I found out that when Jane had driven there, she was still crying. Her heart was so heavy.

We found Jane had passed away a week later. *"...all the days of my life were written in your book before one of them came to be"* (Psalm 139:16b)

On the next Wednesday (at 9:00pm), my daughter Jane called me and informed me that she had received a telephone call from Kenya (from our family). The call let her know that my sister-in-law, Mrs. Josphine Wangechi Maina ("Mama Bilhah") in Kenya, had passed away. After we talked, I immediately made a call to Kenya to speak with my family to let them know that we had received their message about the loss of my sister-in-law. The following day, on Thursday morning, I called my daughter Jane and we arranged that we would hold a memorial Service for my sister-in-law at our church in St Louis, Missouri (United African Presbyterian Church, where I was a pastor). We planned this for the following Sunday (after the morning worship service). I remember that week very well (from Thursday through Saturday). We had a lot of donations come into our church that week (the Presbyterian women in our church as well as friends in our Presbytery had donated items as a community outreach) and we were busy selling the items in our church. I continued supporting the women who were selling the items (as I had done for many years). We had been talking with my daughter about the memorial service. While we were selling the items, I tried calling Jane, but she was not answering her phone (which was unusual for her). Then, on Friday night, I called her again and she was still not answering her phone. I left a message for Jane to remind her not to forget that we were "still holding the memorial service for your auntie." I had also left a message to remind her about the birthday party for her friend Mary Ngendo's son "on Saturday at 6:00pm. You told me you will be the one to bring the cake. Don't forget!"). It had been Jane's tradition to buy birthday cakes for the children in the community – this was a part of her heart of compassion.

I called her again. My husband (her father) Benson had been trying to call her as well. It came time for the Birthday party. I decided to go ahead and go to the party and find out whether Jane was meeting us there at Mary Ngendo's apartment (where the celebration was held). When I arrived, there was no cake and there was no Jane (she was almost never late in bringing cakes for birthday parties). I started now to worry so much, but since I needed to finish preparing my sermon for the next day (and the memorial service preparation to follow), I reasoned, "ok maybe if Jane is in town, we will meet at church." After a short time at the party, I decided not to stay too long and to return home. When I reached the house, I found my husband. He told me that Ben Jr. (Jane's son and our grandson) called and told Benson that he had been calling Jane and that she was not answering his phone calls. I confirmed that the same thing was happening when I tried to call her, too.

In the morning, before I went to Church, we started worrying (but Jane would sometimes go out of town without informing us. We wondered if her not answering the phone just meant she went out of town). Then, we said "let's wait and see whether she will come to church today". Even though the week before she had said she wasn't coming back, we still held out hope that she would cool down and return anyway. We went to church and we started the worship service without Jane. Jane did not show up. This was very unusual because she was the leader of our choir and she conducted the praise and worship for our congregation. Members were asking, "where is Jane?" Nobody really knew anything. The members wanted me to at least to let the church know where she was, but I did not know either. We finished the worship service and it was now the time for the memorial service for my sister-in-law. Still, Jane did not show-up. She was the one who was supposed to read the eulogy. We finished the memorial service and then we had refreshments. Again, everyone was asking about Jane. Her presence was missed by so many people during both the worship service and at the memorial service.

After the memorial service (at about 6:00pm), we sat down in the house. This was the time that Ben Jr. called us (from Denver, Colorado) and told us to go and see whether Jane was in her house or not. We then said we would go to her house to check on her in the morning. We praying and asked God to be with us. We knew that wherever Jane had gone over the weekend, the Lord had taken care of her.

In the morning (on October 12, 2009), I received an urgent call from the hospital. I thought it might about Jane (maybe she was in the hospital?), but it was a call for me to go and interpret for a patient (from the Swahili language into English language - this was a woman in my community who had delivered a baby, but there was a language barrier when the doctors tried to give her instructions. There was a misunderstanding when the nurse tried to take the infant to the nursery. The woman screamed, and she did not understand why they were trying to take her baby away, as this was NOT the custom in Africa). I went to the hospital interpreted for her (this was very early in the morning and she had just delivered a beautiful baby girl).

When I finished at the hospital, we went ahead to Jane's home. Benson and I met at our house so that we could drive together to Jane's house (at Hazelwood where she used to live alone in her condo). We prayed for God to give us peace before we walked out from the house. I had bad feeling, so my husband was the one who drove us to Jane's house. As we drove, we did not talk until we reached her parking lot. We found her car parked the same space she always parked in. We parked our car right next to her car.

We walked to the house. Since I had a spare key to her house, I tried to open the door from the outside, but my key did not open the door. We walked to the back door (and we found the gate was open. I also saw that her door was slightly open). I pushed the door and we went in. Once I stepped in, I felt something in my stomach. I told my husband "there is something here which is not well." I looked on the dining table to see whether there was any note on the table, but there was nothing. Jane had put her umbrella and her jacket on the couch and we saw her bag (from her job) there as well. There so many letters piling up – mail that had been pushed through her door.

Her bedrooms were upstairs, so we began to walk up the stairs. I was in front and my husband was behind me. I opened her bedroom door and I could see that she was on the bed. I looked at her and I touched her and I found that she was cold. I screamed! I was calling my husband, "Dad! Dad! Jane is not here!" I pushed him in the room and I closed my eyes. What I remember is that I left my husband there and I went down the stairs fast (jumping down over two stairs at a time). I was shouting, "GOD! GOD, my LORD and my God! I this so? Do you have the soul of my daughter Jane?"

My husband came after me. He was holding me, and I was not able to speak or to look at him. He had followed me downstairs. I sat down. I was not crying, but what I can remember is saying, "GOD, MY LORD, is this so?" I went back upstairs again, and my husband was still behind me, following me back into Jane's bedroom. I started calling her, "Jane! Jane! Please, if you are going, please say 'goodbye' to me and dad. We are here!" At that time, I took two steps near her dresser and I was in a dark place. I opened my eyes and I could not see my husband. I only saw the face of Jane.

I touched Jane's body again (her face; her hands). She was so cold on her bed. Her cell phone was right there beside her, next to her prayer book. The TV was still on (it was playing a program on the TBN channel and the bedroom light was also on).

After a moment, I remembered our grandson, Ben Jr. (the son of Jane). I went downstairs again. I called Ben Jr. and I told him, "Ben, Jane is not there." He asked me, "where is Dad?" I told him, "he is here." Ben Jr told me to go upstairs and check again on the condition of Jane and to let me know what I found. I came again downstairs and I told Ben, "she not there. She is cold." At this point, he told me to call 911. I gave my husband the phone to talk with Ben. After talking to Ben, immediately I called our daughter Joy in Florida. I heard my daughter's voice, and I was not able to talk again. I gave my husband the phone and he was also not able to talk to Joy, so he handed over the phone to me again and he told me talk to Joy. I took the phone and I told her, "Jane is not there." She said to me, "mom, what are you saying?" She told me to talk to her husband (Joe Njogu). Joy then passed the phone to my son-in-law Joe. I talked to him and he asked me what happened. I did not say more than that, but he also talked to Benson. After a while, my son-in-law called Pastor Paul Macharia (a family friend and pastor of Covenant Church Florissant in St. Louis, Missouri. He was a pastor that demonstrated compassion and worked beyond boundaries. He and his wife, Pastor Eunice Macharia, were wonderful people in our community). Joe informed Pastor Paul about Jane.

After a few minutes, Pastor Paul Macharia called 911. Immediately afterwards, ambulances, police, fire trucks and church people come and showed up at Jane's house. Within a short time, many people from all over the community were on the scene with us. When the emergency services showed up, I was still in Jane's bedroom talking to her and sharing my story of our relationship and life together. I went to her bathroom and I got a wet small cloth and I wiped her face, combed her hair, put moisturizer on her very dry lips put body lotion on her face and body. I knew I would not get another chance to say goodbye to my beloved daughter. Since this was my last time to be together with her, Benson and I decided to use that moment to give Jane our last respects. At that time, my husband started knocking on the door telling me that the medical people were waiting to get into the room. But still I could not open the door. My husband was also talking to God and asking God so many questions over the departure of Jane's life. I gave hugs to Jane and then I opened the door for my husband. I let him in, but his heart was so broken he was not even able to enter in Jane's bedroom. My husband came in and he stood with me, holding my hand until the medical people asked me to step out for a moment. It was a dark dark moment. Benson talked to Jane with me before allowing the paramedics in. We asked Jane forgiveness if we had ever done something wrong to her. We held hands and gave thanks together for her life. We praised God that He had given us Jane for 42 years and remembered what a great daughter she was. Jane had been so obedient and loved Christ very much. She had a special ministry of compassion for others. She was a teacher of the word of God. She was also a great cook and a wonderful support to me in the ministry during my studies and when I became a minister. She was so proud that her mom had become an ordained Presbyterian church minister (and she shared this with others often). She always asked me whether she could sing a song after I preached to support the message I gave. God called Jane home and I would miss her dearly in so many ways – it was like a part of me would be missing from that point on. Before she had come to the United States for further studies, Jane had worked in the Department of Dental Health at the Kenya Medical Research Institute in Nairobi, Kenya. She had a dream to become a Registered Nurse. She had not yet completed this goal, but she had been well on the way in America. Benson and I remembered good memories of Jane.

My husband finally allowed the medical people to come in and we went downstairs. There, we saw SO many people from the community who had showed up to be with us (pastors, members of the church and those from the community came). I walked out, but still I wanted to be in the room with the medical people. I thought and hoped they could possibly do something to revive Jane and maybe make her breathe again.

After a while, the medical people asked us to come in and give them information. Jane's body needed to be taken out, so that they could start the postmortem processes (they needed to do an autopsy to figure out what happenend). We would be informed of the outcome of the cause Jane's death once they found out. According to the records of when we called her, they figured that when she was not answering the phone, she had already passed away. The last known person to talk to her on the phone before she died was her sister Joy Nyawira Njogu (from Florida). Because of this, they believed that she likely passed away on the Thursday before that Sunday.

Later, they discovered that she had had a seizure at night while she was sleeping. During the seizure, she bit her tongue and she had swallowed blood. The subsequent bleeding stopped air from reaching her lungs. This in turn stopped oxygen from reaching her brain, and this was the cause of her death. Although this was the medical reason, we knew that she died because God called her home. The Bible reminds us in John 14, that Jesus went to prepare a place for us. He has appointed our time. When our place is finished, God calls us home, one by one, according to His will. *"When everything is ready, I will come and get you, so that you will always be with me wherever I am. And you know the way to where I am going"* (John 14:3-4)

Pastor Paul Macharia gave us spiritual support and walked with us until the day of Jane's funeral (as did other pastors in the community). My heartfelt gratitude is so strong for them. Writing about the death of my precious daughter, even now, has helped me to process and grieve. I pray that it will also help other mothers who are mourning the losses of their own children.

37. My Daughter Jane's Funeral

After we discovered that Jane had died, the community met together two weeks before her funeral for prayers and fellowship. The pastors in the community would be conducting the funeral (being coordinated by Pastor Paul Macharia, Pastor Frances Karengi, Rev. Dr. Isaac Wanyoike and other church leaders in the community). It was a powerful moment for everyone to come together. Every time they would meet from that point on, they took up donations to support and pay for the funeral. The Presbytery of Giddings-Lovejoy (led by Rev. Dr. Linda Shugert) was very much involved as well.

What I remember is that we looked for the biggest Presbyterian church in the community (which could hold as many people as possible). We were invited to hold Jane's funeral at Landue Presbyterian Church (it accommodated over 650 people who came to Jane's funeral!). The Day of Visitation was held on Friday (before the funeral on Saturday). The Visitation was held at South Webster Presbyterian Church/United African Presbyterian Church (where I was a pastor and had Jane served in different capacities (e.g. Sunday School Teacher, Choir Director, Youth Director, Evangelism Leader and Leader of Hospitality).

When the day came for Jane's funeral, Rev. Dr. Isaiah Muita officiated. The message was given by Rev. Dr. George Gitahi (from Georgia). Pastor Charity Kamau came from Seattle. She said that even though she had never met Jane, she came "because of the way Jemimah talked about Jane." It was very important for her to come and support us during that time. During the service, Ben Ngatia, Jr. told a story about his late mother. He shared about how she raised him up. His story touched so many hearts.

After the church memorial service, we went to the graveside. We needed four police officers to manage all the traffic! I remember it was such a painful moment to see the cars following one another to head to the cemetery on the way to bury Jane's body. It was so difficult to see the coffin being lowered down. I held tightly Ben, Ben Jr., Joy and Rochelle. Benson was holding my hand. I also remember my good friends Sarah Karanja (from Georgia) and Mrs. Rose Muita (from Kansas City) as well as other women leaders. They had to hold me tightly because I was feeling as if I could also jump into the grave and be buried with my daughter, too. It was a very sorrowful moment.

It is God who gave us Jane and it was God who called her home. There is a song, "Ona gutwika uguo mwathani orogo chow" It means "His name is to be praised and glorified!" This reminds me of Job's response at the suffering he was going through, *"…Naked I came from my mother's womb and naked I will depart. The LORD gave and the LORD has taken away; may the name of the LORD be praised"* (Job 1:20)

Writing this book is helping me to deal with those memories. *"There is a time to weep and a time to laugh, a time to mourn and a time to dance.." (Ecclesiastes 3:4)* This process of the loss of my beloved daughter was a preparation for me to be ready. When my own house in heaven is complete, I will go and join my daughter and we will sing songs of praise, "hallelujah, hallelujah amen!"

I want to saw that I am so grateful that Rochelle and my grandson Ben Jr. were already married when Ben's mom Jane passed away. I want to especially thank Rochelle. She held and comforted her husband (my grandson) so much during that time. She was there for us 24/7. She has truly been a blessing to our family! *"Blessed are those who mourn, for they will be comforted" (Matthew 5:4)*

38. Founder of the Stephen Ministry "Care-Giver" Program

When I arrived in St. Louis, Missouri (attending one-year Theological Seminary studies at Eden), I was involved with different programs at Webster Grove Presbyterian Church in the neighborhood. I was introduced to the congregation members by Rev. Dr. John Cochran. He was on staff and a trainer of the Stephen Ministry.

After worship service one day, he set up an appointment for me to meet with him during the week and to share my story. After we shared our stories with one another (he was a good listener), I remember that he had a connection with one of the churches in Africa. I was impressed by his love and the spiritual connection we had. He then prayed for me in my studies at Eden Theological Seminary. At the end of our meeting, Rev. Cochran offered lunch to me where we continued our conversation. We talked about a way forward for being trained as a Stephen Minister.

We met again. In our next meeting, I shared with him how much my heart was touched by the ministries he was doing in his congregation (especially the Stephen Ministry program). I asked him so many questions because he was a Pastoral Care provider in his congregation. It touched my heart to hear how much he was committed to visiting church members in hospitals (and those who were shut-ins in their homes). My mind went back to what I was doing in Kenya as a hospital chaplain (visiting the patients as well as those who were sick at home). We connected very much with the job I was doing in Kenya (before I come to United States for Theological studies). During our sharing, we discovered it was almost the very same role that Rev. Dr. John Cochran was doing in the States in his own congregation.

My hope of future ministry became clear and rose up right there after our meeting! After having lunch together, he offered me an opportunity to let him know who I was. He gave me another appointment to come and see if I could be accepted into his next Stephen Ministers Training (as a Stephen Minister). I remember sharing with him that that would be a blessing - not only to me, but to my entire congregation at Bahati Presbyterian Church East Africa in Kenya (I knew they would all benefit from the Stephen Ministry program).

Rev. Cochran felt was important because I was able to share with him that the program would benefit my whole community in Kenya. He said to me that he would find a scholarship for me be trained.

I was trained as Stephen Minister. Thereafter, I was commissioned. I remember the day of my commissioning there was a celebration. We were praising the Name of God for having opened the doors for me to be trained as a Stephen Minster. Afterwards I became a Stephen Minister at Webster Grove Presbyterian Church.

The dialogue between Rev. Cochran and I continued. He later told me that he would find a scholarship for me to be trained as a Trainer so that when I went back to Kenya, I could start training Stephen Minters in my church (PCEA Bahati Presbyterian Church). You can bet that this multiplied ministry in a congregation that had more than 4,000 members (with one minister). Rev. Cockrand secured the funding for the Trainer's Training and I was to be trained as a Stephen Minster Trainer (by the program team). At that time, I was very involved in that congregation, practicing my Stephen Ministry skills.

We continued meeting with Rev. Cochran once a week. He secured another scholarship for me to attend the Stephen Ministry Leaders Training Course (LTC). It was an intensive course with members from different denominations
(Ecumenical). During the training time, I had an opportunity to meet Rev. Dr. Kenneth Haugk (the Founder of the Stephen Ministry Program). He was one of the facilitators of the training team.

The course was powerful and challenging for me. It was especially important for me because I had been already trained as a Stephen Minister. At the end of the training, each student came away with a training materials kit. I utilized my own kit to take it back to my congregation in Kenya. I soon started training Stephen Ministers there. At the closing day of the LTC, we were commissioned as Stephen Ministry Leader Trainers. It was a big ceremony with a high profile. Credentials and Certifications were presented to each of the students who completed the Stephen Ministry Trainer Course. There was a special dinner served at the Renaissance Hotel (in St. Louis, Missouri).

My story did not end there! It continued long after that. After I went back to Kenya, I had great excitement in bringing the new ministry program back to my congregation. I arrived at my church in Kenya. There I met with the Parish Church Minister (Rev. Dr. Jesii Kamau). I shared with him my excitement about being trained as a Trainer of the Stephen Ministry Program.

Rev. Dr. Kamau was a pastoral care pastor. He welcomed me and told me he was going to initiate a meeting of church elders (Session). The purpose of this meeting was for me to explain and share the vision of the Stephen Ministry.

After I did my presentation to the church elders, some did not understand the vision. However, Rev. Dr. Jessi Kamau tried to clarify to them that pastoral care in the congregation was very much needed. He communicated that the church had many members who needed pastoral care and the church was very short staffed and did have the capacity to meet all their needs alone. *Brothers and sisters, choose seven men from among you who are known to be full of the Spirit and wisdom. We will turn this responsibility over to them and will give our attention to prayer and the ministry of the word" (Acts 6:3-4)*

The problem was that some of the elders believed that there was no way for Jemimah to train people for 50 hours and then be commissioned as Stephen Ministers. This was because they only knew only their own minister (they could not understand training lay people and calling them to be ministers).

After many meetings and conversations, we were not able to come up with a way forward (of how to start training the Stephen Ministers in our congregation). We continued talking with Rev. Dr. Jessi Kamau – he was so supportive and advocated for the program. We agree to change the language so that we could give those trained in Stephen Ministry a title that they could relate to. After long prayers and meditation (and lots of discussion), the spirit of God came to us and we found a name that worked (we could not call them "Stephen Ministers." So, we decided to give them a new name to them. They were to be called "CARE-GIVERS". This was the compromise that worked for everyone.

After a few weeks, Rev. Dr. Kamau called yet another Session meeting. I was invited to speak again to the elders and I explained to them that I was going to train the CARE-GIVERS (not the controversial "Stephen Ministers").

The elders said, "yes, yes! That is good thing that they are not going to be called 'Stephen Ministers'." The elders then voted for me to start the Stephen Ministry program (Care Giver Program) with support of the Bahati Presbyterian Church.

After I was confirmed by the elders and the Parish Minister, I was given time to bring the information about the Stephen Ministry/Care Giver program to the congregation.

Immediately, we organized a conference of church members (for two days). The turnout was very good - many of those who attended the conference signed up and wanted to be trained as a CARE-GIVER in our church. Even some of the elders themselves had come to the conference and signed up for the first class.

Thereafter, I continued the conversation with Rev. Dr. Cochran as well as the Head office of the Stephen Ministry Program (back in the United States), letting them know about both the progress and the barriers we were experiencing.

I started training Care-givers with an initial group of twelve students (both men and women). I had an opportunity to meet with the Presbyterian Ministers and give a lecture at Limuru Theological Seminary. Rev. Dr. Kimani Chege was the minister there who invited me. He had already completed the Stephen Ministry Leaders course (in the United States), and he was eager to invite me to speak. I approached him to ask whether we could team up with him to train Stephen Care-givers. He was more than happy to support the programs and join me in training. After fifty hours of training, we had a good team. When it was all said and done, after commissioning, there were nine care-givers who completed the training.

I sent a report on what we had accomplished, and the Stephen Ministry again offered me a scholarship to send two Care-Givers to the Leaders Training Course (back in America). When they arrived, Rev. Dr. John Cochran was happy to welcome the two Care-Givers to his church and to take them to the LTC. They went on to complete the LTC and they returned to Kenya to train even more Care-Givers. One of the blessings was that the Parish Minister of Bahati Presbyterian Church (Rev. Dr. Jesse Kamau) was one of those two leaders who were sent to the LTC. This was such a breakthrough. He made the training known and his training multiplied the ministry. He became so supportive. He was so encouraging of the members of his congregation to become CARE GIVERS in the community. It was such great moment of joy to escort the two students to the airport and to see them when they got back (after they completed the course). It was a joy to see them fly out and to also welcome them back when they returned. What a great difference the training made! It was a powerful moment when they come back to our program.

CARE GIVERS become popular! Everyone wanted to join the program (they thought they, too, may be given an opportunity to travel to United States of America. It was true some of the students might not have had any other opportunity to travel to USA until they joined the Stephen Ministry program). Indeed, some of them managed eventually to train others and were actually (later) sent to America for further training.

The families (and ministries and congregations) of those who had opportunities to travel to the USA through Stephen Ministry will never be the same. This training truly transformed and strengthened their communities and helped them be far more effective at practicing compassion. In doing that, it changed everyone for the better. Those on the outside could see a difference and they wanted it, too. As a result, several other churches requested that we help their churches to start training their members in different churches throughout Kenya.

At that time, the Stephen Leaders were given permission to train more (they were trained to be able to train others) within the Stephen Ministry program in different congregations. *"You have heard me teach things that have been confirmed by many reliable witnesses. Now, teach these truths to other trustworthy people who will be able to pass them on to others"* (2 Timothy 2:2).

Sometimes, I still reflect on how the Stephen Ministry Program started at Bahati Presbyterian Church. After one year, the church was able to train over one hundred Care-Givers in the community! I give glory to our Mighty God because God continues to use us to make a difference in our communities.

Today, we have many congregations still training Care-Givers throughout Kenya using the Stephen Ministry Program! Today, we have so many church members who have benefited from the Stephen Ministry Program in Kenya.

39. The People Who Have Touched My Life in Ministry

I cannot forget many people who have been walking with me throughout this entire process! I know that our God has been into midst of this journey. I want to thank my family, especially my husband Benson Ngatia (who passed away in 2017), our daughter Jane Ngatia (who passed away in 2009), my daughter Joy Njogu and her husband Joe Njogu, my grandson Benson Ngatia Jr and his wife Rochelle Ngatia, and my sister Cecelia Wanjeri Kamau.

I am grateful for many sisters and brothers in Christ Jesus who prayed for me and my family and for my ministry. Each of you have been standing with me through this process.

I want especially thank Sister Patricia Bombard and Sister Cathy. For the years I lived in Chicago, these women were faithfully praying (often using Rosary Beads). They also payed some of the fees of my visas.

Although I have achieved so much since I came to the United States for studies, I have had many sisters and brothers who went the extra mile to support me (to make sure I got the preparation I needed for God's ministry). There are so many people who have been a great blessing throughout my journey. I would not be where I am without them. *"Carry each other's burdens, and in this way, you will fulfill the law of Christ" (Galatians 6:2)*

I cannot forget to mention a few of the many people who have walked with me throughout my ordination process. Rev. Dr. Linda Shugert was my family pastor. She became the Presbytery Moderator during my ordination (and she is the one who officiated my ordination on November 12, 2005). Rev. Dr. Linda Shugert supported me from day one of my ordination process. She used to go out of her way to support me and to advocate for me. She has reached out to many people on my behalf to places where I could not reach on my own. Sometimes, when my heart was broken, she would come over (day or night) to make sure my voice was heard. She would stand up for me and for my ministry to refugee families and Immigrants from Africa. Rev. Dr. Linda worked very hard (finding means and ways) to help! She nominated me to receive an award from United Women of Missouri (she had been on the UWM board). When I received the award, it said that I was being rewarded because I worked beyond boundaries and I also worked to "rebuild the walls". *"But now I said to them 'you know very well what trouble we are in. Jerusalem lies in ruins, and its gates have been destroyed by fire. Let us rebuild the wall of Jerusalem and end this disgrace?'" (Nehemiah 2:17)*

I fondly remember the Presbytery staff, especially the Stated Clerk of Giddings Love-joy, Rev. Dr. Terry Empling and the Executive Presbyter Rev. Dr. Paul Reiter (who was also my family's Spiritual Director). They worked very hard to protect me from being abused or marginalized by some of the white Presbytery committee members from the Committee of Preparation for Ministry (CPM). They stood in the gap and bridged the way for me to achieve my goal of being ordained as a Presbyterian Minister of Word and Sacrament. They played a big role, which I will never forget. That is what I call a "good fight" just like the disciples when they fought for God's mission to reach out to everyone. *"Above all, you must live as citizens of heaven, conducting yourselves in a manner worthy of the Good News about Christ. Then, whether I come and see you again or only hear about you, I will know that you are standing together with one spirit and one purpose, fighting together for the faith, which is the Good News." (Philippians 1:27)* We are called by God to make a difference. These advocates and true partners in the Lord took care of me for the Glory of God. They advocated for me so that others would not take me (or people like me – minorities and immigrants) for granted just because I was not a part of the majority culture. One thing I remember after my ordination was that my picture was supposed to be hung up and displayed on the wall of the Giddings-Lovejoy Presbytery (among others who also had made history in the Presbytery). This was to document the significant historical event of my ordination and what it represented (that I was the first New Immigrant Woman from Africa to be ordained as a Minister of Word and Sacrament by Presbyterian Church USA). Other ministers who had made history in the presbytery had had their pictures hung up on the wall. I, too, had indeed made history. My picture was taken, but it was never hung up on that wall. Some of the staff did not like that, because all the other pictures on that wall were of white people. Even today as I write this, my picture has still not been hung up on that wall. I have never been given a reason why the portrait they took of me was never hung. I have also wondered the same questions I had heard staff wonder (is it because I'm black? Is it because I come from a "third world" country? Is it because I am a woman? Is it because they didn't know what to do with me?). All I know is that of all the other "history makers" on the wall, I none of them look like me! For me, this is the advice that I want to share with everyone. Even the seemingly small things matter. My brothers and sisters in Christ, we are all the same in the eyes of the Lord. God has callings on each of our lives. The Bible clearly says, *"There is no longer Jew or Gentile, slave or free, male or female. For you are all one in Christ Jesus." (Galatians 3:28)* When we talk about racism in America, many do not understand. However, I have experienced racism personally (many times). I would notice that some of the other ministers would choose not to sit next to me during our Presbytery meetings. Some refused to even shake my hand or give me a hug. I often heard people whisper, "I have never interacted with someone like Jemimah from Kenya, Africa before." Rev. Dr. Terry Empling and Executive Presbyter Rev. Dr. Paul Reiter stood up for justice and they stood up for me! I am grateful that they have been my true allies and partners.

I cannot forget to recognize Rev. Keith and his wife Penny, who were both ministers at Evangelical Lutheran Church Webster Grove in St. Louis, Missouri. They gave me a place to move my church to (out of my house). I had been holding the church with immigrants and refugees (in my home) after the Presbytery voted to sell the building where we were doing our ministry - the place where we were worshiping for many years. Rev. Keith and Penny were touched by my story and they blessed us very much. I want to give God glory and honor because they opened wide their church building doors for the African people to come and praise God. *"…I was a stranger, and you invited me in…" (Matthew 25:35).* In the interim (before moving to Evangelical Lutheran Church Webster Grove), I did not have anywhere to bring the members for two Sundays, so that is why we worshiped in the back of my home. Our house was in a white community - we were the only black family in the neighborhood. Most of my members all were from Africa (and some of them were undocumented, not having the proper legal papers to be in the United States). On the second Sunday of my church worshipping in my home, one of my (white) neighbors called police. When church my members saw the police, they quickly left before the worship was even over! I wanted anyone and everyone to be able to freely and safely worship God (without fear that the government or police might come into our anytime). My members were so afraid. Around the same time, I was a member of a community pastors' Bible study. In my group, I shared my frustration. That was when this pastor generously opened his church for me to move my members from our house to meet at his building instead. I am so grateful for him (and others like him) who affirm and encourage me that I have been called by God (it is God's calling that matters; not the color of skin or even documentation).

I cannot forget to mention the ecumenical Lectionary Bible study group. This group was so supportive. Through it, I came to meet Fr. Gerry Gleb, who was a

Catholic priest. I was introduced to him by another Catholic priest from Uganda. Fr. Gerry became a wonderful spiritual support to my family, especially when God called our daughter Jane home to Heaven in October of 2009. I remember that Fr. Gerry had a knee replacement, but even so, he walked to the funeral to honor Jane's life. I remember that after the funeral, there were not many people coming over to see how we were doing. One day, Fr. Gerry came over. At the time, I was broken. I was crying and asking myself, "why did I bring my daughter to this country?" Fr. Gerry responded to me with compassion. He held my hand and said to me, "Jemimah, even if Jane was in Kenya, God would have still called her home. Do not forget the people who came to her funeral, Jemimah. Many people went back to their homes transformed because they heard the message and the stories of Jane's ministry in the community. So many people came for Jane's funeral and some testified that they had not even met Jane, but they had heard about her because of the ministry she was doing in the community." He reassured me that any time I talked about my children, I would start telling my story starting with Jane's life (because she was my first daughter and again she loved Jesus so much as her Lord and savior in her life). In the community, Jane was known because she would listen and love on families (and she would always remember birthdays for their children). My late daughter Jane was always offering to buy birthday cakes for families - she became so popular from buying birthday cakes for the children. So, Fr. Gerry greatly encouraged me, reminded me of God's will and lifted my spirits as he remembered my dear daughter Jane.

If I did not mention you by name, please forgive me. Know that I am who am today because you paid a special price for me many times. Some of you, I have called in the middle of the night! You have never let me down! What you have done for me, I know you have done for God. THANK YOU!

"Then the King will say to those on his right, 'Come, you who are blessed by my Father, inherit the kingdom prepared for you from the creation of the world. For I was hungry, and you fed me. I was thirsty, and you gave me something to drink. I was a stranger, and you invited me into your home. I was naked, and you gave me clothing. I was sick, and you cared for me. I was in prison and you visited me.' Then these righteous ones will reply, 'Lord, when did we ever see you hungry and feed you? Or thirsty and give you something to drink? Or a stranger and show you hospitality? Or naked and give you clothing? When did we ever see you sick or in prison and visit you?' And the King will say, 'I tell you the truth, when you did it to one of the least of these my brothers and sisters, you were doing it to me!" (Matthew 25:34-40)

When we are gone, who will remember me and you with the deeds we have done in our communities today? My heart is heavy now because there is a lot to be done today in our communities: to feed and nurture those who are thirsty for the word of God. Someone somewhere did something! Many people walked the extra mile for me. That is why I am who I am today. Somebody somewhere stood in the GAP for you and me - that is the reason why we are who we are today. I am called to do something for someone, sharing the blessings that God has given me. Yes, we will be remembered if we will wake up and work for the Glory of God beyond our boundaries, lifting others by hope. Those who are already on the journey (loving and caring for people of God just where you are), please keep it up! Do it with joy, knowing that your name and my name is written in the BOOK of life! *"Do not forget to show hospitality to strangers, for by so doing some people have shown hospitality to angels without knowing it"* (Hebrews 13:2)

As women of God, our prayers are for God to remember us when His Kingdom of God comes. Like the women throughout scriptures, today we recount their stories in the Bible as follows:

Lastly be like Sarah. Age doesn't matter in the eyes of God (there is no "too young" and no "too old"). Trust and believe God. Take Him at his word. Sarah at first disbelieved, but ultimately, she trusted in God and believed His promises (and got to see them fulfilled). All things are possible with God!

"The Lord kept His word and did for Sarah exactly what He had promised. She became pregnant, and she gave birth to a son for Abraham in his old age. This happened at just the time God has said it would. And Abraham named his son Isaac." (Genesis 21:1-3)

Be like Rebekah. Never forget that true beauty lies within. Draw your man closer to God through your character. Isaac married her because she was direct and specific answer to prayer. He trusted His servant to choose his wife based first on God's direction, and not solely on appearance. Rebekah and Isaac are part of the promise of God (and indeed, God would often refer to Himself as "I am the God of Abraham, Isaac and Jacob"). From Rebekah's line would come the lineage of Jesus. God would use the "nation" created in her womb to be Israel (which God would use to show all the nations of the earth that He is the true God).

"And the Lord told Rebekah, 'The sons in your womb will become two nations. From the very beginning, the two nations will be rivals'" (Genesis 25:23)

Be like Ruth, loyal in all your relationships. Walk the extra mile, and don't quit when things get tough. Someday, you will see why it was worth all the effort. Ruth was spiritually strong. She demonstrated loving and trusting in God. Ruth has become a role model to women today.

"But Ruth replied, 'don't urge me to leave you or to turn back from you. Where you go I will go, and where you stay I will stay Your people will be my people and your God my God. Where you die I will die, and there I will be buried. May the Lord deal with me, be it ever so severely, if even death separates you and me.' When Naomi realized that Ruth was determined to go with her, she stopped urging her." (Ruth 1:16-18)

Be like Hannah, who never ceased to pray. It was difficult for her, but she continued praying until got what she was praying for. Her prayers were not in vain. She prayed, and she did not put a time limit on her prayer. She kept on praying, sensing in her spirit that God would do something. Sometimes we get discouraged when we pray and do not see God answering our prayers. We can feel that God does not see our situation or that He does not care. Hannah was in pain, but she still believed that God was in her journey and in her spirit. Sometimes, the enemy can sow doubts into our hearts to try and discourage us. Hannah believed that God would answer her prayers according to His own timing.

"Hannah was in deep anguish, crying bitterly as she prayed to the Lord. And she made this vow: 'O Lord of Heaven's Armies, if you will look upon my sorrow and answer my prayer and give me a son, then I will give him back to you. He will be yours for his entire lifetime, and as a sign that he has been dedicated to the Lord, his hair will never be cut.'" (1 Samuel 1:10-11)

Be like Abigail! Remember how each decision can turn your life around (for good or for bad). Be wise and share your stories. Stand in the gap for others. We are called to listen to the individual stories of others. Some of their stories are painful. Sometimes storytellers have an agenda. In the case of Abigail, her purpose in sharing her story was to save people despite her husband Nabal's foolish choices. The question of Abigail was clearly heard, and she was released to go in peace. Her actions made the different in sparing so many peoples' lives (her husband in particular)! We are called to act on behalf of people in their pain and make a clear way for them to still act justly.

"David replied to Abigail, 'Praise the Lord, the God of Israel, who has sent you to meet me today! Thank God for your good sense! Bless you from keeping me from murder and from carrying out vengeance with my own hands. For I swear by the Lord, the God of Israel, who has kept me from hurting you, that if you had not hurried out to meet me, not one of Nabal's men would still be alive tomorrow morning.' Then David accepted her present and told her 'Return home in peace. I have heard what you said. We will not kill your husband.'" (1 Samuel 25:32-35)

I would like you to remember Esther, bold and courageous enough to stand for the truth. She voiced her opinion and fought the fight for the good of others, even when it meant sacrificing herself. If God has put you in a position, it is for His purpose. Never be afraid to heed to that inner voice of God! Today, we women are called to spend more time with God in prayer. Prayer can move mountains and we have seen the fruits of prayer.

"Go, gather together all the Jews who are in Susa, and fast for me. Do not eat or drink for three days, night or day. I and my attendants will fast as you do. When this is done, I will go to the king, even though it is against the law. And if I perish, I perish." (Esther 4:16)

Be like Elizabeth. Never doubt what God can do! Miracles do happen, even today. Upon learning that she was to become pregnant at old age with John the Baptist, Elizabeth responded (unlike her husband Zachariah), *"How kind the Lord is! He has taken away my disgrace or having no children"* (Luke 1:25)

Be like Mary. She humbled herself before God and was submissive. You do not have to be great for God to use you, but you do need to obey Him. Mary humbled herself and she even sat at her son Jesus' feet to learn from him. If we listen to the voice of God through what the Bible is teaching us, we will be obedient and will continue teaching others to love their neighbors. I admire Mary for all her commitments. God had great plans for her life and her future.

"Mary responded, 'I am the Lord's servant. May everything you have said about me come true.' And then the angel left her." (Luke 1:38)

Be like Mary Magdalene. Never let your mistakes (or others' judgments of you) stop you from experiencing true joys in Jesus Christ. When we follow Jesus, He opens doors for us. He does not only see where we came from, but He sees much deeper into who He made us and called us to be. He welcomes us. Mary Magdalene was one of the very first people to discover the biggest miracle in all of history and the greatest single in event in world history – the resurrection of Jesus, the Christ!!

"Mary Magdalene found the disciples and told them 'I have seen the Lord!'" (John 20:18)

Be like Dorcus. Your talents, no matter how small they may seem, can bring a smile on someone's face. You will never know how much it might mean to someone when you touch their hearts in different ways as you serve them. Dorcas worked closely with the widows. She was visiting them, sharing meals together with them and sharing in prayers and meditation. The widows felt so loved by her. She met their needs of clothing and coats that she had sewn for them. When she died, the women she helped were the same ones who came crying to the apostles, testifying about how Dorcas had touched their hearts. Dorcas is my model when I go to visit the sick and the needy. She reminds me that we often do not have to do much, but if we touch one life, we have done a good thing. These widows remembered and loved her well (so much so that they cried out to the apostles who came and through the holy spirit were able to miraculously raise her back to life again). If you die, are there people (like these widows) that will cry out for your life. What will they say about you and me? I think what we need to do is to take the model of Dorcas and to continue to evangelize in our communities by meeting their needs as we share the Good News.

"Peter returned with them; and as soon as he arrived, they took him to the upstairs room. The room was filled with widows who were weeping and showing him the coats and other clothes Dorcas had made for them." (Acts 9:39)

Be like Lydia! Let your homes be open. Let your heart be big enough to help the needy in your community. Joys are the greatest when shared. Lydia demonstrated that we are called by God and is it clear in our spirits that the Kingdom of God is for us and for our families. We are called to go out into the community and encourage others by loving, sharing and guiding them into true worship of God (in different traditions of worshipping God).

"On the Sabbath we went a little way outside the city to a riverbank, where we thought people would be meeting for prayer, and we sat down to speak with some women who had gathered there. One of them was Lydia from Thyatira, a merchant of expensive purple cloth, who worshiped God. As she listened to us, the Lord opened her heart, and she accepted what Paul was saying. She and her household were baptized, and she asked us to be her guests. 'if you agree that I am a true believer in the Lord,' she said, 'come and stay at my home.' And she urged us until we agreed" (Acts 16:13-15)

From that point forward, the Philippian church met inside Lydia's home. Lydia gathered people and they grew spiritually and in number.

The above women of God remind me of the many ways God has used women powerfully throughout history. Each of them did something which made their names appear in the Bible. When I think of them, I also think about my late daughter Jane. She did not do much according to her age, but the little deeds she did in the community make her name remembered, even today. She made a difference in the lives of people for the glory of God and the kingdom of God.

As you have read the accounts of these women in the Bible, know that God is calling us today just as He did then. I pray that as you have read this book, that you (and me) will pay attention and that we will do what God is also calling us to for His glory.

40. Difficulties and Blessings in my Ministry

Some of difficult experiences I have had in the United State have arisen from trying to understand all the complicated immigrant visa requirements that are for this country.

On my first visit to the United States of America, I was given a scholarship for one year (for my theological studies at Eden Theological Seminary in St. Louis, Missouri). Once I was awarded this scholarship, I was then responsible to apply for my own visa to be able to come. This was so difficult because I did not know where to start in looking for the visa. Since I was working at Kenyatta Hospital, I was under the Ministry of Health (meaning that I was working under the authority of the Kenyan Government). I heard that one of the first things I would need to do was to be cleared by the government before I could start the visa application process (in Kenya, if you are working for the government, you are not allowed to apply for an international visa unless you have a special Letter of Authorization from the Kenyan President's office). So, to start, I first had to be given a letter from the Hospital Director at Kenyatta Hospital (where I had been working as a Chaplain). That letter would enable me to seek the clearance I needed from the President's office.

Praise God, it did not take me a long time to obtain my governmental clearance! This was due in large part to having a friend (Grace Kihara) who worked in the President's Office. When I called her, she told me she was familiar with what I needed and that she even had the proper stamp in her office! She said she was willing to help me and guide me through the process.

The first requirement was an academic prerequisite: I could not be granted the visa unless I had previously studied theology first in Kenya. Fortunately, I had already completed courses (I had previously received my Certificate of Church history, Introduction of the New

Testament and Introduction of the Old Testament).
Additionally, I needed a letter from my denomination
(Presbyterian Church East Africa) for introduction and
affirmation that I was an active member of their church.
This letter was no problem at all, because I was indeed
active in (and a leader of) the women's ministry at Bahati
Presbyterian Church in Nairobi, Kenya. Next, I had to
visit the American Embassy, which I did. After I went to
the American Embassy (and proved that I met all the
requirements), I was given a Student Visa (F-1).

I come to America holding my (F-1). Student Visa. Before
I completed my year of theological studies, I was given
another scholarship for 4 units of Clinical Pastoral
Education (CPE). Since this training was more practical
than academic, I learned that I now had to change my
student visa from F-1 to J-1. The J-1 Visa was a special
agreement between the American government and the
Kenyan government. The requirement of the J-1 Visa was
that I had to leave the United States (and return to my
home country) after I finished the training. If I did not
return to Kenya within the time limit I had been given, I
would be in violation of the agreement. Overstaying a
Visa's time limit puts you at risk of Immigration and
Customs Enforcement (ICE) coming to pick you up and
deporting you (without question). When I was signing the
papers, I did not understand how serious this whole
process was. When came to understand the weighty
significance of this requirement, I had to leave the United
States with immediate effect and return to Kenya to avoid
deportation. I learned that one of the consequences of
getting deported is forfeiting the right to come back to
America again. It was a big deal.

After I completed my studies as a Hospital Chaplain (4 units of CPE), I needed to go back to Kenya to avoid deportation. My family (including my husband and my daughter Jane) were all still living in Kenya at the time. My required return to Kenya turned out to be a great blessing to my community in Kenya! After acquiring the theological training and CPE training, I was now empowered to start training chaplains at Kenyatta National Hospital (and I excitedly began doing so). God used that training in wonderful ways.

Even though I was actively serving in Kenya and multiplying what I had learned so that others could train even more, I still felt that I had not yet completed all of what I had come to America to do. I called a Methodist Pastor from the United States and I asked him to write a Letter of Invitation to come back to the United States - this time with my children, my daughter Joy and my grandson Ben Ngatia Jr.. The pastor sent me a letter to come with my children for the Christmas celebration at his church. When I got the letter, we went to American Embassy and we were issued Visitor's Visas (B-1). It granted us longer stay in the United States. We arrived America and I found schools where I enrolled Joy and Ben Jr. At last, we were able to be in the United States together as a family. Because I was given an "open visa", I was allowed permission to go back and forth to Kenya on the same visa. Because of this, I was able to leave my family in America while I went back to continue training Kenyans in Clinical Pastoral Education at Kenyatta Hospital (where I used to work as a Hospital Chaplain). I started the program (which was successful and was sponsored and supported by the Presbyterian church). I continued to empower and guide the chaplain students at Kenyatta Hospital. I still felt there was a need for me to come back to the United States to get even more education in CPE. Since I already had a visa, I came back to the States and enrolled to take more CPE units. During that time, since I was already a candidate for ordination from Kenya, the Presbytery of Giddings-Lovejoy Presbytery (St. Louis, Missouri) gave me a scholarship to complete my Master of Divinity at McCormick Theological Seminary in Chicago. God used that open Visitor Visa (B-1) to further ministry in Kenya and sharpen my ministry in the United States!

While I was studying at McCormick Theological Seminary, my visa expired! I was told that I had to go back to Kenya, even though my studies were not yet finished. I talked to my Presbytery about it and they then applied for a Religious Visa (R) on my behalf (the R Visa lasts for three years, but it can be renewed on the condition that I traveled back to Kenya every three years). So, when the time came, I went back to Kenya to pursue the R Visa. It was risky because the American Embassy at any time can deny the renewal of my Visas. They are not guaranteed.

I went to Kenya so worried, but I trusted God. All praise and glory to God, my Visa (R-1) was renewed and I was given more three years! I was able to legally work with that visa. After another three years, the Presbytery applied on my behalf and sponsored me for "Permanent Resident" status (this is known as the "Green Card"). It took months and months before I was finally issued that card. This status required biometric data. I was taken in to get finger printed and background checked. It took another several months for my results to come back. During that time of waiting, I felt like I might get arrested or detained at any time. I was afraid I might be deported, even though I had other documents. I was working at the time as an Organizing Pastor of Refugee Families – families who had come from countries in Africa and who spoke the Swahili language. Through this experience, I got a taste of what it must feel like for other immigrants who are waiting for and working for their proper immigration paperwork or visas, and even those from many countries who may not be documented. Refugees are oppressed peoples and they have great needs. I am grateful that God is FOR those who are oppressed! *"You will bring justice to the orphans and the oppressed, so mere people can no longer terrify them." (Psalm 10:18)*

I was reminded of what happened to a family I knew. The father had just purchased their family's first car. He promised to take his family on a road trip (it was exciting, since they finally had a vehicle). "I am going to take you for a trip to go and visit our friend who lives in another state!" he eagerly declared. They started their journey early in the morning. Before they got to where they were headed, they accidentally got lost. Dad could not figure out where they were. He eventually saw a police car roll by. He flagged police car down, so he could ask for directions. The officer walked over to the family car. Dad immediately said to the police, "we are going to this address, but we are lost. Can you help us?" The police officer looked at the address, but before he gave any directions at all, he asked, "where are you from?" The father replied, "from Kenya." The officer proceeded to question him about what he was doing in this country. The father began to grow worried that the police officer might profile him for something or treat him like a suspect. His fears were realized! For a reason the officer never revealed, he asked the dad to step out of the vehicle. He then handcuffed the father in front of his family. His children began to cry, then his wife – everyone still in the car was crying! They did not know what was happening to their dad. Praise God! The tears of the children truly touched this officer's heart. After the officer saw how much distress it was causing his family to see their dad in handcuffs. He soon told the dad he was "free to go". After ALL OF THIS, the officer - who had originally been flagged down by the father in the first place – finally gave out the driving directions! Sadly, stories like these are very common. This man had proper documentation, but he was singled out because he was Kenyan (and looked like he didn't belong). You can only imagine how much higher the level of fear is for those who do not have the proper immigration papers.

I had waited a long time for my Green Card, but I knew that my waiting time was very short in comparison to others' stories I had heard. Praise God, I finally received it! I learned that after obtaining Permanent Resident status, I would need to wait for another five years to begin to apply for Citizenship (which was an even more involved process including being interviewed and meeting many requirements to qualify). During this lengthy waiting time, I was tired and frustrated, but turned to God's promises in the Bible. *"For I know the plans I have for you', declares the Lord, 'plans to prosper you and not to harm you, plans to give you hope and future...."(Jeremiah 29:11)* These words

encouraged my heart! I needed to wait upon the plans
God had for my future.

After five more years (and a long process), I was finally I
was naturalized as a US Citizen and granted American
Citizenship!! I had been in the United States for decades
by this point (23 years, to be exact!). It was like a dream!
For the first time, I could claim and receive benefits (that
US citizens receive) and I was even able to be a sponsor
and apply for a Green Card for my husband! After a year,
my husband received his own Permanent Resident card.
He had worked hard for many years in the United States.
He was now qualified to receive his Social Security benefit
(although he had paid into Social Security over the years,
he could not get anything out unless he had an official
Green Card or US Citizenship). It has been a journey for
many years to get to where God has taken me. Many
people have been with me on this journey of so many
years. They have been standing with me and giving
comfort when I not see past my circumstances.

The following are the stages I went through during my
citizenship process (it took me many, many years):
1. 1992 - Student Visa (F-1)
2. 1994 – Practical Visa (J-1)
3. 1997 – Visitors Visa (B-1)
4. 1998 – Religious Visa (R-1).
5. 2005 – Permanent Residency (Green Card)
6. 2015 - Citizenship of United States of America

"…I can do (endure) all things through him who gives me strength."
(Philippians 4:13)

"...and my God will meet all your needs according to his glorious riches in Christ Jesus" (Philippians 4:19b)

My dear sisters and brothers in Christ, do not give up! Since we are walking with God, there is no mountain bigger than our mighty God!

I have mentioned throughout my book that many times I faced difficulties. After prayer and meditation and in God's perfect timing, the difficulties would eventually result in God's good and in joy. *"And we know that God causes everything to work together for the good of those who love God and are called according to His purpose for them. For God knew His people in advance, and He chose them to become like His Son, so that His Son would be the firstborn among many brothers and sisters. And having chosen them, He called them to come to Him. And having called them, He gave them right standing with Himself. And having given them right standing, He gave them glory."* (Romans 8:28-30) It is a joy to know that there are no mountains higher than the power of God! Sometimes I have felt like I was at the end of the road, but then God came and held my hand. God let me know that He was walking with me - right by my side. I am sharing this because many times I have been in a place where I felt I could not take it anymore. I had become hopeless and I was not sensing that He was walking beside me in my times of trouble, sickness, frustration (and times that I sometimes felt like my friends were not there for me). Many times, I sensed darkness (where I could not see light at the end of the tunnel). My sisters and brothers, as you have read this book, do not forget that there is only One who will never leave you or forsake you! He is our Mighty God who walks with us into those dark places where we cannot see. *"About midnight Paul and Silas were praying and singing hymns to God, and the other prisoners were listening to them. Suddenly, there was such a violent earthquake that the foundations of the prison were shaken. At once all the prison doors flew open and everyone's chains came loose"* (Acts 16:25-26) I myself have felt like Paul and Silas (in my own darkness and "prisons"). God heard my cries and He has answered me. His presence is with me, regardless of whether I can always sense Him. Throughout my journey, when I am in dark places filled with struggles, I always lift my eyes up to God (through prayers and meditation). I have often heard the voice of God saying, "I am with you until the end of this journey." Many times, we feel as if God is far from us, but I know the Bible teaches us that Jesus came so that He could walk with us. He walks with us where we cannot reach. Jesus stands at the gap of any mountains, storms and valleys.

The Bible reminds me that when the people of Israel saw Goliath and then looked at David, they feared because Goliath was a giant and was equipped with weapons and armor. David collected five small stones, but he did not even use all of them – it only took one stone to slay the giant!

"David replied to the Philistine, 'You came to me with sword, spear and javelin, but I come to you in the name of the LORD of Heaven's Armies – the God of the armies of Israel, whom you have defied. Today the LORD will conquer you, and I will kill you and cut off your head. And then I will give the dead bodies of your men to the birds and the wild animals, and the whole world will know that there is a God in Israel! And everyone assembled here will know that the Lord rescues His people, but not with sword and

spear. *This is the LORD's battle, and He will give you to us! As Goliath moved closer to attack, David quickly ran out to meet him. Reaching into his shepherd's bag and taking out a stone, he hurled it with his sling and hit the Philistine in the forehead. The stone sank in, and Goliath stumbled and fell face down on the ground. So, David triumphed over the Philistines with only a sling and a stone, for he had no sword." (1 Samuel 17:45-50)*

I know that God was the one who brought the victory!

41. Lifted by Hope: Overcoming Barriers

After many memories of being alone, I know my God has been good to me both day and night. Many times, the joys of the Lord have come after I have overcome boundaries difficulties. Only after these hard times have I started living a new life. My life has been filled with a lot of joys. I have met people who have been there for me and have supported me in achieving my goals.

From the first day I arrived in United States with my family, I have been supported by many people from different corners of the world. My spiritual journey has been a testimony to the Lord because God has allowed me to meet many committed people who have helped and supported me, especially in my ministry.

"Lord, if it's you' Peter replied, 'tell me to come to you on the water' 'Come' He said. Then Peter got down out of the boat, walked on

the water and came out toward Jesus. But when he saw the wind, he was afraid and, beginning to sink, cried out 'Lord, save me!' Immediately Jesus reached out his hand and caught him. 'You of little faith' He said, 'why did you doubt?'" (Matthew 16:28-31). When Jesus walked on the water, Peter wanted to walk like Jesus (and he did walk like Jesus on the water for a few steps!). But Peter doubted and then he began sinking down into the water. God called Peter to trust him because he had the power to save him. God also has the power to give us to overcome any circumstances.

My message is that when we focus on Jesus, we will finish the journey as God has promised us. My true joy is to know that if I focus on God, I will never forget that God called me by my name (as Jesus called Peter by his own name). He has proven (again and again) that He is a faithful God. He does what He says and He carries our journeys on to completion.

We need to trust God and obey His word no matter what we are going through right now (circumstances change, but God and His word never will). We are called by our names by God. His call is not part-time! We are called full-time! We need to remind ourselves that our God is the Alpha and the Omega. He is the beginner and finisher of our lives! *"Therefore, since we are surrounded by such a huge cloud of witnesses to the life of faith, let us strip off every weight that slows us down, especially the sin that so easily trips us up. And let us run with endurance the race God has set before us. We do this by keeping our eyes on Jesus, the Champion who initiates and perfects our faith. Because of the joy awaiting Him, He endured the cross, disregarding its shame. Now He is seated at the place of honor beside God's throne. Think of all the hostility He endured from sinful people; then you won't become weary and give up." (Hebrews 12:1-3)*

"And I am certain that God, who began the good work within you, will continue His work until it is finally finished on the day when Christ Jesus returns." (Philippians 1:6)

42.   The Gospel is for Everyone

"You are all sons of God through faith in Christ Jesus, for all of you who were baptized into Christ have clothed yourselves with Christ. There is neither Jew nor Greek, slave nor free, male nor female, for you all one in

Christ Jesus" (Galatians 3:26-29).

I have been reminded that the good news about Jesus is very important to learn (basic, simple, easy to understand). When we become Christians through faith and baptism into Christ around the world, the gospel is simple to those who understand and allow God to be their interpreter. Race, gender, and social status don't change our need for God. All that is left is One. The one. Jesus! Our lives are His and thus we are connected to each other. If we have trusted in Jesus, our destination is the same - heaven. Our family is the church. No barriers. No closed doors. We are one in Christ Jesus. Amen!

43.   The Journey Continues

"You must have the same attitude that Christ Jesus had. Though He was God, He did not think of equality with God as something to cling to. Instead, He gave up His divine privileges; He took the humble position of a slave and was born as a human being. When He appeared in human form, he humbled Himself in obedience to God and died a criminal's death on a cross. Therefore God elevated Him to the place of highest honor and gave Him the Name above all other names, that at the name of Jesus every knee should bow, in heaven and on earth and under the earth, and every tongue declare that Jesus Christ is Lord, to the glory of God the Father."
(Philippians 2:5-7)

As you have read this book, I pray that my story has helped you to understand that Jesus did not hang onto His heavenly glory, but He surrendered it to serve and to rescue us. Now, He asks us to follow His example and share His heart. He wants us to treat each other as He has treated us, thinking of their needs and God's will before our own.

Now, that is one revelation I hope I get to see fully happen when the Kingdom of God comes. Amen!